OKA

A POLITICAL CRISIS

AND ITS LEGACY

Harry Swain

OKA

Douglas & McIntyre
D&M PUBLISHERS INC.
Vancouver/Toronto

Douglas & McIntyre
An imprint of D&M Publishers Inc.
2323 Quebec Street, Suite 201
Vancouver BC Canada V5T 4S7
www.douglas-mcintyre.com

Cataloguing data available from Library and Archives Canada
ISBN 978-1-55365-429-2 (cloth)
ISBN 978-1-55365-642-5 (ebook)

Editing by Barbara Pulling
Jacket design by Peter Cocking
Text design by Jessica Sullivan
Photo research by Pronk & Associates
Jacket photograph © Christopher J. Morris/CORBIS
Maps by Eric Leinberger
Printed and bound in Canada by Friesens
Text printed on acid-free, 100% post-consumer paper

We gratefully acknowledge the financial support of the Canada
Council for the Arts, the British Columbia Arts Council, the
Province of British Columbia through the Book Publishing Tax
Credit and the Government of Canada through the Canada Book
Fund for our publishing activities.

Mixed Sources
Cert no. SW-COC-001271
© 1996 FSC
FSC

*In recognition of the discipline and restraint
of the 5th Mechanized Brigade, and of Jenny Jack,
which saved many lives*

CONTENTS

PREFACE

THIS BOOK is written to supply a perspective on the Oka crisis of 1990, from the point of view of someone who worked inside the federal government. To date it has been mostly journalists telling the story, as in the colourful and readable accounts of Geoffrey York and Loreen Pindera on Kanesatake *(People of the Pines)* or Rick Hornung on Akwesasne *(One Nation Under the Gun),* though there have been a few personal memoirs, notably those of John Ciaccia and Doug George-Kanentiio. Bruce Johansen's excellent *Life and Death in Mohawk Country* investigates what happened during the civil war at Akwesasne. Alanis Obomsawin produced a dramatic two-hour movie, *Kanehsatake: 270 Years of Resistance,* for the National Film Board that captures some of the emotions on the Mohawk side of the barricades. The Montreal *Gazette* and the *Globe and Mail,* as well as radio and television broadcasters, followed the story closely once the gunfire began. To one degree or another, these "first drafts of history" tend to be sympathetic to the participants and critical of governments and their agents in the police and the armed forces. An exception is a lengthy chapter in a book entitled *The Real Worlds of Canadian Politics:* "Feather and Gun: Confrontation at Oka/Kanesatake" by Robert Campbell and Leslie Pal, a careful account that uses the Oka story to call attention to the need for deep changes in public policy.

In the summer of 1990, I was the federal deputy minister of Indian Affairs—the latest, in the eyes of some, in a long line of heavy-handed Eurocentric colonial administrators. The advantage of the job was that it gave me a unique view of events, the drama and excitement of which I hope comes through to readers. The downside is equally obvious: as a player, and a representative of a government that had a decided position on many of the issues, nothing I have written will, nor should, be seen as neutral or scholarly. My own views were not always those of the government I served, however, and I have not tried to suppress them here. What happened at Oka is part of the story of Canada, and, more generally of the collision of European and native cultures over the last five centuries or so. There are a number of Mohawk people (by no means all) who will nod their heads, perhaps in private, at much of what I have to say.

I spent my civil service career dealing with microeconomic policy in one form or another, except for five years in the Department of Indian Affairs and Northern Development (DIAND). In the end, economic policy became humdrum for me, even boring. The direction of virtue is always apparent for economists, even if you never get there. In the aboriginal world, and I suspect in the area of social policy generally, the path to truth, justice and right thinking is much less apparent, and conventions of language can conceal yawning gaps in meaning. Every now and then during my time in Indian Affairs I would stumble, in the middle of a conversation in an ostensibly shared language, into some epistemological abyss. The sudden realization, for example, that the malign spirit in the snowdrift over there to whom an Inuit speaker was matter-of-factly referring was not just a figure of speech but an empirical reality—well, that was a new thought to a southern Euro-Canadian. Working across cultural boundaries can be exhilarating. I think of my five years in Indian Affairs as the best years of my working life.

One of my first lessons there, as this book reflects, was that contemporary events have two-hundred-year-old tails. No part of the department's business makes sense without understanding that, and people with no taste for history should not work there. Trying to impose the latest nostrum from a management school text is a recipe for failure—and, in Indian country, an occasion for mirth. In this context, the old Historical Section at DIAND, now the Research and Analysis directorate, is a national treasure, and over the years its people have helped all parties to understand better just where in the grand currents of history they are swimming at the moment. The first two chapters of this book are intended to offer a similar perspective for readers. Every word in them bears on the events of 1990—and of 2010.

History veers from drama to farce to tragedy and back again. People under the pressure of great events are never simply noble, silly, scared, humourless or accident-prone. They are human: they are all of these things. What makes behaviour in a crisis so interesting is the compression of events. There is little time to check facts, untangle mysteries, assess new players or invent new modes of institutional response.

So it was with the story of Oka. All sorts of people were drawn into the affair, many surprised to be there, all of them with fragmentary histories of past entanglements, and all of them with views that corresponded imperfectly to the world and to the views of the other players. Ignorance, uncertainty and risk waited at every turn. Speed and strain affected events. The Canadian Army understood better than anyone the costs of haste and the value of sharing information with adversaries. Slowing things down—buying time—was often the most constructive step anyone could propose.

A NOTE ON TERMINOLOGY

"INDIAN" IS the erroneous European name for the original inhabitants of the Americas. It is the term used by the department I worked for and the law I administered. The word "Indian" has become incorrect in certain quarters, even slightly antique. But it continues to be used, notably among those inhabitants of the Prairies who regard themselves as treaty Indians. Other terms have their problems too. "Aboriginal," a term widely used in Australia, is a historically recent import preferred by some, but, like "native," its scope can be too broad for precision. "First Nations" is popular, but it is a collective term, and it tends to be synonymous with the old "bands" of the *Indian Act.* It is also tied to a particular political organization, the Assembly of First Nations. Tribal names are less contentious, though the word "tribe" itself is used principally in the United States. The Mohawk people, or Kanienkehaka (Kanien'kehá:ka), meaning "people of the flint," are properly understood as the easternmost of the Six Nations of the Iroquois Confederacy. In this book, I use Mohawk or Kanienkehaka to refer to this nation, Iroquois for the larger grouping of which the Mohawk people are so prominent a part, and terms like Algonquin or Cree to refer to other major groupings, trying to be as specific as possible. I use "Indian" to refer to persons recognized under the *Indian Act* and "aboriginal" to mean all, including non-status

Indians, Métis and Inuit people, who are meant to come within the ambit of Section 35 of the Canadian Charter of Rights and Freedoms—the *Constitution Act, 1982.* "Indian country" is partly real—reserve lands and other territories over which Indian communities have rights—and partly metaphorical. In the latter sense, it means that archipelago of territories where Indian custom and communication prevail, along with an Indian sense of humour.

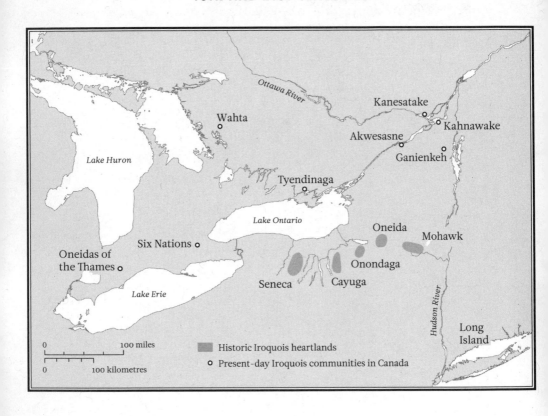

THE IROQUOIS WORLD,
16TH AND 21ST CENTURIES

Ottawa River

Kanesatake

Wahta

Kahnawake

Lake Huron

Akwesasne

Ganienkeh

Tyendinaga

Lake Ontario

Oneida

Mohawk

Six Nations

Onondaga

Oneidas of
the Thames

Seneca

Cayuga

Lake Erie

Hudson River

Long
Island

0   100 miles

0   100 kilometres

Historic Iroquois heartlands

o Present-day Iroquois communities in Canada

IROQUOIS,
FRENCH AND ENGLISH

THE IROQUOIS must be the most written-about
people in the Americas. The literature devoted to
them—little of it produced by them, unhappily—is enormous, and
for good reasons. Iroquois mastery of unconventional warfare terrified European newcomers, and the Iroquois political structure fas-
cinated them. The young Benjamin Franklin may have carried some
Iroquois ideas forward into the constitution of the new and revolutionary United States. Iroquois ferocity in war was widely known
and feared. Crucially, their location alongside one of the principal
routes of the fur trade, together with an instinct for monopoly that
would have made Adam Smith smile, brought the Iroquois into an
amazing series of wars and alliances with each of the European
powers—French, Dutch, English and American—who contested for
territory in the New World, as well as with neighbouring Indian
nations who also wanted to control European access to the furs of
the interior.

On linguistic grounds, as well as from some of their origin stories, it seems the Iroquois were squeezed out of a homeland in the
southern Plains, west of the Mississippi, and up the Ohio Valley.[1] At
the time of European contact, the Iroquois nations occupied a broad
swath of territory south of Lake Ontario, in what is now upper New
York State, as well as parts of southern Ontario. From time to time

they descended the Richelieu River and expanded along the shores of the lower St. Lawrence, though this brought them into conflict with the Algonquins, Montagnais (Innu), Nipissings and others who inhabited the wooded territory to the north.

Relations between the French and the Indians of North America were unstable, characterized at different times by mutual dependency, paternalism and belligerence. In 1534, when Jacques Cartier sailed into the Baie de Gaspé, he encountered people later described as St. Lawrence Iroquoians.[2] Over the protests of their chief, Donnacona, Cartier raised a cross claiming the land for the king of France and kidnapped two of the chief's sons, promising to return with them the next year. This event is the earliest documented evidence of French-Indian relations. It is also the first historical evidence of Iroquois occupation in Canada—many miles to the north and east of the territories they would occupy in later years.

Cartier returned in 1535 with the two young men, Dom Agaya and Taignoagny, who had learned rudimentary French over the winter. The boys directed him up the Gulf of St. Lawrence to the small village of Stadacona (near present-day Quebec City), where they were reunited with their father. The boys also told Cartier of a larger settlement farther upriver. Leaving two of his ships at Stadacona, he took his smallest upstream to Hochelaga (Montreal). A thousand men came to the shore to meet him. Cartier observed cornfields, a settlement of longhouses surrounded by a wooden palisade and, from the top of the mountain he called Mont Réal, the great Lachine Rapids, which put paid to any easy route to China. After two days he retreated to Stadacona, where he and his men spent an uncomfortable winter. They were saved from miserable deaths from scurvy by Donnacona's sons, who showed the French how to prepare infusions of cedar tea.

Cartier had encountered a large, settled and quasi-horticultural community of Iroquois. In at least three sites in the lower St. Lawrence, in the mid-1530s, people speaking an Iroquoian language were well established in permanent settlements. Relations between the Iroquois and the French were wary but not without a certain reciprocity. They were not helped by Cartier's second kidnapping, in the spring of 1536, of Donnacona himself and a number of children. Save one young girl, none of the people taken survived to return with Cartier on his third voyage, in 1541. Donnacona, who likely died in 1540, was buried in France.

Cartier's third voyage saw the establishment of a French settlement a few miles upriver from Stadacona, where he found a large number of Iroquois to be of somewhat menacing aspect. Rediscovered in 2006, this first French colony of Charlesbourg-Royal, where the Rivière du Cap Rouge debouches into the St. Lawrence just above Ste.-Foy, experienced the usual hardships and was abandoned in 1543. Another sixty-two years would pass before the French essayed a second settlement in the new world, at Port Royal in the Annapolis Basin, and sixty-five before they reappeared in the lower St. Lawrence, under the command of the redoubtable Samuel de Champlain.

In the sixty-five-year gap between Cartier and Champlain, the Iroquois had disappeared from the lower St. Lawrence Valley and returned to their traditional homeland in what is now northern New York State. Whether this was due to intertribal warfare or the effects of European diseases cannot be known—either explanation is plausible. There were a number of trading contacts, mostly below Tadoussac, among Basque whalers, French fishermen and natives in the intervening years, and plenty of opportunities for the transmission of those diseases, endemic in Europe, that were so devastating for unprepared populations. In sum, the St. Lawrence lowland appears to have been a long-time marchland between the Algonquin peoples of the boreal north and the Iroquois, who were infiltrating slowly from the southwest.[3]

The major event in the period between the first two French expeditions may have been the coalescence of five of the Iroquois nations into a confederacy, the Haudenosaunee. Around 1570, or possibly earlier, the Mohawks, or Kanienkehaka,[4] the Senecas, the Oneidas, the Onondagas and the Cayugas formed a league under the charismatic leadership of Dekanawidah. The adherence in 1722 of the Tuscaroras made them the Six Nations. Together, they controlled most of northern New York State.

In 1608 Champlain established a small settlement at Tadoussac, at the mouth of the Saguenay, then pushed upstream to Stadacona, which he immediately started to fortify. The local Indians were Ochasteguins (later called Hurons by the French), Algonquins, Montagnais and Etchemin, with all of whom he established friendly relations. The Algonquins suggested that Champlain prove his friendship by aiding them in their war with the Iroquois. And so, in the summer of 1609, a small mixed party ascended the Rivière des Iroquois, now the Richelieu River, and mapped Lake Champlain. This was contested territory, and the local inhabitants had wisely settled some distance from the navigable streams. The war party searched the lake but found only remnants of settlements.

Suddenly, late one evening in July, Champlain, with two French *harquebusiers* and sixty Algonquins, encountered some two hundred Iroquois near Ticonderoga. The Iroquois threw up a temporary fort while the invading party tied their canoes to poles offshore. A night of catcalls, insults, boasting, songs and elaborate threats from both sides ensued. In the morning, the two sides deployed. Amid volleys of arrows, Champlain, wearing light steel armour, loaded his gun. "I took aim with my arquebus and shot straight at one of the three chiefs, and with this shot two fell to the ground and one of their companions was wounded who died thereof a little later. I had put four bullets into my arquebus."[5] His two companions fired from the flank. Astounded by their first encounter with gunfire and dismayed by the loss of their leaders, the Iroquois fled. The victorious Algonquins seized shields, food and a dozen prisoners, the first of whom died a gruesome death that evening at the hands of his captors. Thus was the tone of French-Iroquois relations set for the rest of the tumultuous seventeenth century. Indeed, the echoes of that discharge can be heard faintly today.

The energetic Champlain pushed farther west.[6] A stockade was built at Montreal in 1611, and by 1613 he had ascended the Ottawa River as far as Allumette Island, where he met the Algonquin chief Tessouat. In 1615 Champlain brought four Récollet priests on a voyage from France. In due course, the Roman Catholic Church would be given nearly 30 per cent of the lands granted by the French

Crown in New France.[7] The consent of the inhabitants was not at issue, in common with European practices of the time, which saw territories and their inhabitants routinely change sovereignty through acts of war, marriage and purchase. For the French, the concept of *terra nullius*—empty land—that so outrages later writers simply did not arise.

Over the next century and a half, until the conquest of Quebec by the English, French immigration to the St. Lawrence Valley slowly proceeded. A partly agrarian but soon fur-dominated economy grew up, replacing the early dreams of gold and diamonds. Through the fur trade, the fundamental nature of the French relation to the land and its inhabitants took shape: exploitive, mercantile, Christianizing, adventurous, and not especially territorial in the sense of agricultural settlement. The French colonial administrators were keen on establishing in New France a clone of the feudal and agricultural society of their homeland and tended to see the conversion and settlement of the Indians as part of that process, though saving souls was a good thing all by itself. The French settlers, however, soon realized that the returns from killing beaver to make European hats far outshone the meagre rewards of farming in a cold, cold climate.

Iroquois lands, at the time, abutted the St. Lawrence River and perhaps the lower Ottawa. The Iroquois controlled completely the land north of the Mohawk River and much of the territory west of the Hudson. Their earliest European commercial alliances were with the Dutch, who were ascending the North (Hudson) River in search of fur. Initially, the easternmost Iroquois nation, the Mohawks, fell upon the beaver in their own territory, as did the Mahicans and other tribes east of the Hudson. But by 1640 the Iroquois lands south of Lake Ontario were trapped out. That led the Iroquois to attempt, savagely but unsuccessfully, to interpose themselves as middlemen between the Hurons and the French.[8] The beaver frontier was on its inexorable way west. French voyageurs and Indian guides undertook ever more heroic explorations of the river systems of the continental interior in their search for new hunting grounds.

Indians became symbionts in this predatory game, doing most of the trapping and a great deal of the paddling in return for European manufactures, including alcohol. Those who collaborated with the coureurs de bois collided with others who resented their intrusions into traditional hunting territories. The greatest rewards went to tribes who positioned themselves as principals in the fur trade, not just as hired labour. For the Iroquois, the strategic problem was that the great highway into beaver country, the Ottawa River–Lake Nipissing–French River route to Lake Huron and beyond, was controlled by others. Nipissings controlled the central Ottawa from their base on Allumette Island, and beyond them, in the rich lands running from Georgian Bay to Lake Erie, were cousins of the Iroquois, the Hurons and the Neutrals. From the time the beaver was exterminated south of Lake Ontario, around 1640, to a peace of exhaustion in 1700, the Iroquois warred against the French and their native neighbours to control this trade. The most horrifying of the wars, the one that cemented the Iroquois reputation for ferocity and cruelty, was the raid of 1649 into Huron territory, which shattered that peaceful society and scattered its remnants over a quarter of a continent. The fiery end of the missionary priests Brébeuf and Lalemant underscored for the French the nature of their great adversary and the distance the Iroquois would go to establish control of the fur routes.

The ordinary ebb and flow of hunting societies was accelerated during this time, with greater incentive for warfare, mostly low level but occasionally exterminatory, and greater risk of the transmission of European diseases. A further handful of French missionaries also died excruciatingly in Iroquois hands. The lower Ottawa remained the key to the continental interior and its beaver pelts, and the Iroquois warred on all who contested control of this choke point. Uneasy relations—wars and marriages, trade and dispute, French farms and Iroquois raids—between the French and the Iroquois continued, punctuated now and then by ceremonies of reconciliation and treaty-making.

A great conclave at Montreal in 1700 involving the French and the Five Nations finally proved reasonably durable. By the middle of the eighteenth century, the focus had shifted to the contest between the French and the English, with both sides bidding for the support of the still-fearsome Iroquois. Under these conditions, bilateral agreements between culturally distinct groups became more important—to settle wars, to make treaties, to profess friendship and to open routes and settlements to traders. The Iroquois custom of using belts of wampum expanded greatly. These patterned belts, made of small white and dark purple shells threaded onto strings and woven together, were presented to underline the special weight of a speaker's words and were often used to seal treaties. An especially important style of belt for the Iroquois was the two-row wampum, presented to successive European settler groups to memorialize the Iroquois version of an agreement with the new settlers. In the two-row wampum, two nations are likened to vessels going down a river in parallel, each keeping its own laws and traditions, both travelling in peace and friendship but never meeting, neither interfering with or imposing its laws on the other.[9]

The Iroquois were not *sauvages*. Their hideous practices with respect to enemies and prisoners fully matched those of medieval and renaissance Europe. In governance terms, the Iroquois were in some respect more advanced. The 1648 Treaty of Westphalia, which recognized the integrity of principalities and indirectly licensed the Hobbesian war of all against all, fell a long way short of the ideals of the Iroquois Confederacy.

Somewhere between 1390 and 1570—authorities differ[10]—when the savagery of intertribal warfare had become all but intolerable, there arose a leader who proposed what came to be called Kayane-rakowa (Kaianerakowa, Gayanashagowa), the Great Law of Peace. The history is oral and has magical elements. It was recorded in two different versions, in 1900 and 1916.[11] The story is important; the account I provide here is based on the 1916 version, but the precepts of governance and honourable behaviour it sets out are common to both. Those precepts echo through the wars of the seventeenth and eighteenth centuries to the present day, and they had a huge effect on the way Mohawks thought and acted during the Oka affair. That few of these precepts were widely appreciated by the larger society meant mutual incomprehension and unavailing negotiation throughout that long summer. In summary, the story is as follows.

Dekanawidah, the Peacemaker, an Ontario Huron born of a virgin near the Bay of Quinte, is found by bereaved Onondaga chief Hayonhwatha (Hay-yonh-wa-tha, Hahyonwatha, Hiawatha). They cure the cannibal Adodarhoh (Ta-do-dah-ho, Tadodaro) of his evil ways, and the three of them propose a Great Law to the warring five nations. Under the law, the Onondaga are the Firekeepers. The Mohawks are "the heads and the leaders of the Five Nations Confederacy." Adodarhoh and the Firekeepers must agree with the council of the Confederacy and may make only small decisions independently.

Questions are first debated and agreed among the Mohawks and the Senecas, the "elder brothers," the Keepers of the Eastern and Western Doors of the Confederacy respectively, then passed to the Oneida and Cayuga *royaner,* or lords. (Chiefs would be the present-day word.) Only if there is disagreement do the Firekeepers vote, and at first vote only to pass the question back. A decision is confirmed only on consensus. In extreme cases of council waywardness, after the Council of Women has met and the war chief has warned the errant lords three times, those lords may be executed by war club.

The lords are appointed by women having the hereditary right to do so, signified by the possession of certain strings of shells. A lord may be deposed by the war chief of his nation for failing to attend meetings of the council, for trying to "establish any authority independent of the jurisdiction of the Confederacy of the Great Peace," or for murder, but he may not resign without permission from the other lords. The Confederate lords may elect a man showing special ability and interest as a "Pine Tree sprung up for the Nation"; he cannot be deposed but his title is not hereditary.

On the death of a lord and the accession of a new one, a ceremony of condolence is held. The grieving clan is condoled, and so in a sense is the new chief, who must take on the burdens of leadership and exemplary personal behaviour. A person who is a "condoled chief" has been the object of this community sympathy.[12]

Society is matrilineal: "Women . . . shall own the land and the soil."

Peace is to rule inside the Confederacy. The modern phrase "burying the hatchet" comes from this time: "I, Dekanawidah, and the Union Lords, now uproot the tallest pine tree and into the cavity thereby made we cast all weapons of war. Into the depths of the earth, down into the deep underearth currents of water flowing to unknown regions we cast all the weapons of strife. We bury them from sight and we plant again the tree. Thus shall the Great Peace be established and hostilities shall no longer be known between the Five Nations but peace to the United People."

Sovereign independence is bedrock. "If at any time any one of the Confederate lords chooses to submit to the law of a foreign people he is no longer in but out of the confederacy, and persons of this class shall be called 'They have alienated themselves.' Likewise all such persons who submit to laws of foreign nations shall forfeit all birthrights and claims on the Five Nations Confederacy and territory." Alien persons or nations may be adopted, but only temporarily, and only as long as they obey the law. In fact, adopted nations have an obligation to spread the Great Law to other nations, and this obligation is to be noted in the treaty that establishes their adoption. Treaties in turn are woven into and symbolized by wampum belts.

THE GREAT LAW seems to me to be largely procedural, in that its text concentrates on the legitimacy of those who are to rule and on the processes that lead to decisions and the resolution of disputes. It is not statutory, in the modern sense of encoding rules about civil or criminal behaviour, but it does imply a great many things about ethical relations in society. For instance, there are elaborate songs and ceremonies invoking gratitude to the Creator for all the wonders of the natural world, and there is a hugely democratic spirit at the core of the Great Law. In addition to the back-and-forth, consensus-oriented debates of the chiefs, there are procedures for importing the views of the Council of Women and—perhaps exceptionally—for expert or especially esteemed voices, even voices from outside the Confederacy, to be heard. Action by what in modern

terms would be called the "executive" must await council's decision—none of this "act now and ask forgiveness later."

In some respects, the Great Law foreshadows the famous New
England town hall meetings, but in a disciplined and hierarchical
manner that allows the accommodation of many communities in
important matters. In others, it recalls the Japanese process of corporate and governmental decision-making, with its emphasis on a
prolonged examination of a question by successively senior ranks
before, finally, the top man carefully articulates the consensus that
has been reached. The Great Law is arguably much more democratic
than the representative governments of twentieth-century Canada.
The downside of the process is that it could take quite some time for
a decision to be reached.

The Iroquois Confederacy still exists today, centred at Onondaga,
New York. It retains an important moral authority, even though its
power has been vitiated by the imposition of elected Indian governments by both Canada and the United States, and lately by the rise
of other forms of aboriginal organization. Asserting a connection
to the traditional forms is one means by which such organizations
establish their legitimacy.

Toward the end of the colonial wars in the United States, the
Iroquois were much subdued and under serious pressure to take up
European-style farming. Those wars had left Iroquois society battered and subject to two of the great causes of deracination, alcohol
abuse and domestic violence. In 1799, a sixty-four-year-old Seneca
prophet named Handsome Lake, himself much debilitated by alcohol and disease, had a series of visions, later systematized as the
Code of Handsome Lake.[13] The code, *Gaiwiio (Kariwiiowi),* bears
some resemblance to Christian precepts, and unlike the Great Law
concentrates not so much on political process but on what consti-
tutes good behaviour. This includes abstaining from alcohol, family violence, abortion and gambling, as well as being scrupulous
in caring for children and respecting what today would be called
children's rights. In the words of Onondaga faithkeeper and chief
Oren Lyons, "The message was how to deal with the white man...
you must not use the strong drink, the liquor. One was witchcraft:

they said it came over on the boat, and to stay away from that. One was the Bible . . . The fourth one was gambling. They said that those things will destroy your people unless you deal with them."[14]

Handsome Lake spent the remaining sixteen years of his life preaching these revelations, principally among the western Iroquois. For much of the remaining nineteenth century, there was otherwise quite a void in Iroquois political life. The old Law had mostly been forgotten, and defeats in the U.S. Revolutionary War and marginalization by the flood of white settlers into upstate New York had deeply discouraged the Iroquois. A teacher who offered a promising view, one asserting that earthly poverty would in time be replaced by an everlasting life of ease and content, Handsome Lake found real resonance in the communities in which he preached. But his influence did not reach east of Akwesasne.

BY THE EARLY eighteenth century, Montreal was a solidly established, relatively prosperous fur-trading colony sheltered by wooden walls and surrounded by Indians. Trade goods of iron and steel, as well as guns and brandy, were decisive in attracting people to the settlement. As early as 1671, "eight Mohawk families came to Montreal Island and erected longhouses at the foot of 'le Mont Royal' near the present-day corner of Fort and Sherbrooke streets."[15] Fragments of clans and tribes traded the frequent starvation of the hunting life for scraps from the European table, often provided by priests who combined relief with attempts at conversion. By 1683, the Indian village, called La Montagne, had more than two hundred inhabitants, including Algonquin, Wendat (Huron) and Dakota people as well as Mohawks. The Sulpician order of Catholic priests had set aside four arpents (about 3.5 acres) for the Indian village and "a chapel, a presbytery, a school for boys, and another for girls."[16] But a disastrous fire blamed by the priests on a drunken Indian man destroyed La Montagne in 1694 and led to the relocation of the community to Sault-au-Récollet, at the eastern end of Montreal Island.

Soon even that seemed too close for comfort to the French. About 1715, the superior of the seminary renewed his efforts to isolate the Indians from the sellers of ardent spirits and other debauchers of Indian morals by proposing they move to one of their hunting grounds near the mouth of the Ottawa River. As recalled by Chief Agneetha, the principal leader of the Mohawks at the new site, in a 1787 speech to the Superintendent of Indian Affairs,

> Again our Priest, in conjunction with the clergy of the Seminary of Montreal, told us we should remove once more with our families, for it was no longer proper that any Indians should live on this Island [of Montreal]. If we would consent to go and settle at the Lake of Two Mountains we should have a large tract of land for which we would have a Deed from the King of France as our property, to be vested in us and our heirs forever, and that we should not be molested again in our habitations.[17]

Accordingly, Philippe d'Orléans, regent for the seven-year-old Louis xv, wrote to Governor de Vaudreuil and Intendant Begon on June 15, 1716:

> His Majesty agrees that the Indian Mission which at present is located on the Island of Montreal be moved off this island and placed on the north shore adjoining the lands granted to S. Duguay and ascending the Lake of Two Mountains. He wishes that Messieurs Vaudreuil and Begon concede in this area three leagues square of land for the placement of the Mission, on condition that as soon as the Indians leave it will revert to the king and that ... the expenses of this relocation, as well as those of constructing the new fort, will be borne by the Seminary of Montreal which will be compensated by the land at present occupied by the Indians [at Sault-au-Récollet] which the Seminary will be able to dispose of.
> His Majesty, also following the advice of Sieur de Vaudreuil, accords to the Missionaries a half-league of land by three leagues in depth adjoining the Indians, on condition that when the Indians abandon their lands, this land will also revert to His Majesty.[18]

The grants were conditional on the Sulpicians building a church and manse and a stone fort. No mention was made in the document of the alienation, permanent or temporary, of any of the land set aside for the Indians, still a tribally heterogeneous group. Instead, it was clear that the Sulpicians were to be recompensed by the gift of the valuable property at Sault-au-Récollet, on Montreal Island. Of the two pieces of land, the smaller, half a league wide by three leagues deep on the north shore of the lake, was conditionally granted to the Sulpicians. The larger adjoining tract, three leagues by three, just to the west, was to be enfeoffed to them as a place where the Indians might live and farm. It was to be home for the Indians as long as they wanted to live there. Should the Indians ever leave, the land would revert to the King of France. This was not an offer of fee simple ownership. In other words, the Sulpicians had no rights to the larger block of land at all, but rather obligations regarding the spiritual and temporal welfare of the Indians, obligations that were to be financed from the proceeds of the vacated lands at Sault-au-Récollet.

In the autumn of 1716, before a single tree had been felled or an Indian moved to the Lake of Two Mountains (Lac des Deux-Montagnes), the Sulpicians complained to the governor that the costs of building in stone were so onerous that they should be given perpetual ownership of both tracts. The governor wrote to the regent. The regent agreed, but only if the stone fort was built within two years in accordance with some grand military engineering plans he thoughtfully enclosed. Well, then, seven years, please, Sire, the Sulpicians responded. The regent agreed. Although the stone fort, prime object of the shrewd regent's design, would never be built, the Sulpicians thereafter acted as owners. Based on the seven-year promise, they sent priests thirty miles upriver, trailing tracts and rations, with the first Indian settlers in February 1721. The Indians still believed the larger tract of land would be theirs, as originally promised. Chief Agneetha again:

Although it was very inconvenient to us to be quitting our homes and small clearing, yet the desire of having a fixed property of

MONTREAL AND THE OKA GRANTS

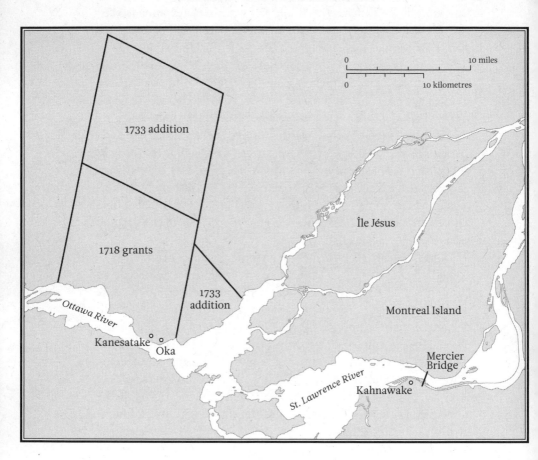

our own induced us to comply, and we accordingly set out, and took possession of the land, and as was the custom of our forefathers we immediately set about making a [wampum] Belt... by which our children would see that the lands were to be theirs forever, and as was customary with our ancestors we placed the figure of a dog at each end of the Belt to guard our Property and to give notice when an enemy approached.[19]

Years passed, but no start was made on the fort. The superior kept complaining about the cost. According to DIAND's John Thompson,

In 1731 an agreement was reached. The Seminary would not be required to construct a stone fort and would be compensated for costs already incurred in moving the mission and building several small dwellings for the natives. Two years later the Seminary was granted additional land to the east of their existing seigneury, with a river frontage of 2.5 leagues. They built a stone church surrounded by wooden walls on the point. The wooden walls were replaced by a stone wall nine years later. A house for the priest, another for the French farmers employed by the Seminary, and another house outside the walls for the Soeurs de la Congregation, as well as a watchtower, completed the establishment at Lac des Deux-Montagnes mission.

Two years later [in 1735], when King Louis XV gave his approval to the Sulpician land grant, he gave them an additional three square leagues extension to further indemnify them for their expenses... Thus without having to build a stone fort which they had use to augment their original concession—one-half league by three leagues—the gentlemen of the Seminary of St. Sulpice gained, over a period of 20 years, title to 15 times that amount of land. This included the three square league tract conceded by the King to the Mohawks of the mission by letter in 1716 and called "their lands."[20]

The additions in 1733 and 1735 created a grand seigneury of about 265 square miles in total.

In 1764, after the capitulation that ended the Seven Years War, the lands and the settled village of Kanesatake (Mohawk for "on the hillside") were reconfirmed as having been granted to the Sulpicians—the Sulpicians of Paris, not of Montreal—under the same unusual conditions.[21] The situation at Kanesatake was tricky, as the Sulpicians of Montreal were not a separate body corporate, merely an extension of Paris, and did not therefore have the legal capacity to own land in their own right in now-English Canada. A strong argument could be made, and was, that the Sulpician territories in Quebec now belonged to the British Crown, In fact, two attorneys-general of Lower Canada, Sewell in 1804 and Stuart in 1828, after careful study, concluded "that the Seminary's rights and titles had not survived the conquest and subsequent to the conquest vested in the British Crown."[22] The Indians much preferred this view, seeing no reason to have priests between them and the Crown. The interference of the Black Robes in their spiritual life was one thing, but the bossiness of the priests with respect to allocations of wood, pastures and house lots was quite another. Firewood was critical in a Quebec winter, and attempts to restrict access to it were resented. In legal terms, a decision in favour of Crown ownership would have brought the lands at Oka (Algonquin for "pickerel"), the entire grand seigneury, under the umbrella of the Royal Proclamation of 1763[23] and laid a duty on the successive British colonial and Canadian national governments to protect the lands against usurpation.

Such a conclusion, however, was at cross-purposes with colonial policy. As in India, a handful of redcoats were supposed to govern thousands of locals; locals, moreover, whose customs were quite different from those of the English gentry—these were the days when officers bought their commissions, with proceeds from family estates—and whose loyalty to the British Crown could never entirely be taken for granted. The value of a policy of assuagement of local establishments became apparent during the Rebellion of 1837, when important parts of the French community either sided with the English or refrained from any real aid to the sans-culottes of the Ottawa Valley and elsewhere. It was in the wake of this sobering event that the Sulpicians of Montreal, harassed continually by the complaints and disobedience of their Indian charges at Oka, petitioned the government of Lower Canada for a legal reconfirmation of the land issue. The colonial government obliged, passing in 1839 an ordinance that was re-enacted in 1840.²⁴ This statute overturned the earlier opinions of the Crown's most senior law officers and conclusively vested ownership in the Montreal Sulpicians, subject to some obligations to their sub-grantees, and *en passant* declared them to be a body corporate capable of holding the titles. The Indians were understandably unconvinced by this high-handed exercise of *raison d'état,* which certainly would not meet the standards for honourable behaviour by the Crown of a century and a half later. They continued to press their case, to resist the instructions of the Sulpicians regarding the use of the pastures and forests of the seigneury, and to express dismay when the Sulpicians, now unencumbered by the regent's stipulation that their expenses should come only from Sault-au-Récollet, sold off pieces of the seigneury in order to pay for the religious instruction and governance of the Indians. Troubles continued.

And so, to recapitulate this essential bit of history: French concerns about security in 1715–21 led to the Indians on Montreal Island being induced to move thirty miles away by the promise of having their own indefeasible lands, from which they would never have to move again. The Church, having intervened to protect those they saw as innocent children of God "not capable of keeping the things most necessary to them,"²⁵ ensured in the process that step by step, decade by decade, land that had been set aside for the Indians instead accrued to the Church. The Indians were never consulted. Arguably, decent intentions became sharp dealing, and, once land sales to non-Indians began, theft.

2

UNDER A
NEW SOVEREIGN

THE GREAT struggle between England and France for imperial mastery in the Americas had broken out in 1756. Two years later, General Jeffrey Amherst, supported by the youthful Major General James Wolfe, took the mighty fortress of Louisbourg, in Cape Breton—the key to the control of the St. Lawrence and hence all of New France. In 1759, at the ripe age of thirty-two, Wolfe led British troops up the cliffs west of the fortress of Quebec and there, on the Plains of Abraham, defeated Montcalm. Both generals lost their lives, but France lost an empire.

The Indians were not for the most part directly involved in these European colonial battles, but events in the aftermath had consequences for them that continue to this day. In 1760, for instance, General James Murray, Wolfe's successor and a notably successful colonial administrator, wished to mollify the Indians around Montreal and promised them "the free exercise of their religion, customs and trade with the English" in a note that, in 1990, was determined by the Supreme Court of Canada to be a treaty and hence the source of constitutionally protected rights.[1]

In 1763, again with an eye to the creation of allies, the British government issued its famous Royal Proclamation, which among other things required Indians to be treated with before their lands were opened for European settlement. This far-reaching, unilateral statement became a founding constitutional document of Canada.

It guided the efforts of colonial governors and, after 1867, administrators in the fledgling Canada, in their relations with the original peoples. Civil servants preceded the wave of agrarian settlement from Ontario westward, making treaties with the Indians that were intended to produce amicable relations, assure the Indians at least part of their traditional territories in perpetuity and, after 1870 or so, provide for basic material, educational and medical requirements.[2]

A further result of the Seven Years War of 1756–63 was the *Quebec Act* of 1774, another statute now part of the Canadian constitution, through which the British conquerors promised the defeated French the continued practice of the Roman Catholic faith, the use of the French language, the continuance of land tenures flowing from grants of the French sovereign, and French legal norms. Language, religion and especially land tenure are at the heart of the Oka story of 1990.

It is not going too far to say that another consequence of the Seven Years War was the U.S. Revolutionary War of 1776–83, whose proximal cause, after all, was the imposition of new taxes by a war-impoverished home government.[3] That civil war caused the English on either side of the St. Lawrence to search for allies among the Indian nations—nowhere more so than among the warlike and aggressive Iroquois who inhabited the marchlands between the old and new sovereignties. The Iroquois Confederacy was split, with some adhering to each side and others declaring it was not their fight at all. But the Mohawks fought mainly with the British—and so, in the end, came north in defeat as, in effect, some of the early Loyalists. The British promised the Mohawks expansive grants of land in Ontario, principally in the Grand River Valley, home of their great ally, Chief Joseph Brant. The Jay Treaty of 1794 between England and the United States, which in the standard fashion of eighteenth-century European principalities settled postwar matters between the belligerents and provided for the continuance of peaceful commerce, included language that allowed Indians to pass freely across the new international boundary.

The new and revolutionary United States, no longer bound by proclamations from London, adopted a novel theory of its own relations with the original peoples. After a good deal of low-grade skirmishing and some outright ethnic cleansing in the original thirteen colonies, it fell to Chief Justice John Marshall, in two U.S. Supreme Court judgements in 1831 and 1832,[4] to define Indian peoples as "domestic, dependent nations"—with a degree of surviving sovereignty, to be sure, but ultimately subject to the legislative powers of Congress. It also followed that since these peoples were nations, however qualified, war could be declared on them. And it was. The six decades from Marshall to Wounded Knee marked a period of colonial warfare, forced migrations of Indians away from the farming lands favoured by the white settlers, and military subjugation. However sharp the dealings of Canadian administrators, there was no Trail of Tears, Blackhawk Rebellion or General Custer north of the border. A peculiar result is that Mohawks in twenty-first century Canada can claim with literal truth never to have ceded land or lost a war—north of the St. Lawrence, anyway.

IT WAS NOT in the interest of the new colonial masters in Canada to stir things up in New France, and the Sulpician Ordinance of 1839 was but one of a series of British acts of appeasement. The priests, for their part, apparently believed that their only duty was to the religious instruction of the people at Kanesatake, with perhaps a little welfare for the most exiguous cases in the worst winters; otherwise, they felt free to manage and even dispose of the lands they had been awarded as a means of defraying the expenses that these duties, and their own upkeep, required.

When an itinerant Methodist preacher wandered up from the States in 1846, some Indians saw adherence to the Protestant faith, and the use of the language in which it was presented, as a way of cocking a snoot at their French oppressors. To this day, many Mohawks prefer English in a province determined to make French the language of everyday affairs, and Catholicism is but one strain of several in the religious lives of Quebec Mohawks.

The original migrants to Oka were a mix of Mohawks, Algonquins, Nipissings and a handful of others. Over time, resentment against the dominant Mohawks led to the Indians at Kanesatake becoming, through both emigration and marriage, more and more Mohawk. Sulpician high-handedness with people they saw as children did not decline. In 1881, a group of unhappy Mohawks accepted the offer from the Sulpicians of a subsidized migration to a place far away from Oka. A location at Doncaster, some distance north of Montreal, was selected and even acquired, but as raw Canadian Shield it proved unsuitable. After some time a site at Gibson, now Wahta, in Muskoka was deemed agreeable, and about thirty-nine families moved there, much to the relief of the Sulpicians. But their relief was short-lived. The remaining Indian population continued to press the case for their ownership of the seigneury of the Lac des Deux-Montagnes, and they took their case to court in the 1890s. They lost, appealed, and lost again. Finally, in 1910, the federal government in Ottawa sponsored an appeal to the British Privy Council, paying the costs for both sides and ensuring that the advocates for the Indians were fully competent. The English Law Lords, trapped by the ordinance of 1839, reluctantly agreed, in *Corinthe et al. v. Seminary of St. Sulpice* (1912), that the Sulpicians owned the land. But they thought the Indians were getting a raw deal.

> [The Law Lords] desired, however, to guard themselves against being supposed to express an opinion that there were no means of securing for the Indians in the Seigniory benefits which Section 2 of the Act shewed they were intended to have. If this were a case in which the practice of the English Courts governed, their Lordships might not improbably think that there was a charitable trust which the Attorney-General, as representing the public, could enforce.[5]

Such a concept did not, however, exist in French law, and French law, courtesy of the *Quebec Act* of 1774, was guaranteed a continuing authority.

During the drawn-out adjudication of *Corinthe,* the seminary was disposed at one point to negotiate a settlement, since the courts had made it clear that the mere alienation of the land to whites did not extinguish the Indians' rights to use the land or the Sulpicians' obligations to care for them. In 1905, the Sulpicians offered to transfer the remaining 4,000 (of an original 170,000) acres of land to the federal government, reserving to themselves the church and its dependencies, much of the woods and the farms rented out to whites, as well as leaving undisturbed in their possession the whites who had bought land from the Sulpicians in the past. The Indians, through the Department of Indian Affairs, made a counter-proposal in 1914 that Indian Affairs supported but the Department of Justice did not. So things continued, with the Sulpicians selling more land, including property that until then had "been considered common lands of the Indians and which was used by them for pas-turing their cattle and horses, and as wood lots,"[6] finally turning over 1,556 acres to the federal government in 1945, less than 1 per cent of the original seigneurial grants. Some of the commons, hav-ing passed into private hands, was acquired by the municipality of Oka. Only a patchwork of lands remained for the Kanesatake band. The lands were never formally made into a reserve under the *Indian Act,* and remain to this day Crown-owned lands "set aside for the use and benefit" of the Kanesatake band under Section 91(24) of the *Constitution Act, 1982.* The Indians, living cheek by jowl with their French neighbours, had long started to intermarry, so to checker-board land holdings were added checkerboard genetics.

Sulpician attempts to regulate wood-cutting and pasturage, and to severely punish transgressions, seem at this remove to have more to do with an assertion of Church dominance than a concern for Indian welfare. In 1899[7] and again in 1924, the Canadian govern-ment, in its own acts of colonial paternalism, decided to impose an elective form of government at Kanesatake (and elsewhere) under the *Indian Act,* despite the fact that the absence of a reserve at Kanesatake made the action legally questionable. Onto an already discontented population, split by language and religion, the fed-eral government overlaid another source of division, and enforced it through the power of the purse and the RCMP. An elected band council became the recipient of federal funding and attention, while the old Longhouse system was left with only its consider-able moral authority intact. The traditional system's continuing relevance has been demonstrated in many ways since then, including very low rates of participation in provincial and national—not to mention band—elections.[8] A consequence of the many pressures from the two "founding" peoples of Canada was the growth of factionalism in the Kanesatake community.

EACH OF the main Kanienkehaka communities has its own distinct history. Kahnawake began, oddly enough, with a handful of Christian Oneidas who were persuaded to settle on the Jesuit seigneury at Prairie de la Magdelaine, on the south shore of the St. Lawrence opposite Montreal Island, in 1667. "With only a half a dozen families in 1667, it grew to nearly 500 people a little more than a decade later as Oneidas, Onondagas, Hurons, and, increasingly, Kanienkahaka joined the new community. In 1673–74 alone there were 180 newcomers. That many who came were adopted war captives only contributed to its diversity and dynamism."[9] The community split, however, and in 1676 most of its members moved a few miles upstream, Jesuit mission in tow. Onondagas and Hurons began to leave, and the community became more and more Mohawk.

In the 1680s, with the French and the Iroquois Confederacy at odds over control of a fur frontier that had moved deep into the Mississippi watershed, the people of Kahnawake found themselves with conflicting loyalties. Their traditional religion had been diluted with French Catholicism, and they were developing a brisk illegal trade between French Montreal and English Albany. The community's sympathies lay increasingly with the French, to the point that the Confederacy expelled them in 1684. Three years later, warriors from Kahnawake joined in Denonville's raid on the Senecas, a treachery that was repaid by a serious onslaught on Montreal in 1689. Many of the settlers on the south bank, French and Indian alike, took refuge in fortified Montreal as the Senecas and their allies burned and butchered in the neighbourhood. The relationship between Kahnawake and the French grew even closer, but it was more nuanced than their position as military allies would suggest. Kahnawake representatives to the Confederacy pleaded that their enemies were not the entire Confederacy, only the Senecas. When skirmishes occurred in the period after 1689, Kahnawake warriors, as part of larger mixed groups, would avoid firing on their Iroquois cousins on the other side. English pressure on the Confederacy led eventually to a treaty with the French, under which the Confederacy promised to remain neutral between the French and the English. The treaty did not apply to Kahnawake, which remained firmly in the French camp.

In the wake of the Seneca siege, the village relocated several more times, all within the same general area, before settling in 1716 on the land it now occupies across the St. Lawrence, south of Montreal. Grants totalling more than 40,000 acres were made to the Society of Jesus to support the Indians and the society's missionary work. In a decision strikingly at variance with what happened at Kanesatake, Indian title was established to this land by General (now Governor) Murray after the fall of Montreal in 1760, a decision confirmed by his successor in 1762. But then the usual dismal pattern of events kicked in. White farmers began to encroach on the land, and white men filtered into the community and married Indian women. A Métis community began to grow. A century later, Kahnawake had shrunk to less than a third of its original size— 12,328 acres in 1890—and increasingly serious resource struggles turned community members against each other. Firewood was insufficient and was concentrated in the hands of land-owning families, families who, moreover, tended to have strong admixtures of white or Métis blood. The old ease of incorporation and acculturation after capture was working less well in the more settled, constrained world of the late nineteenth century.

Long before then, around 1750, a number of families from Kahnawake had moved some sixty miles upstream to found a new community at Akwesasne, "the land where the partridge drums," a place where several rivers flow into the St. Lawrence. Like the land around Kahnawake, this was a rich region. The St. Regis and Raquette Rivers, as well as lesser streams, descended from the Adirondack foreland, crossing game-rich forests that, once cleared, became attractive farms. The great St. Lawrence, with its islands and swamps, provided fish and birds. There were few competitors for the land, as large-scale white settlement was still several decades away. Even the international boundary was undefined, since the land was all part of British North America. It was the success of the Revolutionary War that slowly brought calamity to Akwesasne. Boundaries were drawn through the territory, and Loyalist refugees from the new republic began to stream northward.

The late nineteenth and early twentieth centuries were not all bad. In 1884–85 some sixty Mohawk boatmen guided Sir Garnet Wolseley's forlorn expedition up the Nile to rescue Chinese Gordon.[10] Young men from Kanesatake, Kahnawake and other Mohawk communities discovered an affinity for high steel. Starting in 1886–87 with the CPR's St. Lawrence Bridge, which bisected Kahnawake, these men learned entirely new skills. Commuting to New York and other skyscraper cities in the U.S., they developed a reputation for fearlessness and skill in riveting together the steel skeletons of the new America. The work was hard on family life, and dangerous, but it paid well and became a source of pride. When changing building technology after World War II began to limit opportunities in this field, binational "native American" men found an outlet for adventure and for the display of valour and toughness in the U.S. armed forces. Many had served with distinction in Canadian and U.S. forces during the two world wars, a tradition that continued in Korea and Vietnam.

The expropriation of land for the railway was not the only encroachment on the already small Kahnawake community, by then increasingly hemmed in by the fast-growing Montreal suburb of Châteauguay. Roads, bridges and power lines from hydroelectric plants all took land away from the people there. Then came the 1960s, with social ferment, flower power, serious reaction against a U.S. foreign policy many thought had gone astray and the appearance of the American Indian Movement. Centred in the Upper Midwest, the tough language and actions of AIM raised Indian consciousness across the continent.

By the mid-1970s, with the Vietnam War winding ingloriously down, high steel in decline and recession gripping North America, a number of young Mohawk men were decanted back into their communities, skilled at arms but jobless. One of the things they found was a new spirit of Kanienkehaka irredentism growing up around the teachings of Louis Karoniaktajeh Hall, whose uncompromising *Rebuilding the Iroquois Confederacy,* published in 1970, galvanized a number of angry followers. Hall called for a rededication to traditional religion, for support of Warrior Societies, for the Europeans to get in their boats and go home, for the execution of Iroquois who did not agree with him, and for an insistence on all practical (and some not so practical) ways of maintaining an Iroquois nationality independent of the governments of the United States and Canada.

Meanwhile, attacks on Iroquois nationality and territory continued. Both Canada and the United States had imposed widely resented electoral systems and backed them up by refusing financial dealings with electorally unrecognized factions. In 1959, the building of the binational St. Lawrence Seaway sliced 1,358 acres (net 1,106 acres; 252 acres were given back after construction)[11] of land from the small reserve at Kahnawake and flooded it. It was not just the land that was lost; the shore-based fishery and recreational uses also disappeared. In the face of community hostility, policing became sporadic, centering on big raids following long periods without routine patrolling. At Kahnawake and Akwesasne, police raids in 1968 alarmed all Kanienkehaka, and the times were ripening toward some sort of confrontation.

It finally came in 1974, when a group of traditionalist people from Kahnawake and Akwesasne seized a state park at Moss Lake, New York, claiming it as a first step in restoring the Confederacy of old. The story has been told in some depth elsewhere.[12] In summary, Governor Hugh Carey dispatched his attorney-general, Mario Cuomo, to negotiate an end to the occupation. Cuomo had few carrots and no sticks, however, since in what has become a common pattern on both sides of the border, police were loath to enforce the law. The commanding officer of the New York State Police, Tom Constantine, had been in charge of the restoration of order at Attica state prison in 1971, and he wanted no further mass bloodshed in his career. A lengthy period of desultory negotiation ended with

Mohawk acceptance of an alternative piece of state-owned land, not a state park, in the Adirondack hills west of Plattsburgh, close to the Canadian border. The Mohawks named it Ganienkeh. The "Ganienkeh Manifesto" describes a self-sufficient commune operating as the "Independent North American State of Ganienkeh" under the Great Law of the Confederacy.[13] Despite ups and downs as people have coped with subsistence living in an inhospitable place, Ganienkeh has survived ever since. The U.S. government has tacitly ceded sovereignty. When a U.S. Army National Guard medevac helicopter innocently flew over the territory from Vermont in 1990, carrying an injured man, it was shot down over Ganienkeh. The helicopter auto-rotated down to a semi-controlled landing outside Ganienkeh's borders. A doctor aboard was injured. He and the other passengers were rescued, and the hull of the helicopter was recovered—but no police or military authorities were allowed onto the territory where the gunfire came from, nor were they permitted to interview possible witnesses.

In Canada, by the 1980s the long history of the federal government dictating the type of government Indian bands should have had given way to deference. Even though the *Indian Act* allowed the minister to intervene, most incumbents rubber-stamped whatever system of "election" a band wanted, under the pretence that these were traditional band customs. So, for instance, in response to a question in the House from Lise Bourgault, M.P. for Oka, about whether the minister had the power under the *Indian Act* to restore the "democratic" system that had existed before 1979, Bill McKnight said, "It would be totally inappropriate for the federal government or this Minister to interfere with the elections or customs of the Indian government of the Oka Band."[14] Later, McKnight's parliamentary secretary, Stan Schellenberger, nailed the door shut. Not only was it inappropriate, Schellenberger said, but since the land was not formally a reserve, the *Indian Act* did not even apply. Canada had come 180 degrees from 1924, when the RCMP was used to force *Indian Act* elections on Mohawk communities.

In other Canadian Mohawk communities, relations were often grumpy. At Tyendinaga, east of the Bay of Quinte, a dispute in the

1980s over the occupancy of some land on the edge of the reserve was the cause of local friction and a source of worry for the area M.P., Jack Ellis. At the Six Nations reserve, near Brantford, the inadequacy of local regulatory powers held by the band council under the *Indian Act* was a continuing thorn in the community's side, as was the inadequacy of critical infrastructure. These deficiencies were properly laid at the feet of the federal government.[15]

In 1973, the Supreme Court, in the *Calder* judgement, failed to agree that aboriginal rights had been extinguished in Canada. Immediately following this ground-shaking case, the people of Kanesatake undertook the substantial effort of raising a claim to the old Sulpician lands.[16] In January 1975, in conjunction with Kahnawake and Akwesasne, the Kanesatake band filed a comprehensive claim asserting continuing aboriginal title to lands along the St. Lawrence and Ottawa Rivers, including the Sulpician seigneury at Lac des Deux-Montagnes. The claim was rejected by the minister of the day, Judd Buchanan, in May 1975, on the grounds that the Mohawks had not maintained possession of the lands since time immemorial but had occupied the land alternately and concurrently with the Nipissings and the Algonquins. Further, Buchanan said on the advice of the Justice Department, any aboriginal title that may have existed had been extinguished first by the kings of France and second by the British Crown, through the Crown's granting of title to white settlers. But the finality of the Justice Department's dictates bothered the minister, and he offered to negotiate with a view to acquiring lands so that Kanesatake would be a more-or-less contiguous community.

A second claim,[17] filed by the Oka band in 1977, contains extensive legal arguments from U.S., Commonwealth and Canadian jurisprudence concerning aboriginal rights, despite an earlier characterization of the claim as "specific," that is, based on the breaking of post-contact promises and treaties. Aboriginal rights, in contrast, descend from pre-existing occupance "since time immemorial."[18] The federal government again rejected the claim as an aboriginal rights matter, since the Mohawks had not inhabited the area on a continuous basis even during historical times. Rather, they were sporadic inhabitants of territories contested by Nipissings,

Algonquins and others. There is evidence of Iroquois presence in the Oka area in the seventeenth century, but the claimants did not assert that they were the sole or even dominant people there at the time. Likewise, the government rejected the claim as fitting within its specific claims policy, saying that the assertion of broken promises had been dealt with by the Lower Canada ordinance of 1839 and subsequent litigation, culminating in the reluctant decision of the Law Lords in 1912. But the palpable injustice of this (from the federal point of view) necessary legal conclusion was tempered by a recognition that something had to be done. Bill McKnight's rejection letter of October 1986 offered to negotiate a solution with the Kanesatake band. Frank Vieni, the department's regional director-general for Quebec, with the assistance of negotiator Yves Desilets, set to work on a framework agreement on land assembly for the community of Kanesatake.

3

THE DEPARTMENT
OF INDIAN AFFAIRS

THE RELATIONSHIP between Indian communities and the Department of Indian Affairs and Northern Development is something like that between Canadian banks and the Department of Finance. As are banks, reserve life is governed by federal acts and regulations that are often resented by those they affect. The evolution of the rules is slow and only partly driven by the consent of the governed. For the federal government as a whole, the two departments are expected to be, and are, the principal sources of knowledge and policy advice about their respective domains. Both departments view their "subjects" as, in some sense, their creations, and neither department is wholly objective or unconflicted in its view. The realities of life on the ground in Iroquois communities are a product of an odd sort of codependency. And of course, DIAND was a principal player for the federal government in the events of 1990.

In 1987, three years before the Oka summer, DIAND was experiencing a quiet crisis of its own. The department's expenditures seemed always to exceed its estimates, and for reasons that the central agencies—Treasury Board, Finance and the Privy Council Office—understood poorly. After all, this was the only department of the federal government that had national, provincial and municipal responsibilities, and the central agencies had no experience with the latter two. Moreover, the 1982 Charter of Rights and Freedoms was starting to bite in fiscal as well as rights terms. Section 15, for instance, forbade discrimination in a way that meant Indian Affairs could not depart too greatly from provincial funding norms for such non-federal fields as education and welfare without running the risk of a Charter challenge.

Heedless, the Treasury Board imposed tight control—always, for example, approving amounts in estimates that insiders knew would be exceeded by year's end. The standard allowance for inflation rarely kept up with real costs in small and remote communities, and adjustments for population growth never matched the demographics of aboriginal Canada, whose young people were the fastest-growing segment of the whole national population. This ongoing situation meant that conditions could easily be extracted when DIAND came back, cap in hand, in the second half of the year for supplementary estimates.

Micromanagement by central agency bean-counters is not generally conducive to high service quality. In this case, the matter was exacerbated by the response of departmental management, which bought off angry central agents by imposing ever stricter procedures inside the department. When I arrived as deputy minister in September 1987, even small expenditures in districts thousands of miles from Ottawa had to be approved by a cascade of officials up to, and often including, the august assistant deputy minister for Finance and Administration. As this person believed that good government meant minimal expenditure and a perfect paper trail, DIAND in the mid-eighties was characterized by financial constipation.

My predecessor had licensed his ADM Finance and Administration to rule with a whim of iron and permitted little delegation of authority to the three-quarters of the department who were, and are, spread thinly across the vast archipelago sometimes called Indian country. I resolved to turn this process on its head. We set in motion a consultation with all of our staff, asking for their best ideas about how to do what the department was supposed to do in the most brilliant fashion possible. The story is told elsewhere,[1] but one of the early outcomes was a delegation of authority to the field that was the farthest-reaching in the civil service. John Murray, our hand-picked new ADM Finance, and his sidekick, Alan Williams, wrote, and slipped past the Treasury Board hawks, an entirely new and modern way of serving our communities.

Nor was this all that was going on at the time. There was also a great, if largely submerged, debate about what the department was supposed to be. Emerging notions of Indian self-government meant that the close supervision of reserve affairs by old-fashioned Indian agents was no longer appropriate, even if this was what the *Indian Act*—and the central agencies—seemed to demand. Some political voices—irresponsible ones, in my view—including at least one minister of Indian Affairs, said the whole concept of the department was an embarrassing throwback to Victorian days, and that it should simply be abandoned. Some in the department also felt that way, but most people were just confused.

The only vision held out by David Crombie, the first Tory minister of the new Mulroney era in 1984, was for the last person left to shut off the lights. This arresting vision was not shared by his colleagues. The question of what part of the federal government would carry out DIAND's constitutional obligations is overlooked in this simple scenario.

Crombie was suspicious of his department. Many thought that the appointment to Indian Affairs of the popular ex-mayor of Toronto was some sort of joke played by Brian Mulroney on a former contender for the Tory leadership. Whatever the case, Crombie had little experience of rural or Indian life, and he was horrified by what he found. He travelled widely in Indian country, often accompanied by his political staff rather than by departmental officials, scattering promises that the department could not fulfill and, all too often, knew nothing about. When in due course chiefs and councils complained about non-delivery, they naturally did not minimize the extent, cost or precedential nature of Crombie's promises. In his first major cabinet shuffle in 1986, Mulroney replaced Crombie with a much steadier pair of hands, Bill McKnight.

A grain farmer from Wartime, Saskatchewan, McKnight was well suited to the job. He and his wife, Bev, counted Indian people among their friends and neighbours, and they had long been aware of Indian cultural norms and social conditions. They had also fostered Indian children on their farm from time to time. McKnight's respect for others, his sense of humour and his unwillingness to promise what could not be delivered quickly led to his being seen by aboriginal people as a straight-shooter.

On January 30, 1989, McKnight was called to rescue another portfolio in trouble, National Defence, where his experience in aboriginal Canada would serve the government well in the turbulent year and a half to come. His replacement, Pierre H. Cadieux, was a lawyer from Vaudreuil, a riding situated between Kahnawake and Kanesatake. Cadieux was new to cabinet, and like most ministers who walked through the department's doors for the first time, was a deeply surprised human being. But a few months were enough to convert him from dismay to getting his teeth into our challenging files. The same shuffle brought us Kim Campbell and Shirley Martin, an experienced politician from the Niagara peninsula, as ministers of state, or junior ministers. Campbell, from Vancouver, was seen by Mulroney as a rising star. Her assignment to DIAND was explicitly for training: she was instructed to learn about the duties of a cabinet minister from the experienced senior civil servants in the department.[2]

Indian Affairs employed about 5,200 civil servants in 1987. About 22 per cent were self-declared aboriginals,[3] 55 per cent were women, and about 40 per cent—department headquarters was on the Quebec side of the Ottawa River—were francophone. Many had joined because of personal commitment to the advancement of native peoples. Northerners and rural people found the department congenial, as it offered good employment in the remote parts of the country they preferred. All knew that even if DIAND was abolished, a new bureaucracy would be required to transfer resources to and support new Indian governments, and to perform the many land and resource management functions that had nothing to do with aboriginal peoples as such. Thus a disparate, committed and high-spirited group of people were consistently told by their political masters what all knew to be a pack of self-serving lies.

Another curious contradiction: Indian Affairs had the reputation among high-fliers in other departments of being the graveyard of ambition. Good people didn't go there, it was said; the problems were intractable, and bright policy sparks were soon extinguished. Yet, looking around the table at the regular Wednesday breakfast meeting of deputy ministers, I was often struck by how many of them had spent a crucial stage of their service in Indian Affairs. Such pillars of the civil service establishment as Arthur Kroeger, John Tait, Reid Morden, Huguette Labelle and even the Clerk of the Privy Council, Paul Tellier, were graduates. At one point during my tenure as deputy minister, we counted fifteen graduate degrees and two Rhodes scholars among our eleven-person executive committee. At least two members of that group went on to lead other departments. There were many senior officials in Federal-Provincial Relations, the Privy Council Office, Justice and elsewhere for whom working at DIAND had been a formative experience. Only the financial central agencies maintained their innocence.

Initially, my innocence was as one with that of the other economic central agency types. So I took advantage of being a Privy Council Office executive and asked the desk officers there and in Treasury Board for their views on Indian Affairs and the problems I'd likely have to face. This was uncommon, and the officers responded with enthusiasm. PCO's Judy Ferguson, in particular, gave me both a well-considered briefing note and a good conversation. Likewise, I resolved to call on those predecessors as DIAND deputy minister who were still extant. Paul Tellier offered me his views with his usual force and vigour.[4] Arthur Kroeger, Ernest Côté, Bruce Rawson and Gordon Robertson, among the most senior and respected civil servants of the postwar era, were warm and generous with their advice.

The key players in the department the summer of the Oka crisis were Fred Drummie, Ruth Cardinal, Rick Van Loon, Roger Gagnon, Frank Vieni, Vieni's fellow regional directors-general and me. Cardinal was the director-general of Communications. Like many others in Ottawa that summer, she was on holidays when the simmering pot boiled over, and she and her team would work very long hours to counter rumours and get out the facts.

Fred Drummie had been the associate deputy minister of Indian Affairs since February 1984. Trudeau's last appointment before leaving office, Drummie was a wise, experienced and frequently funny number two around whom much of the department's work flowed. The relationship among the two or three order-in-council appointees who head departments is often fraught. There are few good models of how to share responsibility at that level, and many examples of failure. The Privy Council Office nevertheless persisted with the process, since its advantages in smoothing transitions, bringing new senior people up to speed quickly and providing senior service to departments that often—especially in the second Mulroney government—came with fleets of junior ministers, were compelling. My senior by eight years, Fred Drummie could reasonably have expected to succeed to the top job. But the New Brunswick Tories in the cabinet remembered that Drummie had worked for New Brunswick premier Louis Robichaud back in the sixties and assumed that Drummie was therefore a closet Liberal. Under Lowell Murray and Gerry Merrithew, then and later, Drummie never got an independent command. Too bad: it cost them.

Shifts at the deputy minister level are usually swift. Shortly after the completion of the free trade negotiations with the United States in September 1987, a terse press release announced that I would be the new deputy at DIAND, starting the next Monday. In the few days available, the new person has to clear off his or her old desk, meet the new minister and senior staff, get briefed by the Clerk of the Privy Council and the number two about the department and their expectations, and prepare to step into a whirlwind. The department, meanwhile, is full of rumours about the new appointee—Is he or she any good? Nice guy? Anyone ever work with her?—and of people frantically reviewing the briefing books to make sure they are up to date.[5]

Drummie called me at home the night of the press release, welcoming me and promising all assistance in getting up to speed. We had known each other for some years, as is common in the senior ranks of the civil service; we had both been members of the late, lamented Temporary Assignment Pool under noted economist Rod Dobell in the Treasury Board in the 1970s. Within a week of my formal arrival, Fred proposed that we operate as one: that is, that there be one "office of the deputy minister" inhabited by two people, one of whom was slightly more senior and considerably less knowledgeable.

I had been thinking hard about how to manage this relationship, especially as there were two associate deputy ministers in the department. The other was Jacques Gérin, an even more senior figure, who had served a full term as deputy minister of Environment Canada before being cut to pieces by one of the monumentally incompetent ministers of the first Mulroney government, Suzanne Blais-Grenier.[6] It was unstated but clear that Gérin, having been demoted and placed in charge of the Northern Affairs program, was on his way out. (He subsequently had a stellar career as chief executive of one of Canada's largest engineering firms.) In the end, in discussion with both Drummie and Gérin, it was decided that the appearance of equity should give way to reality. Yet for the remaining months of his public service career, Gérin was an unfailing source of wisdom and good cheer.

So Fred Drummie and I embarked on the rarest but potentially most productive of relationships. It wasn't hard for me; after all, I had the rank, and both the department and the system looked to me as top dog. Fred had to swallow his ego and be a faithful partner. For the next five years, we split the job. We did not specialize, in the sense of either one of us taking certain files exclusively. Instead, we split the work as circumstances required, making time to talk to each other several times a day so we both knew what was going on. This arrangement had real advantages. For the most part, Fred and I did not travel together, so there was always a deputy minister at headquarters. Our ministers rarely felt neglected. We could usually field a general when we needed to in the interdepartmental wars (useful when others sent colonels). Holidays were more easily planned. But such an arrangement works only when backgrounds are sufficiently distinct, so that the partners have something to learn from each other. In this respect, the advantage was on my side. Fred's experience, particularly as head of the old Personnel Policy Branch of the Treasury Board, was invaluable. Treasury Board makes the rules civil servants play by and is the only body entitled to break them. Fred's unparallelled knowledge of the administrative system was key to the reputation DIAND later developed for managerial smarts.

Roger Gagnon and Frank Vieni were the two senior francophone officers in the department. Gagnon, assistant deputy minister for self-government, would represent Canada in some of the summer's negotiations and before UN bodies in Geneva. For a man whose emotional attachment to Quebec was stronger than it was to the more abstract idea of Canada, representing the national government in negotiations with Quebec and the Mohawks posed some interesting problems of conscience. Roger and I talked about these from time to time, and when it came to action, he played a straight bat all the way. Frank Vieni headed the department's Quebec office, where his long experience of both Indian politics and the Quebec bureaucracy were invaluable. None of us at headquarters could have made sense of the complicated factions at Kanesatake without Frank's guidance. To him fell a lot of the detail work of the dealings at Oka, including negotiating for the purchase of land.

Fred Drummie and I invented slogans to try to make our new way of doing things memorable. For example, we said we wanted "down and out management." This meant that decisions were to be made as far down the hierarchy, and as far away from Ottawa, as was consistent with the officer involved having the information necessary to make an informed judgement. It meant, in turn, that headquarters staffs had to make sure people in the field were well informed and trained. Distinction in line management became the key to promotion, not just brilliance in writing briefing memos. A corollary was "Don't buy a dog and bark too": in other words, don't assign someone a task and then lean over their shoulder doing it for them. More important was "Everyone a student, everyone a teacher." Even the grandest mandarin had much to learn, and ought to learn it. And no matter how mundane the job, the incumbent had something unique to teach colleagues and an obligation to do so. It was a lot of fun overturning the power relations within the department. At the same time, we made financial management a job for everybody. There were no further ugly surprises at year's end. By 1990, we had won the Treasury Board's gong for best-managed department in the government. This may have said more about the rest of the government than about DIAND, but it was a source of considerable satisfaction to us.

The transformation of the department was not complete by the time of the Oka affair, but it was well underway. In consequence, when the curtain rose, we had a cast of reasonably energized people who knew their jobs. Those who had to step up and manage the crisis full-time could do so confident that the department would not drop a stitch in normal program delivery elsewhere in the country.

ON FEBRUARY 23, 1990, Pierre Cadieux learned the consequences of failing to hold an unreasonable government line on post-secondary education spending in 1989. Suddenly Cadieux was the Solicitor General. In his place was the Honourable Thomas E. Siddon, previously minister of Fisheries and Oceans and Member of Parliament for Delta in his adopted province of British Columbia. We did not consider this good news. We were less than two weeks away from a crucial meeting with the Council for Yukon Indians, a meeting expected to be the capstone on seventeen years of off-and-on-again negotiations over the council's comprehensive land claim. Success would mean the immediate signing of an agreement-in-principle; failure would mean the collapse of the negotiations, perhaps for a very long time, with knock-on consequences for other treaty negotiations. The Indian Affairs minister would have an inescapable role as deal-closer, in the name of the Queen, and the part had to be played to perfection. Siddon, however, had the reputation of a man much taken with his own brilliance. I had watched his performance in Cabinet over several years from my privileged position in the Privy Council Office and had seen little to set him apart as a leader in that rarefied company. His best performance, one that used some of his scientific training, was in negotiating a resolution of competing hydroelectric and fishery interests over the Nechako River salmon run. A former university professor in the demanding field of aero-acoustic engineering, Siddon had once worn his academic robes onto the floor of the House. Mulroney, reacting to the laughter of the members opposite, turned around to see Siddon preening and laughing in his academic finery. Furious, Mulroney hissed at him to leave the chamber and never appear in those robes again.

Siddon at least looked ministerial. Tall and white-haired, he was always ready with a smile and an outstretched hand. The question for us was whether there was any substance behind the politician's grin.

As is customary in cabinet shuffles, the deputy ministerial phones lit up. I called Peter Meyboom, Siddon's deputy in Fisheries, to get a line on the new man. One thing stood out. "In four years with Mr. Siddon," said Peter, "I never once called him by his first name." Meyboom's streak of Dutch Calvinism was obviously running counter-current to a politician's normal desire to be loved. Hmm, I thought, maybe we can use that.

The dynamic of treaty negotiations requires that the day-to-day work be done by a negotiator, in this case the brilliant and eccentric Mike Whittington, under the supervision of a controller and master strategist back in Ottawa, in this instance Rick Van Loon, then the assistant deputy minister for self-government. Years before, Van Loon and Whittington had co-authored a standard text on Canadian political science. (No more astute pairing has been achieved before or since.) Both men were alarmed by the recent turn of events. After a slow start in the portfolio, Cadieux had followed his litigator's instincts to become engaged and enthusiastic over the Yukon negotiation and was thoroughly briefed in the voluminous arcana of its grinding history. Now he was missing in action, replaced by a minister with a reputation, deserved or not, as a lightweight and a popinjay. Seventeen years down the drain...

The first several days of the new minister's term began straightforwardly. There were people to meet, briefings about the business of the department, a new political staff to be settled in, files and memorabilia to be shifted from one office to another. On March 8, I suggested that it was time for a private meeting with Van Loon and Drummie. We met in Siddon's spacious office in the East Block. I opened with a splash of cold water. "Tom," I said, underlining that Siddon wasn't in Fisheries any longer, "you have a week to learn precisely what you must do in Whitehorse. You will take instructions from Van Loon here, who understands more about these matters than you or I ever will. If you don't, you will go down in history as the man who blew the first treaty negotiations since James Bay." Wise or not, my words had the desired effect. Siddon was surprised, to say the least, and sobered to be addressed in so blunt a fashion. But he understood that events, rather than logic or politesse, ruled history, and he set about to learn the file.

The Yukon is a small place, and distant from the centre of things. In 1990, the fourteen bands grouped together under the Council for Yukon Indians banner numbered only 7,000 souls in total, and the whole Yukon, at 28,000 people, had the same population as Penticton, B.C. But since the days of the Klondike gold rush, it has been part of the Canadian soul. The bands were inclined to do a deal, an historic and important one from the viewpoint of federal policy. If agreement could not be reached there, the prospects for more difficult cases would decline enough to call into question the whole of post-Calder policy. So the stakes were high, and officials nervous, as we gathered in Yukon Hall on Saturday, March 17, 1990.

In a room about forty feet on a side, with dozens of Indian men, women and children lining the walls, Siddon and his officials occupied one side of a hollow square of tables and the chiefs the other three. The body language was not promising. Grim-looking Indian men leaned against the wall, arms crossed. The minister sat flanked by Whittington and me. Facing us were fourteen chiefs and Elijah Smith, the universally respected Yukon elder who had led the CYI through all its years of struggle.

There were five issues left to be settled, for each of which the new minister had been provided with the final, and expected, federal position. "I don't care what else you say," Van Loon had told Siddon in briefings, "but you have to say the specific words—the bottom line—from your briefing book."

Siddon began the meeting by asking Smith to say a prayer, a courtesy in Indian country not always observed by white visitors. The Indians had prepared well. For each of the five issues they chose one of their best speakers. Each spoke movingly to the CYI position for five minutes. Siddon, somewhat to our surprise, made no wisecracks or comments. He took notes, like a good university student. The speeches continued. Finally it was Elijah Smith's turn to sum up.

"Well, Minister," he said, "I guess we'll see what you're made of. I've been at these negotiations for eighteen years now, and you're the twenty-second minister I've seen." An appreciative chuckle went round the room. Everyone knew a master orator was just warming up. "Now, Minister," Smith said, "I've been reading the newspaper, and I see Canada has just forgiven the debt of some small Caribbean countries a long, long way away. A hundred and eighty-two million dollars, it said. So how is it you want to charge some Canadians thirty-five million dollars for negotiating costs—just for standing up for their rights?" There was more—all brilliantly put, all unassailable.

Finally it was Siddon's turn. Instead of making a speech himself, he looked closely at his notes and then started around the room. To each of the speakers, his message was the same. "Chief," he would say, "if I understood you correctly, you said that..." After summarizing the chief's argument, Siddon would regretfully conclude that he had come to the end of his negotiating space on that issue, offer a minor final concession, then turn to the next speaker. The atmosphere in the room started to shift. As Siddon addressed each chief, showing that he had heard and understood the argument before regretfully but conclusively stating the expected final federal position, the body language in the room began to change. Scowls changed to puzzlement, then smiles. Folded arms unfolded. People slouched against the wall began to lean forward so as not to miss a word. The deal was done, and the final price was paid in the coin of respect, the most important currency of all.

Nobody had briefed Tom Siddon to take this approach. He carried the day on his own, and from then on, we knew we had a winner on our side.

4

ANARCHY AT AKWESASNE: THE MOHAWK CIVIL WAR

By Christmas the Commissioners had drawn all but one section of the line. They made numerous trade-offs along the way. Barclay [the British commissioner] conceded the Long Sault islands near Cornwall, and the Americans compensated by giving up the strategically important Grand Isle, later named Wolfe Island at the head of the St. Lawrence.

The loss of the Long Sault islands angered a group of businessmen from the eastern district of Upper Canada who published a letter criticizing Barclay and Thompson. The commissioner responded by noting that the islands in question were notorious as 'the principal depots for smuggling along the whole Frontier.'[1]

AKWESASNE IS a geographer's delight and a police officer's nightmare. Straddling the Canada–U.S. boundary as it does just south of Cornwall, with its Canadian side cut off from the rest of the country by the mighty St. Lawrence and split between Ontario and Quebec, and the Canadian parts connected only by water, it appears divinely designed for smuggling.

As in other Mohawk communities, authority at Akwesasne was split as the 1990s dawned. There was a traditionalist Longhouse, led by the Mohawk Nation Council of Chiefs and aligned with the Confederacy in Ohsweken on the Six Nations reserve in southern Ontario, and there were elected councils on both sides of the border, the St. Regis Mohawk Tribal Council on the American side and the Mohawk Council of Akwesasne in Canada. Since 1979 there had also been a "Tri-Council," a body through which the two elected governments tried to coordinate their policies and actions. Separate U.S. and Canadian entities were necessary as receptacles for federal funding and, in the case of the St. Regis council, relations with the state of New York. The existence of the elected councils seemed to contradict the view of the Confederacy as a continuing sovereignty that did not recognize the imposition of extraterritorial power on Iroquois lands. But in this, as in other ways, was Mohawk pragmatism expressed.

Akwesasne had suffered the same fate as Kahnawake in losing land to the St. Lawrence Seaway in the late 1950s. It also experienced some special problems with the construction of large plants by General Motors, Reynolds Aluminum and Alcoa immediately upstream. These plants grossly polluted the shorelines, the Raquette River and local groundwater with polychlorinated biphenyls, aluminum and other industrial wastes. Fishing and hunting no longer produced edible food. Ducks turned up with 300 parts per billion of PCBs in their systems, and crops, pastures and garden vegetables were rendered unsafe by airborne industrial waste. The activities that had once produced modest incomes and wholesome local food all but disappeared. The problem of gaining an adequate income, never easy on Indian reserves, worsened through the 1960s and 1970s.

In May 1979, longstanding ill feelings between traditionalists and those supporting the elected Mohawk governments boiled over.[2] A land ownership dispute on the U.S. side led to a "spontaneous" attack on a police post. The Mohawk Nation people, led by Loran Thompson, felt that the New York State and tribal police forces were illegally occupying Confederacy land. After the raid, "the Mohawk Nation built a makeshift fortress on Raquette Point. They built at least six bunkers and added two large meeting halls to the homes in the area."[3] The traditionalists called for recognition of the St. Regis reservation as a sovereign territory whose economy would be based on agriculture, not government grants. A relatively gentle police siege went on for more than a year, with occasional confrontations and symbolic gunfire. The Mohawk Nation's core membership, about 70 people, had sympathizers in the broader community, but even by their own claims that group was never more than 1,035 of about 10,000 people living in Akwesasne at the time. One of their lawyers was William M. Kunstler, renowned for his support of radical causes in the U.S.

Modern Indian radicalism, if it can be said to have a single starting point, began with the founding of the American Indian Movement in the slums of Minneapolis in 1968 by Dennis Banks and George Mitchell.[4] AIM and the incendiary teachings of Louis Hall led swiftly to a resurrection of the Warrior ethos in Iroquois country. Under the Great Law, all Iroquois men constitute a kind of citizen militia, always on the lookout for danger and liable to be summoned for protective duties in times of trouble. Such Warrior Societies traditionally operated only under the authority of the Confederacy. Each community would normally have a War Chief, whose powers were mostly latent but could be greatly expanded in times of emergency. In 1990, the War Chief at St. Regis was Francis Boots, but he operated without Confederacy sanction.

In fact, Boots and others associated with smuggling and gambling were denounced in a remarkable statement by the Mohawk Nation Council of Chiefs in January 1990, a document that was widely noted, and one that I forwarded to Indian Affairs Minister Pierre Cadieux and his junior minister Kim Campbell.[5] Referring to the Mohawk Sovereignty Security Force (the Akwesasne local of the Warrior Society) and the Mohawk Nation Office at Kahnawake, the chiefs said that the Haudenosaunee had denied these groups official status, on the grounds that both organizations were "characterized by violence, hatred and greed." The statement named a number of individuals active in gambling and smuggling at Akwesasne (who turned up later as leaders and militants at Kanesatake), noting that they were former Longhouse adherents gone bad. "We confirm the decision made by our brothers at Ohsweken in August of 1988 that those individuals who persist in illegal activities such as smuggling and illegal gambling put themselves outside the sacred Covenant Circle and leave themselves open to the laws of a foreign nation."

In the case of one of these "foreign nations," court judgements based on precedents running back to Chief Justice Marshall's U.S. Supreme Court decisions had stimulated congressional action. When the Seminoles of Florida set up gaming outside the rules established by the state, they were stopped by local police. The ensuing lawsuit led, after a lengthy journey through the courts, to a landmark decision of the Fifth Circuit of the U.S. Court of Appeals.[6] The blunt and broad decision of both the lower court and the Court of Appeals was that state regulatory power could not be enforced against an Indian tribe. The decision flowed from an earlier Minnesota case in which the U.S. Supreme Court had said that the state could not impose property taxes on an Indian reservation.[7] In general, only the U.S. federal government could legislate in those areas. Only if a state made the matter criminal and general would its laws hold. The principle was affirmed in a separate U.S. Supreme Court decision in 1987.[8] Congress, its hand forced by the court decisions and continuing controversy, enacted the *Indian Gaming Regulatory Act* in 1988. Its purpose was to encourage economic development and strong tribal government while protecting Indian gaming from criminal influences, but it bowed to strong representations from the states in saying that the ensuing regulatory regime had to operate within the framework of a state-tribal compact. According to a U.S. tribal source, "States lobbied vigorously for IGRA and for the compacting provisions over tribal objections. IGRA requires tribes to negotiate with states concerning games to be played and regulation while it ensures that tribal governments are the sole owners and primary beneficiaries of gaming."[9] In fact, states did not easily accept the necessity of negotiating as equals with other sovereign groups and demanded revenue sharing and other concessions as the price for compacts. IGRA, which was intended to settle matters, became instead the field on which lobbyists and favour-seekers sold friends and enemies for advantage. The prize was worthwhile. The Indian gaming industry grew to astounding proportions: from an estimated legal gross revenue of $100 million in 1985 to $16.7 billion in 2005.[10]

Of course, the Mohawks had not waited for IGRA. In the mid-1970s, Mohawk entrepreneurs began selling tax-free cigarettes and gasoline to Mohawks on the St. Regis reservation. Meeting little official opposition, they expanded their market to non-aboriginals living nearby. The idea of tax arbitrage between reservation and non-Indian lands began to take root. In Congress and in state legislatures, people saw this as not that bad an idea: conservatives thought it might reduce the welfare bill, and liberals believed it could endow the tribes with own-source incomes. In the early 1980s, the U.S. federal government started to take the view that the establishment of casinos on Indian land could be a route to economic development. Moreover, it was a route Washington and the states could regulate and profit from—if not through direct taxation of the establishments or of Indian incomes, there would be a fiscal benefit through an easing of welfare costs. According to Rick Hornung, a journalist later invited to St. Regis by the gambling faction to tell their story, "The United States government encouraged its aboriginal populations to buy a piece of the American dream by developing high-stakes bingo parlours and casinos designed to attract large amounts of white money."[11] In 1983, five years before IGRA, the St. Regis Tribal Council licensed its first high-stakes bingo operation.

Doug George, an anti-gambling traditionalist, also went on to produce a book about the events. According to George (later George-Kanentiio), "In the spring of 1984 the new economy was brought to Akwesasne in a plain black Chevrolet van driven by Philip Deering, a resident of the Mohawk community of Kahnawake... Mr. Deering was accompanied by Thomas Delaronde, one of the leaders of the Ganienkeh community... The residents there were looking for a way to make an income, with bingo and tobacco having great appeal."[12] Deering and Delaronde were members of the U.S.-based Iroquois Land Rights Committee, which had held discussions in a number of communities regarding the improvement of the

Iroquois situation through land claims and novel economic activities. They were seeking the approval of Doug George, editor of the influential *Akwesasne Notes* and the community's main newspaper, *Indian Time.*

The issue proceeded upward in leisurely traditional fashion. A year later, the Grand Council of the Haudenosaunee established a trade and commerce commission that would, among other things, establish rules governing tobacco and gasoline sales, as well as gambling operations, so that these activities would benefit the communities financially and not result in great concentrations of wealth. But opportunity waits for no council. By then a number of members of the Iroquois Land Rights Committee were already in business, and, as George-Kanentiio writes, "not about to subject the sources of this newfound wealth to any external government, including their own."[13] By the spring of 1986, with the horse well out of the barn, the two elected councils drafted common policies to govern the new activities, which were already dominating the economic life of Akwesasne. These policies too were ignored. By 1989, seven bingos and casinos were operating without agreement from either the Mohawk Nation Council or the state government. Law enforcement agencies knew well the efficiency of such enterprises for laundering money from businesses that were even more unsavoury, but enforcement languished in the absence of clear political will established in statute.

New divisions in the community began to cross-cut the existing fissures in religion and governance. Some Mohawks, often followers of Handsome Lake, saw gambling, but not necessarily smuggling, as against the Great Law. Some saw the movement of goods across the border not as smuggling but as an aboriginal right. Others, basing themselves on the Great Law, saw both gambling and smuggling as prohibited under traditional law. Some people saw all such businesses as wonderful opportunities, free from competition, since the police forces could be counted on to suppress them outside Mohawk territory. Opponents foresaw only trouble from taunting the authorities and from endorsing the growth of concentrated, dubiously legal wealth, as well as connections to shady people from Las Vegas and Miami, in weakly governed communities. People holding all of these views could be found in each of the governing organizations, though of course they were not evenly distributed among them. Those benefiting from large flows of new income were quick to argue the righteousness of their conduct and to find laudatory references in traditional teachings. They were also quick to denounce the cautious and law-abiding as collaborators and "apples"—red on the outside, white on the inside. A fractured community became even more fractious once lubricated with money.

In these early years, the mid-1980s, the issue was principally high-stakes bingo and, slightly later, casino gambling. New bingo halls sprang up along Highway 37, which ran through the south end of St. Regis, and busloads of tourists, some from Montreal, were brought in to engage in a little voluntary taxation. The owners of these enterprises, rightly thinking their properties might be in danger from affronted community members, hired tough young Mohawk men to protect them. These underemployed young men, many with training in high steel or the U.S. military, wanted to think well of themselves: they were not just thugs, bouncers and bodyguards, they were freedom fighters. Borrowing liberally from Iroquois tradition, they styled themselves as the Mohawk Sovereignty Security Force, or, informally, as the Akwesasne Warrior Society. Their task, as they saw it, was to protect the community from outside forces—whether the community liked it or not. In practice, they became mercenaries for Tony Laughing and other casino owners, and in short order an independent political force on the reservation.

The combination of intimidation and assertions of effective self-policing was mostly successful. The New York State Police rarely went on to the St. Regis reservation, and then only in brief raids, in great force. As for smuggling across the St. Lawrence, both the RCMP and the Ontario Provincial Police (OPP) were unconvinced that popular opinion would support vigorous efforts against "victimless crime," so they paid it little attention. Anyway, enforcement would mean coordinated effort on both sides of the border, since the Canadian and U.S. forces had to stop at the line. This involved planning, communications and inevitably leaks. Enforcement rarely worked.

The Mohawk entrepreneurs who ran the gambling business soon discovered that even more money could be made by taking advantage of Akwesasne's unique geography. The taxes on Canadian cigarettes were much higher than on those in the U.S., due in no small measure to a well-organized anti-smoking lobby in Canada. Health advocates saw ever-higher taxes as the strongest weapon in their armoury, and at budget time successive ministers of Finance could be counted on to see sin taxes as the least unpopular way of raising cash. By the late 1980s, a Canadian carton often cost more than three times as much as one in the U.S. A small trade in excise stamp-free U.S. cigarettes had existed for some time, but its prospects were limited by Canadians' different tastes in tobacco. In 1985–86, someone had a brainwave: why not export tax-free cigarettes from Canada and smuggle them back?

According to RCMP intelligence, the big Canadian tobacco companies, all headquartered in Montreal, began to ship large quantities of unstamped cigarettes to addresses of convenience set up in northern New York by the Buffalo Mafia.[14] This organization wanted mules to ship the contraband back to their cousins in Montreal, and they approached the casino owners and their bought-and-paid-for Warriors. The Mohawks, through gambling, now had sufficient capital to insist on being principals rather than mere smugglers for hire, and soon the St. Lawrence was buzzing with Donzis—cigarette boats!—whisking cases of smokes to anonymous semis waiting on the Canadian side, or sometimes all the way down to Kahnawake.

Montreal is not a city so impoverished that it has but one criminal organization. While the Mafia had close connections with many of the *dépanneurs* in the metropolitan Montreal area, so did other criminal organizations. Vietnamese gangs, for one, had their own distribution networks, and these often extended to metropolitan areas hundreds of miles away. Others, like the biker gangs, were more interested in drugs and especially weapons. Their struggles for market share were not as well regulated internally as those of the ethnicity-based organizations.

On the U.S. side, the Akwesasne Warriors had become very well armed indeed. Though New York State regulates arms, enforcement is more assiduous in the downstate areas. And of course, state regulation is bounded by the famous provision of the U.S. constitution that guarantees the right to bear arms. There is no such right in Canada, where sporting arms are heavily regulated and personal ownership of pistols, revolvers, automatics and assault weapons is all but forbidden. What more could an unarmed Hell's Angel or Rock Machine member want? And so to the high-volume movement of cigarettes was added a low-volume but lucrative trade in small arms. The Asian gangs, not just the Vietnamese, also had special concerns. Many of their countryfolk wished to enter the United States informally, and a small volume of people going south joined the manifests. Some liquor, too, though dollar for dollar it was a lot heavier than cigarettes.

The fight about border crossing rights would be brought to a head by Grand Chief Mike Mitchell (Kanentakeron) of the Canadian elected council at Akwesasne in a case that started on March 13, 1988, and thirteen years later, after wins in the federal court's trial and appeal divisions, resulted in an adverse judgement of the Supreme Court of Canada.[15] Mitchell, warning authorities beforehand, had brought a truckload of blankets, bibles, motor oil, food, clothing and a washing machine into Canada. The goods were for the most part intended as gifts to the Mohawks of Tyendinaga. Canada Customs told Chief Mitchell he would be charged $142.88 in duty and let him pass. In discussing the case with me, Mitchell argued principally that his right to transport goods without interference was founded on the recognition of aboriginal rights in the Jay Treaty of 1794.

This treaty between Britain and the United States, an example of the kind of eighteenth-century agreement commonly made to wrap up wars and allow the combatants to get back to making money, acknowledged the right of Indians to freely pass and re-pass the new boundary with their goods "not in bales." I have always agreed with those who feel that these treaties were abrogated by subsequent wars and agreements, and the Treaty of Ghent of 1815, which ended the War of 1812, was nowhere near as generous to Indians.[16] No matter: the case was ultimately decided on aboriginal rather than treaty rights. The Supreme Court found that there was "negligible transportation and trade of goods by the Mohawks north of the St. Lawrence River prior to contact. This trade was not vital to the Mohawks' collective identity."[17] Therefore, the court said, there was no aboriginal right. In addition, a minority concurring opinion by Justices Major and Binnie took an interesting new look at the old theory of the two-row wampum, saying that the purpose of Section 35(1) of the Charter was to bring about a reconciliation of the interests of aboriginal peoples with Canadian sovereignty, not the entrenchment of separation.[18] There was confusion about Jay Treaty rights during the events of 1990, however, as the court of first instance did not render judgement until 1997. Even in 2001, the Supreme Court did not directly attack Chief Mitchell's assertion that his citizenship was "not of Canada but of the Haudenosaunee (Iroquois) Confederacy with its capital in Onondaga, New York State."[19]

BY THE FALL of 1987, staff in the Department of Indian Affairs had begun to hear stories about smuggling and gambling at Akwesasne. Gambling was confined to St. Regis, the U.S. half, and was not our direct concern. But gambling had divided the community and rendered ineffective the authority of the band council on the Canadian side. DIAND was worried that gambling and smuggling involved some of the same people and that the rapid accumulation of tens of millions of dollars in the hands of a few U.S.-based entrepreneurs might have a divisive and radicalizing effect on the community. Stories of the circular trade in Canadian cigarettes and the rise of gambling entrepreneurs came from Mohawks in the affected communities who were aghast at what they saw as the corruption of their young men and the rise of powerful criminal organizations in their communities. These stories were relayed to us by field officers in both the Ontario and the Quebec regions of the department, and occasionally recounted directly to senior officers. It is no secret that most Indian people are strongly conflicted in what they think of the Department of Indian Affairs. For some it is the hated personification of colonialism and deracination. For others it is an instrument, however imperfect, for helping Indian communities. People who would never talk to the police sometimes talk to the department.

There was even, according to stories we heard from Mohawk sources, a small movement of people being smuggled north, notably Miskito refugees from the U.S. war against the Nicaraguan Sandinistas. This last piece of information has a quality of urban myth about it, but it was cited with pride by more than one Warrior as proof that not all of their work was mercenary and illegal. A modern underground railroad, saving innocent people from the horrors of the U.S.'s Central American puppets! What could appeal more to the muddle-headed north of the border?

The persistence, detail and multiple sources of these stories were worrisome. They were mixed with stories of the rise of the Mohawk Warriors, an organization of militant but underemployed young men, some with training in the U.S. armed forces, who had acquired guns, ammunition, and a deep belief in the continuing independence of the Mohawk nation and their duty to defend it. Some of these young men were working as mules smuggling cigarettes across the river; others protected the casinos in St. Regis from the incursion of "foreign" New York State police. In 1987 DIAND had also been told of a 1979 raid on an Army National Guard armoury in Ohio that resulted in the theft of many M-16 rifles and large quantities of distinctive .223 "zipper" ammunition, though the story is still uncorroborated. I discussed all of these rumours with the minister, Bill McKnight, and with his successor, Pierre Cadieux.

Around the same time, Fred Drummie and I decided we ought to make the acquaintance of the newly appointed commissioner of the RCMP, Norman Inkster. Given the uncertainties of the day, we thought it would be useful to have some sort of personal relation with the head of Canada's national police force. So, through his office, we invited Inkster to lunch at a downtown Ottawa restaurant. No agenda, we said, just a chance to get acquainted. Relations between cops and bureaucrats are traditionally distant and infrequent, and neither Inkster nor any of his people knew us. Somewhat suspicious, he turned up for what we had intended as an under-the-radar lunch in full blue uniform. As he was well over six feet, with a military moustache under the brim of his polished visor, Inkster made quite an impression on the quiet little Queen Street eatery.

The pace of rumour—police intelligence sometimes falls under this rubric—increased as 1988 progressed. There was the Ohio National Guard story. Rumour had it that at the core of the Warriors were mature men radicalized by contact with the American Indian Movement, expert in the use of small arms and booby traps through their training in the most macho of the U.S. forces, the Marines. There were kernels of truth in all of this, but also a great deal of over-egging. Post-Oka writings by Mohawks and others have offered a more nuanced view.[20]

By mid-1989 official Ottawa was paying attention to Akwesasne. Several departments besides Indian Affairs were by then aware of the large-scale tobacco smuggling and the well-armed nature of the smugglers. On September 5, for instance, I attended a meeting at the Privy Council Office that included two assistant commissioners of the RCMP, the Deputy Solicitor General and an ADM from External Affairs. The RCMP reported that, over the weekend, traditionalists had overturned and burned a Warrior car full of cigarettes, and said the OPP would assist the Akwesasne police if things got out of hand on the Canadian side. The New York State Police were reportedly ready to enter the reservation only in the case of a shooting. The RCMP were preparing to take over the Canada Customs post should the Customs union down tools. But the Mounties' bottom line was "Should we lose men to enforce the *Customs Act*?"[21]

The minister, Pierre Cadieux, had a hunch the cigarette trade that tied Akwesasne to Kahnawake and, to a degree, to Kanesatake might escalate into "something bad." He and his political assistant, Dick Labelle, spent a lot of time on the issue, "trying hard to find a solution to the leadership problem" as a prologue to settling things

down, but Cadieux was moved to the Solicitor General's portfolio the following February in a shuffle that "did not anticipate the
summer!"[22]

The descent of Akwesasne into anarchy has been examined in
detail, though no published account pays much attention to the role
of the government, police or armed forces of Canada. Each of the
three principal authors takes a different slant.[23] Hornung's perspective is sympathetic to the Warriors and their gambler godfathers.
Professor Johansen's leans to the anti-gambling factions. George-
Kanentiio, the only Mohawk and Akwesasne resident among the
three, was so vocal in his anti-gambling stance that his views, published in *Indian Times,* attracted violence toward him and his family. (George-Kanentiio's general history of Akwesasne is the best
in print, though he is inaccurate on some details of the momen-
tous spring of 1990.) In brief, arguments became insults; insults
led to pushing and shoving, which escalated to rock-throwing
and destruction of vehicles, and then to gunfire and arson. Road
blockades sprang up around the casinos on the St. Regis side. The
New York State Police would not intervene, and the authority of
the Mohawk police was undermined when it became clear that the
Warriors outgunned them considerably and moreover appeared
willing to engage in gunplay, beatings and arson. By early 1990, law
and order at Akwasasne had more or less broken down. By the time
barricades went up on March 23, two to three thousand people had
evacuated the community.

It must be said that none of this social breakdown could have
happened without a vigorous demand side to the illegal trade. As
Akwesasne descended into horror, the blue-rinse bingo babes still
arrived by bus from Montreal, Ottawa and upper New York State,
and Canadian consumers still bought cheap cigarettes at reserve
smoke shops and off-reserve convenience stores. Had cigarettes
been classified as addictive drugs, the U.S. might have gone after
the suppliers, but the U.S. government has never concerned itself
much with the buyers of drugs, even when they are American citizens, preferring to make war on suppliers in distant lands. Canadian police, unsure if there was any popular support for enforcing

the law, failed to do so. At least the OPP and the Sûreté du Québec (SQ) could argue that the law in question, the *Customs Act*, was federal. The RCMP had no such excuse.

In a narrowly contested election in 1989, the Mohawk Nation Council's three chiefs on the U.S. side had become two-thirds pro-gambling. Although Harold Tarbell, the anti-gambling chairman, was re-elected, he lost control. Feelings among the pro- and anti-gambling factions hardened. On March 23, 1990, the anti-gambling group set up four road barricades. The gambling entrepreneurs and their Mohawk Sovereignty Security Force (MSSF) goons reacted with gunfire and arson, and soon there were only two barricades remaining. Those barricades, however, were strategically located across Highway 37, at either end of the gambling strip, and they were continuously manned. The customers were cut off. The challenged Warriors found themselves siding with the New York State Police, whose duty it was to keep the public highway open. Considerable intimidation by the anti-gambling faction, as well as rose-tinted thinking in Albany, was required to keep the state police from taking down the barricades. George-Kanentiio quotes from logs that were kept at the barricades:

March 24: Warriors smash state trooper windshield

March 24: Warrior shoots at Nation chief's home

March 25: Radio CKON receives threat of arson

March 26: Warriors shoot at antigambler gas stations, fuel tanks, and at building with young people inside

March 26: Warriors drop off fake bomb at Akwesasne Police station

March 26: Warriors fire assault weapons at the people

March 28: Warriors plant bomb on school bus

March 31: Warriors throw Molotov cocktails at Methodist church... [and] at Mohawk Council of Akwesasne administration building...

April 9: Warriors shoot at New York State Police

April 12: Warriors ram Akwesasne Police cruiser

April 14: Warriors issue hit list of over 200 Mohawks...

April 19: Warrior gunfire injures woman at barricade[24]

Eventually, conditions became so unbearable that a truce was called, and male members of both factions met. A long and emotional discussion took place. Both sides realized all too acutely that their "enemies" were brothers and cousins, aunts and mothers. In the end, the two factions decided to put their concerns before the community, and in the meantime lay down their arms and disband the MSSF. The gambling issue would be set aside until peace came to the community. Although the MSSF men had to take the agreement to their leadership, they were confident that war had been averted. Their confidence was ill placed, however. According to Doug George-Kanentiio,

> Many of the men decided to stay at the meeting hall to await the approval of the peace plan by the MSSF leaders. They were taken by surprise when they received word that not only was the peace offering rejected, but it was outright condemned with the vilest · of profanities. The MSSF leaders were outraged that their members, the men whom they had paid, armed, and drugged, were making decisions that could well affect their casino and smuggling operations without their consent.[25]

By April 1990, peace, order and good government had disappeared from both sides of Akwesasne. Armed gangs lit up the nights with gunfire and arson. Postal service stopped. Businesses closed. School boards would not let their bus drivers go on reserve. Roads were barricaded. More people fled, leaving their homes to looters. As conditions worsened, both elected councils appealed for help. Chief Harold Tarbell of the St. Regis Tribal Council pleaded with Governor Mario Cuomo to send in the National Guard, as did Tom Siddon, by now the Canadian minister of Indian Affairs and Northern Development. On April 25, all three councils urgently requested law enforcement help from Major General L.P. Flynn, commander of the New York Division of Military and Naval Affairs. Three days later, on April 28, Cuomo, who had been occupied in drafting legislation to bring St. Regis gambling under New York authority, finally gave in. On the Canadian side, Grand Chief Mike Mitchell appealed to Tom Siddon and to Prime Minister Brian

Mulroney for similar help. The RCMP and the Canadian Forces immediately began contingency planning.

At DIAND, we met all day April 25 with officers who knew the land and the issues and with our ministers.[26] Tom Siddon and Shirley Martin, minister of state for DIAND, worried about public communications and about whether Georges Erasmus, national chief of the Assembly of First Nations, or Harry LaForme of the Indian Commission of Ontario, might issue helpful statements. A planned session with Ken Hughes's Standing Committee on Aboriginal Affairs was postponed in order to make time for meetings with Chief Mitchell and Chief Erasmus. A source in the Chiefs of Ontario office provided warnings that the Mohawks had all the RCMP frequencies and were monitoring unencrypted transmissions, and that there was a tentative plan by the Warriors to seize the Customs port at the International Bridge at Akwesasne. Chief Mitchell provided us with a detailed situation report from Akwesasne: 2,000 people were trapped there, and some were missing; outside police forces had informed community leaders that they would help only with emergencies and the RCMP would only assist the provincial forces should they request help; twenty vehicles had been destroyed; the tribal police were boxed in at St. Regis; and there was heavy fire from machine guns, automatic weapons and grenades.

I called Mark Krasnick, the head of the Ontario Native Affairs Secretariat, to make sure we were all working along the same lines; he repeated the rumour that the Warriors were planning to seize the Customs port. Likewise, I spoke to Canada's ambassador in Washington, Derek Burney, to see what pressure could be applied on the U.S. side to stop the shooting. Shirley Martin called Ian Scott, attorney general of Ontario, and Sam Elkas, public security minister in Quebec, to encourage a more active peacekeeping role by the provincial police forces. At the Privy Council Office, Ward Elcock was gaming options for the involvement of the Canadian Forces, rules of engagement, and command.

On April 26, the prime minister formally instructed the Canadian Forces to prepare to assist the three Canadian police forces: the Ontario Provincial Police, the Sûreté du Québec and the RCMP. The critical assumptions regarding the role of the forces were that they would assist the law enforcement agencies with equipment and logistics and help with any evacuations that might become necessary. Two DIAND officers, Gordon Shanks and Mike Phillips, had been on the spot since 1:45 that morning, helping to coordinate assistance among the federal agencies and Akwesasne Mohawks. One of those efforts, with help from House Leader Don Boudria, had been the opening of the residential facilities at the Transport Canada Training Institute in Cornwall for Mohawk refugees. Operating out of the local marina office, staff also rented space for refugees in local motels. Gerry Kerr, DIAND's regional director-general in Toronto, faxed a letter to the city of Cornwall guaranteeing payment of emergency expenses. Later that day, according to my notes from the time, Shanks and Phillips reported, "Nothing last night—Warriors don't work in the rain!"[27]

Tom Siddon and I met with Joe Clark (External Affairs), Don Boudria, Pierre Cadieux (now Solicitor General) and Don Mazankowski (deputy prime minister). Clark was excited: "This would never happen in Western Canada!" He felt it was useful to involve the U.S. The last thing we wanted to do, by inaction, was to invite the United Nations to meddle, so Clark was tasked with turning up the heat in Washington and Albany, and he promised a response within the hour. Mazankowski asked Cadieux to coordinate the efforts of the RCMP and the SQ. Ward Elcock at the Privy Council Office became the operational coordinator for all of us. At CFB Petawawa, RCMP Emergency Response Teams began familiarizing themselves with the army's light armoured vehicles, armoured personnel carriers and communications equipment. Unheard in the background, except in DIAND, was the granting of an injunction by the Superior Court in St.-Jérôme, Quebec, to the town of Oka regarding a minor barricade on a dirt road in a pine forest.

On April 27, elements of the Second Combat Engineering Regiment, based at Petawawa—and fliers from 450 Squadron at Ottawa—gathered in Cornwall in civilian clothes to do a detailed reconnaissance of the Canadian side of the community. The forces' Special Investigations Unit worked on resource requirements. The day before, the prime minister had confidentially ordered Bill McKnight, as minister of National Defence, "to prepare contingency

plans to support operations by the RCMP, OPP and SQ."[28] Fording
sites for armoured personnel carriers and landing sites for helicopters were identified. Overhead, CF-5s took air photos and the U.S.
deployed its "national technical means": satellite and air imagery.
The police intelligence summary on April 28 identified the number
of Warriors as varying day to day from between 300 and 500 men,
many of whom had U.S. Marine Corps or Vietnam experience. They
were armed with grenades; AK-47, AR-15 and M-16 assault rifles;
9mm Uzis; and miscellaneous shotguns and revolvers. The Warriors
were estimated to have 125,000 rounds of ammunition for these
weapons and had been shooting off 600 to 800 rounds per day.
According to police intelligence, they also had two .50 cal heavy
machine guns, an M-72 light anti-tank weapon and high-quality
communications gear, including the capacity to jam police and
army frequencies. In addition, the Warriors had two 265 hp speed-
boats, in a nice touch named *Pride* and *Joy*.

By April 30, the Department of National Defence had worked
out contingency plans should they be called on to assist the police
forces. When the five forces—RCMP, SQ, OPP, NYSP and FBI—met
that day, Canadian military involvement was still seen as unlikely.
But that night all hell broke loose. There was a nine-hour gun
battle centering around the house of David George, Doug George-
Kanentiio's brother. Arson was committed on several homes, and
an RCMP patrol boat took rifle fire from a speedboat.

George-Kanentiio's account of events is riveting. His brother
Davey had built a home on the Canadian side of the line in Snye,
backing on the river. The Warriors decided to take the house,
declaring their intention to kill its occupants if necessary. Eleven,
later thirteen, of Davey's brothers and friends gathered under the
command of Richard "Cartoon" Alford, a seasoned AIM member who had been at Wounded Knee in 1973 and had a good deal
of other experience with armed opponents. Cartoon set up fields of
fire and directed his small platoon against fire from a much larger
force just on the other side of the Canada-U.S. line. The result was
the biggest gun battle in Canada since the Riel Rebellion—and one
that succeeded in repelling an invading militia for the first time

since 1814. The defence led by Cartoon, plus the surreptitious arrival of the former chief of the Akwesasne Police, Ernie King, with fresh ammunition, turned the tide, but not before the deaths of two men. Mathew Pyke was one of a large group bringing relief to the George house on May 1 when he was mortally wounded by a shot in the back. The Warriors delayed the ambulance that was to take him off-reservation, possibly contributing to his death. Harold "Junior" Edwards was killed at about the same time, probably on the U.S. side of the line, but his body was deposited up the road from the George house, on the Canadian side. No one has ever been charged with these deaths.[29]

The Canadian Army's role at Akwesasne was partly reconnaissance but mostly logistic support for the Canadian—and sometimes American—police forces. Besides specialized vehicles and communications gear, the army brought in a field kitchen that served "four meals every 24 hours to as many as 200 members of the QPF, RCMP and some New York state troopers—a colourful presence in their purple ties, Smokey-the-Bear hats and mirrored sunglasses."[30] Army personnel prepared medical facilities for the worst possible scenarios but were thankful to have to deal with only minor injuries. One-third of their cases involved poison ivy.[31]

At DIAND we monitored developments hourly, making sure our field officers had any resources they needed, including delegated authority to make necessary decisions and expenditures on the spot. On the evening of May 1, a hundred state troopers entered Akwesasne, with no resistance from the shocked community, and stopped traffic, seized all the firearms they could find and closed the seaway bridge until 5:00 the next morning, when it was light enough to see what was happening. The four police forces, not including the FBI, worked together with little regard for the international border. At half past midnight on May 2, twenty-six SQ and ten RCMP officers entered Akwesasne from Dundee, Quebec, and another thirty SQ and twenty RCMP officers entered from Cornwall. The RCMP opened the Akwesasne Police Force station. The officers there were relieved by fifty SQ and twenty RCMP officers wearing "soft hats"—i.e., not riot gear—at 8:00 AM. Canadian Forces logistical support at that point consisted of sixteen armoured personnel carriers double-manned at the Cornwall armoury, two ten-passenger helicopters (one medevac-equipped), secure jeep-mounted communications equipment, a light vehicle ferry and the field kitchen. By the end of the day, 425 police officers from four forces—not including the Akwesasne Indian police force, which was in complete disarray—supported by 200 army people were committed and in place. Akwesasne was locked down tight. Too bad it had taken two killings and two thousand refugees to do it.

On May 3, the overnight report was that a calm meeting of the community had taken place at 10:00 PM and that the Confederacy chiefs would be meeting over the weekend. The community quite sensibly wanted the police to disarm everybody. The SQ agreed to disarm anyone they saw with a gun but would not search any premises; they further said it was the RCMP's job to find cigarettes and drugs, since enforcing the *Customs Act* was not their responsibility. The SQ did not know how long they would be in position but guaranteed the New York State Police that they would give twenty hours' notice of departure. By midday, the confidential meeting of all five police forces and their civilian masters I had scheduled for the Dorval Hilton the following day had become public. I worked up some speaking notes for it anyway. Suggested agenda: (1) Police presence: how long? Terminate under what conditions, and with how much advance notice? (2) Options for longer term. (3) Next steps: what continuing process, noting that Mohawks had to be involved: who, how? And (4) How to handle the press.

The meeting in Dorval on May 4 was a zoo. None of the organizations at the table had a common approach to anything, and there was no unified Mohawk community. New York officially expressed annoyance at Canada, but having made their point subsided and were very professional thereafter. The U.S. Bureau of Indian Affairs and the State Department were both dead at the top: there seemed to be an inverse correlation between rank and IQ. The political appointee who ran the BIA seemed concerned mostly with looking good before the TV cameras. No force would show its cards to any other, especially with civilians present, but all exhibited a strong unwillingness to act.

The Canadian police forces were more worried about arms smuggling, but the U.S. forces saw this obsession with guns as yet another peculiarity of the Canadians. I already knew the views of the Canadian police, but I was struck by the degree to which the Americans, including the FBI, stuck to the line that no laws were being broken in the U.S.—including, unbelievably, state laws about carrying arms and running unlicensed casinos—and that smuggling, if it was happening, was a Canadian problem. But it was really Tom Constantine, the head of the New York State Police, who came closest to the truth. The head of the sanguinary police assault at Attica in 1971, Constantine had no wish for another bloodbath. All of the forces knew that a straightforward assault at Kanesatake or Kahnawake would be violent, and none felt that the public or their political masters, despite what some of them were urging at the moment, would be grateful after the fact. The problem was that they could think of no other tactic.

At least our field officers reported that it had been a quiet night and a beautiful day, and they were encouraging Chief Mitchell to open the band office and start the process of getting things back to normal.

Slowly, things did indeed return to normal. The whole community was shocked at what had happened. Independence, in the sense of being a self-policing entity, had failed catastrophically. Proud people had had to admit they needed help. Inside the community there were arguments, tears and voices blaming everybody but themselves. But gradually emotions subsided, amidst a general feeling that things should never be allowed to get that far out of hand again. Disturbances continued, but less frequently and at a lower level. The road barricades on Highway 37 were not re-erected, though RCMP and SQ roadblocks were fired on in mid-June. On May 16, in a belated act of political correctness, the army changed the name of their intervention from Op FEATHER to Op AKWE-SASNE.[32] In a referendum on June 20, 1992, Mike Mitchell was returned as Grand Chief for the Canadian side.

5

"ALL FOR A BLOODY GOLF COURSE!"

WHILE AKWESASNE was descending into civil war, the old story at Oka was reheating. Relations between Kanesatake and the town of Oka were deteriorating as choice waterfront properties were filled in by the fancy houses of Montreal exurbanites. The checkerboard of lands that remained for the Kanesatake band lay within the municipality of Oka. The town itself was just east of those lands along Quebec Highway 344, on the pleasant shores of Lac des Deux-Montagnes. For the municipality, dotted as it was with Mohawks living on federal land, conformance with local bylaws became an issue. In 1986, as one example, Jean-Roch Simon, a Mohawk who occupied one of the in-town properties, had decided to redevelop it as an apartment building. His plan did not conform to the town's zoning, and a row ensued. Simon's argument was that his property was on federal land set aside for the use and benefit of the band, of which he was a member, and was thus out of municipal jurisdiction. Naturally, the town did not see it that way. They refused to let Simon connect to the town's sewage line. A court fight started, but Simon did not have the funds to beat city hall.[1] Feelings were badly bruised on both sides. Today the lot is vacant, the original house having long been demolished.

The previous year, the band had taken advantage of a federal program to build a detoxification and drug treatment centre to

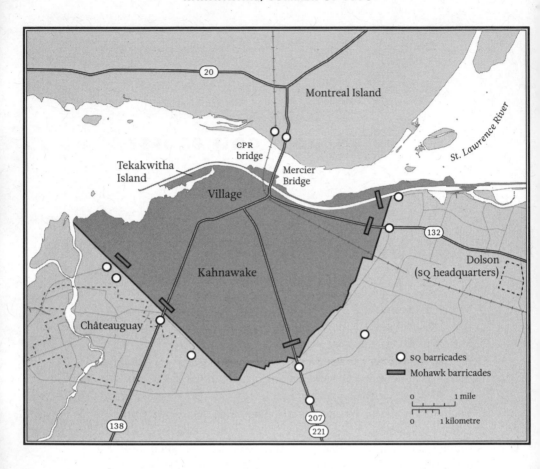

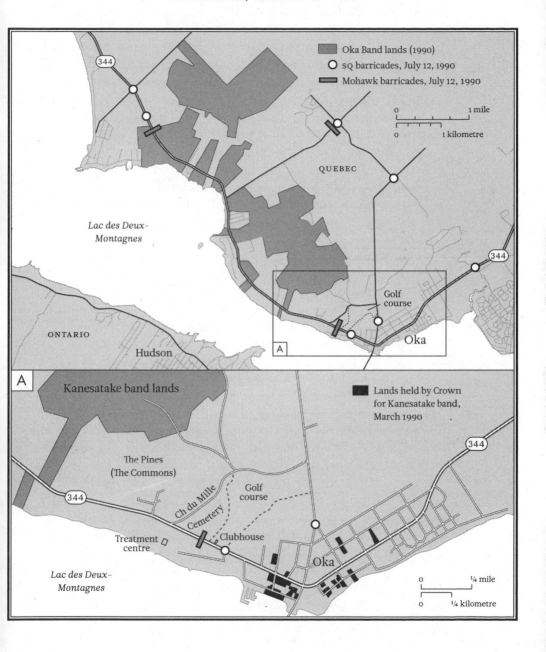

serve aboriginal people in that part of west Quebec. They notified the town that the centre was to be across the road from the Commons, on a property that ran from Highway 344 down to the river. Local shoreline owners were aghast. Such a facility would devalue their properties; there would be drunken, drug-crazed Indians threatening their tranquil existence. They organized themselves as the Regroupement des citoyens d'Oka (RCO) and protested, but to no avail. The centre was built. The Mohawks noted acidly that no permission had been asked of them, nor account taken of their views, when the town had built La Maisonnée d'Oka in 1982, a nearby treatment centre for non-native addicts and alcoholics. The fact that La Maisonée had caused no difficulties for its neighbours did not reassure the RCO. These and similar episodes underlined a growing distrust between the two communities.

IN 1945, WHEN the federal government bought the remaining seigneurial lands from the Sulpicians, it failed to buy the Commons, on the grounds that the land was uninhabited. The seminary, after selling part of the Commons land to investors from France, sold the rest to the municipality in 1959. The Indians objected. The town, uneasy about its title, followed the example of 1839 and sought to have a senior government, in this case the National Assembly of Quebec, pass a private member's bill confirming its title and allowing the lease of the land for sporting and recreational activities. The bill passed easily, as the member who introduced it was not only the member of the National Assembly for the area in question but also Premier Paul Sauvé, the leader of the government. The only such bill to pass in Sauvé's short government, it had all the earmarks of a private deal. The Indians protested to the federal government, which had a year to disallow the new act, but Citizenship and Immigration (responsible for Indian Affairs at the time) and Justice batted the file back and forth long enough to run out the clock. In 1961, over continuing native protests, land was cleared for a nine-hole golf course.

Indian objections were based on the fact that most of this land, as well as some of the adjacent land, was part of their ancient

Commons, called La Pinède or the Pines, used for two and a half centuries as pasture and woodlot. Indeed, in the late nineteenth century, the band had planted a forest of pines and hemlock to stabilize the shifting glacial sands that used to blow into Oka. For many years, two clearings on this large, quiet property had been in use by band members, one as a cemetery and the other as a summer picnic and lacrosse venue. Nevertheless, a piece large enough for the initial nine holes was sliced off the eastern edge of the Commons and cleared. A clubhouse was built just yards away from the cemetery.

The unhappy conclusion to the land claims filings of 1975 and 1977 had become a matter of record in May 1984. Later that year, with a new Tory government in office, David Crombie was troubled by the palpable injustice of the decision and began to study the file. He was nearly ready to act when the cabinet shuffle came. His successor at DIAND, Bill McKnight, was also pricked by the inability of Canada's laws to respond to the ambiguous legal file, the deeply felt continuing sense of grievance and the practical difficulties posed to community development by the scatter of properties available to the band. As the Oka band said in the 1975 letter accompanying their claim,

> The fact is that no land cession treaty has ever been made with the Mohawks of Quebec as in large parts of Canada. Nor have the Mohawk people ever been granted specific rights or benefits because of settlement of lands by non-Indians over the years. Nor is the Federal Government able to point to any specific legislation extinguishing Indian rights. The result is that insofar as the Mohawk people of Quebec are concerned, their land claim is an unsettled matter... We cannot stress strongly enough that the Mohawk people deeply possess this sense of grievance and injustice in respect to their general land claims. In this context, it is irrelevant whether the Indian people possess strong or weak legal arguments in support of their claim. It seems to us on grounds of equity and of justice, there should at least be negotiations between the Government of Canada and the Mohawk people in order to deal with the grievances and sense of justice.[2]

In his letter to the band in October 1986, McKnight offered some crucial words: "Nevertheless, as discussed with Mr. Crombie, I am willing to consider a proposal for alternate means of redress of the Kanesatake Band's grievance which you indicated should be prepared in the near future." The minister's innate caution, however, compelled an honest addition: "As you know, if substantial funds are involved, the proposal would be subject to review by Cabinet before I would make any commitments."[3] McKnight was nevertheless speaking with the same understanding of the limits of the law in attaining justice that the Law Lords of the Privy Council had expressed in 1912.

The prospect of something actually happening galvanized the factions at Kanesatake. In the fall of 1986, the band was governed under a semi-phony custom or "traditional" system. DIAND's policy was to allow elections under the 1951 version of the *Indian Act,* under traditional systems predating the Act or under "custom" arrangements based on tradition but updated for modern times. The custom system in effect since 1969 at Kanesatake, called the Six Nations Traditional Hereditary Chiefs, was based on selection by clan mothers and eschewed voting in favour of consensus. Alas, consensus was about the last thing the system produced. The Longhouse people insisted that they were a separate sovereignty and protested the appropriation of some of their terms and titles by the Hereditary Chiefs. On the other end of the spectrum, various groups demanded electoral democracy.

Trying to determine who could legitimately speak for the community was as much a puzzle for the House Standing Committee on Aboriginal Affairs as it was for the department.[4] No sooner had McKnight's letter been sent than Lise Bourgault, the Member of Parliament for the area, delivered a petition signed by many band members demanding that the minister cease negotiating with the Hereditary Chiefs and hold elections to select a democratic government. This was perhaps to have been expected. Since 1969, referenda had been held or attempted, chiefs and councils had changed several times and various courts had pronounced. Only lawyers had benefited. The truth was that the factional fighting reflected

deep-seated divisions within the community, between modern-
izers and traditionalists, Christians and Longhouse people, various denominations of Christians themselves and families, clans
and individuals struggling for power over the substantial flow of
funds—$2.6 million in 1989-90—coming from the department.[5]

Even a minister doing his best to figure out what the community
wanted had trouble finding a way forward. In subsequent testimony
to the House Standing Committee on Aboriginal Affairs, Tom Siddon explained, "No fewer than seven groups came forward claiming to represent the legitimate interests of the community... These
groups include the Kanesatake League for Democracy, the Committee for Change, the Mohawk Council of Kanesatake, C-31 Status
Indians, the Six Nations Traditional Hereditary Chiefs and the traditional and unofficial Longhouse groups, which are separate."[6]

In 1987, the golf club at Oka bruited the possibility of expanding
to eighteen holes. The next spring, surveyors arrived, stimulating
the Mohawks to interfere with their work by nightly removing the
day's survey stakes. In turn, Mayor Jean Ouellette and his council
procured the first of several injunctions against Mohawk interference. Simultaneously, the Longhouse chief, Kanawato Gabriel, sent
McKnight a letter warning of violence by younger men who were
reaching the end of their tether regarding the land situation.[7] The
department began quiet consultations with the community.

In March 1989, the mayor announced that the town had
acquired an option on land just west of the clearing in the Commons owned by the French investors, Maurice Rousseau and his
brother Jean-Michel. The town had a deal with the Club de golf
d'Oka to expand the course and to rim it with fifty high-value new
homes on land to be retained by Rousseau. There had been no consultation with the band. The RCO, whose membership overlapped
that of the golf club, strongly supported the mayor, who was himself a twenty-three-year member of the non-profit golf club.[8] As
recorded in *The People of the Pines,* "When an angry townsperson
at the March 1989 municipal council meeting demanded to know
if the mayor had consulted the Mohawks before making his plans,
Ouellette merely shrugged. 'You know you can't talk to the Indians,'

the mayor replied."⁹ Ouellette subsequently ignored an anti-golf-expansion petition from the white citizens of Oka, a demonstration march by the people of Kanesatake and reservations expressed by Quebec's Environment ministry. A symbolic August cutting of the first tree was thwarted by a large crowd of Mohawks.

Quite independently, the Sûreté had decided that illegal bingo was a threat to public order. According to military historian Timothy Winegard,

> The volatile situation was made worse by a high profile SQ raid. On 29 September 1989, during negotiations over the golf course expansion, between 50–75 SQ members, with the aid of a helicopter, forcefully raided the Kanesatake Riverside Bingo. The raid resulted in seven arrests and eight more searches. In the past, Mohawks had had run-ins with the SQ over hunting, fishing and traffic laws and distrusted them immensely. The SQ was seen by the Mohawks to be a racist arm of an oppressive Government of Quebec.[10]

The raid was predictably followed by a complaint to the Quebec Human Rights Commission and a local demonstration. Its result was only to deepen community mistrust of the SQ.

Meanwhile, negotiations between DIAND and the band were underway. Frank Vieni, Quebec regional director-general, had long been frustrated by the impossibility of sensible community development on the fragmented lands, and he was encouraged by McKnight's letter and the promise of funds. Yves Desilets, an officer in the Quebec regional office who reported to Vieni, was assigned as the federal negotiator, some general objectives were set out for discussion and the planning firm Pluritec was engaged by the band to assess the land needs of the community for the next decade. It was clear to all that the work was of an interim nature, in that the grand claim to hundreds of square miles of Quebec was not being addressed. Rather, it was to be a practical attempt, without prejudice to some eventual process that would resolve the larger issue, to assemble sufficient land for community development in a contiguous settlement. Pluritec concluded that something between twenty-seven and forty-five hectares would be needed to meet the minimal requirements of the community for housing, health and employment for the period to 1996. It did not pronounce on the Commons, but Vieni persuaded Oka's mayor and council to delay their plans for the golf course expansion until a general land plan could be agreed upon.

Governance continued along its rocky road. Crawford Gabriel, who had been the leader of the Hereditary Chiefs, had been fired by the clan mothers in January 1989 and replaced as grand chief by Clarence Simon. Simon then appointed two members of the Longhouse, Raymond Gabriel and Gabriel's son Allen, to be the band's negotiators on the land unification project. After long and difficult negotiations, and under the Hereditary Chiefs' letterhead, a draft agreement on the principles of land unification between DIAND and the Mohawk Nation of Kanesatake was put to the community on September 19, 1989.

The Gabriels went house to house, systematically gathering the views of Kanesatake residents. By Christmas, they had talked with most people, and they reported that four out of five favoured the Pluritec proposal. The traditionalists, alarmed, caused the clan mothers to strike pre-emptively, before the council could ratify the result. In January 1990, they dismissed Grand Chief Clarence Simon and installed George Martin. Simon and his council balked and refused to stand down. According to Timothy Winegard,

> The financial affairs of the band were frozen. Teachers and other band employees weren't paid. The Simon Council initiated a house to house survey to demonstrate popular support for Simon. Public meetings were held and resolutions passed. Perhaps the most intriguing document of the period is a resolution approved by a meeting at the Kanesatake School Gym on February 17, 1990 which denounces the clan system and calls for "a process whereby all members of Kanesatake will have an equal voice in the choice of our leadership through election." The signatories included former Grand Chief Crawford Gabriel and former Grand

Chief Clarence Simon as well as several other former chiefs who had been beneficiaries of the former system. The crisis passed with the recognition of the new chief and council by the Department of Indian Affairs. The band administrator was fired by the new council and there was no money for Allen Gabriel to carry on with land unification. Indeed, in early March 1990 the new Grand Chief George Martin informed the other parties that the framework agreement was not going to be ratified and suggested that there be an indefinite deferral of negotiations.[11]

That was enough for Mayor Ouellette. Angered by what he saw as bad faith bargaining, he lifted the suspension of the golf course expansion project on March 9 and announced that construction would start that spring. A Mohawk demonstration at the clubhouse that afternoon met with indifference. When heavy equipment began to appear, a number of Kanesatake women, conscious of their role as keepers of the land, arranged for a small barricade to be erected by men from the community on the Chemin du Mille, a gravel track running through the Commons, and started to camp in the clearing nearby. An ice-fishing shack was donated.

In Mohawk communities, the Longhouse generally represents the old Confederacy and thus has, potentially, both spiritual and temporal powers. In some communities, the Longhouse has retreated from day-to-day administration and become more specialized in the religious role, eschewing anything to do with electoral systems. At Kanesatake, the Six Nations Traditional Hereditary Chiefs had governed without overt opposition from the Longhouse, most of the time,[12] until 1989, but they had also been under deliberate attack, most of that time, from the democratic opposition. Kanesatake had not one but two Longhouses, as well. One, with some thirteen members in 1990, was led by Samson Gabriel, a condoled chief of the Six Nations Iroquois Confederacy. The other, led by Walter David Sr., was a breakaway, an even more fundamentalist group with about thirty-six members. It was members of the David Longhouse who placed their lawn chairs in the forest at Oka, adjacent to the first green, and with broad support from the community began their peaceful protest on March 10, 1990.

For all the grumpiness and acrimony at Kanesatake, however, official Ottawa took little notice. I sent Pierre Cadieux and Kim Campbell a copy of a remarkable manifesto from the Akwesasne Mohawk Nation denouncing gambling and Warriors, and in the same vein we spent an hour's briefing time with the new minister, Tom Siddon, on Mohawk governance problems.[13] But that was about it. The rest of the government paid no attention. A lengthy deck prepared for deputy ministers in March 1990 on the social policy agenda of the Mulroney government did not mention aboriginal Canadians at all.[14] Earlier, in May 1989, an interdepartmental meeting on the burgeoning high-stakes bingo business had had trouble taking the subject seriously. As one official put it, "To have no taxes and complain about the absence of tax shelters . . . !"[15] In September of that year we had managed to convene a meeting of senior officials at PCO to discuss smuggling at Akwesasne and Kahnawake, but the same old bottom line came from the RCMP: "Should we lose men to enforce the *Customs Act?*"[16]

The occupation of the Pines by a small camp of women, children and faithkeepers and a makeshift blockade on an infrequently used gravel road gathered little attention outside the community. Even at Kanesatake, the protest camp played a subordinate role in the political struggles within the tiny Mohawk world. It had taken Grand Chief Martin more than three weeks after his predecessor was deposed even to get into the band office. The territory was then retaken by Simon's supporters. On April 6, Martin's supporters retaliated and took the office again. Simon, remarkably, called in the SQ, who evicted the Martin people. Two weeks later, to demonstrate disagreement about the utility of the protest camp, someone torched the fishing shack. But the barricade on Chemin du Mille was reinforced.

Amidst these comic opera follies, something more ominous was afoot. Awareness of the Kanesatake resistance to Ouellette and the golf club was seeping through all the Mohawk territories. When the crisis at Akwesasne ended in blood, tears and a substantial police occupation, a number of Warriors found it expedient to answer a call to defend Mohawk land rights some distance away. Suddenly a pulse of well-armed young men with little local knowledge but a substantial political agenda began filtering into Kanesatake. Unknown to them, RCMP and SQ officers were tracking Warriors not just from Akwesasne but also from Ganienkeh and Kahnawake who were bringing truckloads of camping equipment, food, communications gear and weapons into the community.[17]

On May 1, the day after the shooting stopped at Akwesasne, the town asked a contractor to remove the barricade on Chemin du Mille. The SQ, which had been monitoring events closely by car and helicopter, had planned a raid for the next day, but they were dissuaded by John Ciaccia, the Quebec minister of native affairs. All three levels of government met with representatives of all factions in Kanesatake about half a mile northwest of the focal point in the Pines, but the meeting settled little. Shortly after, a distress call from Kanesatake went out to Warriors in all the Iroquois communities. About a hundred, including the veterans of Akwesasne, arrived in the next few days. Some camped in the Pines; others were billeted around the community.

Back in Ottawa, the department was still digesting the events at Akwesasne. Siddon and Martin were briefed on the gunfights, the deaths of Pyke and Edwards, police operations and weapons seizures. They were not told, because National Defence had not told us, that starting five days before, elements of the Second Combat Engineering Regiment, in civvies, had started scouting the Canadian side of Akwesasne further to their orders to begin contingency planning.

A few Mohawks, principally from Kahnawake, had shown up at the "secret" May 4 meeting at the Dorval Hilton to make sure the press understood their point of view. Continuing inaction by the police led to an acid comment from DIAND's ADM for self-government, Roger Gagnon, to the effect that the RCMP was ineffective at all levels below the commissioner. Mobile Command stepped up their surveillance with fresh air photos of Kanesatake and Kahnawake, incorporating these communities into their contingency planning. On the Mohawk side, newly arrived Warriors at Kanesatake were put to work digging trenches and building fortifications against an expected police raid. Between sixty and a hundred more Warriors were reported as being in training at Ganienkeh and Kahnawake for an armed confrontation.[18] Mayor Ouellette repeated his request of March 9 for the SQ to take down the barricade on Chemin du Mille, but nothing happened.

May and June were contentious months within the Kanesatake community. There were disagreements about the use of arms. Some said weapons were indispensable; others claimed that since the Mohawks could never win an armed confrontation, weapons should be eschewed entirely. Still others said that even unused weapons would have powerful attention-getting and symbolic value. The role of women—as keepers of the land, and even as clan mothers—was hotly debated, along with many other issues. Some traditional people like Samson Gabriel, Allen Gabriel and Curtis Nelson found it necessary to leave the Pines, at least temporarily, as hard-line Warriors asserted power. Toward the end of June, Longhouse and Mohawk Council people met together with Tom Siddon in Ottawa. But Siddon, on the advice of Justice and our department, focused on the council, ignoring the Longhouse people, and on land unification; he refused to talk sovereignty. The Mohawks were miffed.

In the middle of this developing story, a farcical distraction arose. Canada's information commissioner, Inger Hansen, threatened to sue DIAND for not publicly releasing Justice's opinion about the land claims at Oka. The department was directed to claim solicitor-client privilege. Hansen demanded that we sever everything not directly related to the conclusions and publish it. Justice responded that waiving privilege on part raised the risk that a court would find we had waived it on the whole. The commissioner, about to retire, wanted to go out with a win. Correspondence ensued, with each letter requiring many hours of legal and executive time.

None of the events at Oka got any traction at the most senior levels in Ottawa. The Meech Lake Accord was collapsing, much to the dismay of the prime minister and the Quebec premier, and on June 23 it was given its quietus through the combined efforts of Premiers Filmon and Wells, assisted by Manitoba Cree MLA Elijah Harper. None of the Mohawk leadership recognized the enormous emotional effect of this event on Mulroney and Bourassa. They should have: Meech was dominating the media, and one of the first rules of conflict is to understand your opponent.

Tom Siddon persevered with the developments at Kanesatake, alone but for his Quebec colleague John Ciaccia. Neither their cabinets nor their caucuses were much aware of the increasingly dangerous situation, but to the degree they were, there was not a lot of sympathy for the Mohawks. Local federal M.P.s Monique Landry and Lise Bourgault strongly represented the views of their white constituents. On June 28, Siddon met with Ouellette and his town council. The minister urged mediation and the acceptance of the band council as the legitimate governing entity. Ignored by the town council, Siddon subsequently wrote to them, urging again that they meet the band council for a face-to-face discussion of their different points of view. The real views of the town were revealed the next day, when mayor and council sent their lawyer, Luc Carbonneau, back to the Quebec Superior Court in St.-Jérôme to get another injunction to remove the roadblocks. Judge Anthime Bergeron somewhat reluctantly granted it.

At the last Wednesday morning breakfast meeting of deputy ministers before I was due to leave on holidays, a main topic of conversation was fallout from the collapse of Meech Lake. Paul Tellier, who had been as deeply involved and as committed on the file as his boss, Brian Mulroney, reported the prime minister as having said that the government needed to return to some serious thinking on native policy. There would be no retribution for the role of aboriginal people in scuttling Meech, Tellier said. I was asked to think about the possibility of a royal commission. Two days later, on Friday, July 6, Quebec Public Security Minister Sam Elkas announced during a radio interview that the Mohawks in the Pines had four days to obey the injunction or action would be taken. Elkas then went on holidays in the Eastern Townships. His warning was seen as a turning point by the Mohawks, who redoubled their work on trenches and fortifications.

At this point there was another stab by the fickle finger of fate. The Quebec Human Rights Commission, which had been in intermittent touch with the community at Kanesatake and the Quebec government, thought they saw an opportunity for defusing an increasingly dangerous situation. On Saturday, July 6, they sent a telegram—a telegram!—to both Ciaccia and Siddon warning of the risks and advocating the appointment of an independent committee to study the land claim. Ciaccia got his copy, but somehow the telegraph company failed to deliver Siddon's copy. The QHRC did not think to follow up with a phone call or a fax. Too bad: the probability of the tactic working was low, but it was not zero. The main effect of this lost chance was to give subsequent chroniclers of events a stick to beat the feds with. York and Pindera remark with contempt in *People of the Pines* that there was "no reply [from Siddon] for four months," a cheap shot considering they had not checked with the department or the minister's office.[19]

John Ciaccia was becoming really concerned. Alone among non-native observers, he saw that the initiative had passed into the hands of the mayor of Oka, and he had the experience to know that an attempt to enforce the injunction was likely to cause a riot. On July 9, Ciaccia wrote at length and with some passion to Mayor Ouellette, recapitulating some of the long history of Kanesatake and warning about applying the strict letter of the law in a volatile situation.[20] Meanwhile, the native affairs minister asked the people in the Pines to meet with him to find a non-violent solution. Their spokesperson, Ellen Gabriel, a telegenic and well-spoken young woman, refused to meet him: she was holding out for "nation-to-nation" talks and would only meet with the federal government. (I was still on holiday in Europe, but would not in any case have engaged in serious talks on the precondition that Canada and the Mohawks were separate sovereignties.) Yves Desilets approached the Longhouse people on a similar mission. Even though he represented the Crown federal, his overtures were also spurned.

Mayor Ouellette replied to Ciaccia's letter in scathing terms the next day, claiming the minister did not understand native affairs. The mayor refused to meet with the minister, saying that Ciaccia's letter had left nothing for them to talk about. What Ouellette did not say was that he had made a formal request to the SQ that same day to enforce the injunction with no further delays.

In Quebec City, Robert Lavigne, director-general of the SQ, requested equipment from National Defence Headquarters: night goggles, bulletproof vests, eighteen armoured vehicles, wire gloves and cutters.[21] Jacques Lacaille, the Mohawks' lawyer, was working feverishly on an appeal of the injunction when he was interrupted by a demand from the SQ to discuss some vandalism to the car of a local dentist and prominent member of the RCO. Lacaille never got to court. Late that night, one of the Warriors, Crazyhorse, was tipped by an SQ dispatcher that there would be a raid in the morning. Overnight, the Mohawks put finishing touches on new bunkers, booby traps, suspended fish hooks and pipe bombs.

Just before 5:00 in the morning on July 11, a fleet of SQ cars and trucks rumbled through Oka. Sleepy Mohawks at home and in the Pines were awakened and warned. By 5:30, three "tactical intervention teams" of five men each, reinforced by riot police with shields, helmets, sticks and revolvers, plus command and emergency units—altogether about a hundred people, all in black and all wearing body armour—had assembled on the highway at the south edge of the Pines. A smaller group circled around to the northern entrance. At 5:45, a few shots were heard from inside the Pines, but they were apparently not aimed at anyone. Simultaneously, community people from Kahnawake moved to seize the Mercier Bridge, followed hastily by Warriors. The bridge, one of only five connecting Montreal to the south shore of the St. Lawrence, carried over 70,000 cars per day, many of them filled with commuters. Most accounts have the bridge seized at about 8:30, in retaliation for the events unfolding at Kanesatake. However, the initial seizure was at 5:45 AM, a hair-trigger response to the expected raid intended to divert police efforts and support the people in the Pines.[22]

The account by York and Pindera of the next few hours is the best available. Most of it stands up to the detailed scrutiny of the inquest and the trials that followed. As the Mohawks' dawn tobacco-burning ceremony was going on, an SQ officer stepped forward with a megaphone. "We want to talk to your leader. Have your leader approach the lines immediately." The women came forward, open-handed to show they were not armed. The two groups stopped a few yards apart. The black-clad policeman demanded again to see their leader. The women said everyone was a leader; there was no single leader. Flustered, the policeman thought that repeating the demand more loudly would change the answer. It didn't. Eventually Ellen Gabriel and faithkeeper John Cree came forward and explained something of the nature of Mohawk democracy. The policeman said he would give the women five minutes to decide what they were going to do. No, replied Gabriel and Cree, the tobacco-burning ceremony would require another forty-five minutes.

With considerable aplomb—and knowing that the woods behind them were full of armed and prepared Warriors—the women started making coffee and sandwiches. Some took hot ashes from the fire and sweetgrass and went up to the police line, burning the sweetgrass and sprinkling the ashes at the feet of the police. A few insults and demands that the police go away flew from Indian mouths, answered by visible nervousness on the part of some of the officers. Losing patience after the better part of an hour while the Mohawks completed their prayers, the sQ demanded that the occupiers of the Pines approach the barricades, evidently so they could be seized. The women did not fall for that. As the impasse continued, the police fired two canisters of tear gas into the crowd, on orders from Assistant Director-General Marc Lizotte. In the almost still morning air, the gas drifted away from the Indians and back on the police, but not before many of the women were dosed.

In the confusion, the sQ began a flanking movement around the west side of the clearing and the lacrosse field. About 7:00 they began to use concussion grenades. The popping of tear gas canisters and the sharp crack of the grenades became general, but so far there had been no use of guns by either side. Confusion mounted as clouds of tear gas covered the entire area. The sQ donned gas masks, which did not improve their ability to see what was going on. At one point, around 8:50, four members of a sWAT team leapt over the Mohawk barrier to try to seize a Warrior who had gotten incautiously close. The Warrior sprinted north, police in pursuit, toward and beyond the lacrosse field. An intense fusillade began—initiated by whom, no one will ever know. Some ninety-three rounds were fired in twenty to twenty-four seconds, according to calculations by the subsequent Gilbert inquiry, with more than half coming from the SQ. In the blaze of fire, Corporal Marcel Lemay, father of one and with another child on the way, his left arm uplifted, was shot in the armpit above his bullet-proof vest by a high-velocity 5.25mm bullet that tore up his aorta, esophagus and heart, its fragments lodging behind his right scapula. His life ended instantly.

By 9:15, the breeze was consistently blowing tear gas back on the SQ, who were in full retreat down Highway 344 toward the town. They left behind half a dozen squad cars and the payloader they had brought in to dismantle the barricades.

News travelled fast. By 9:30, a meeting of Warriors was convened at the Akwesasne home of Francis Boots, their war chief. The men had an inconclusive discussion about seizing the International Bridge at Cornwall, which crosses Akwesasne; it was occupied for about ninety minutes, but the Warriors went home when instructed to by the Ontario Provincial Police.[23] The news travelled to Alberta, where Tom Siddon was on holiday; he spoke to his chief of staff, Jack White, and to Fred Drummie. And the first piece of news management in a summer that would see a lot of it was underway: the Mohawks at Kanesatake told the media that Lemay had been shot by his own side.

The name of the person who pulled the trigger on Corporal Lemay will likely never be resolved in law.[24] Many people, especially (but not only) Mohawks, still believe the Mohawk version of events. The story that he had been shot by his own people was all over the media later that day and was not denied by any official source at the time. An investigation of the site, an autopsy and eventually a coroner's inquiry would be required to sort out what happened.[25] The SQ, perhaps fearing that the Mohawk claim was true, but more likely because of errors made by senior planners, did everything in their procedural power to stymie the work of the inquiry, which they managed to stretch to five whole years. After a painstaking investigation, and with the assistance of the country's best experts in firearms, the distinguished jurist Guy Gilbert, acting as coroner, concluded in 1995 that Lemay had been shot at a range of about ninety metres by aimed fire from a prone rifleman.[26] The bullet that killed him was of a military type—.223 cal full metal jacket—that, although manufactured in Canada, had been rejected by the military because of a tendency for the metal jacket to come off in flight. The entire lot had been sold to the U.S. and had filtered into retail markets south of the border.

The other continuing mysteries of July 11 are the identity of the person who gave the order to raid the Pines and, more generally, why the SQ tactics were so clumsy. The minister responsible for the police, Sam Elkas, certainly had no sympathy for armed insurrectionists, but Elkas was at his cottage when the raid occurred and was alerted after the fact by a member of his staff. Elkas's senior staff, including his deputy minister, Jacques Beaudoin, himself a former director-general of the SQ, were completely in the dark. Nor were John Parisella, Bourassa's chief of staff, or Bourassa himself informed of the raid in advance. The decision was taken by the police themselves. SQ Director-General Robert Lavigne, in testimony before the Gilbert inquiry, explained that while there were no established rules, he would normally ensure that the minister of the day was not surprised by hearing about important police actions through the media. Commissioner Gilbert expressed dismay that such critical communications should depend so strongly on personality, even as he cited Lord Denning on the necessity to avoid political interference with the administration of justice.[27] In the event, however, Lavigne had not informed his minister. Questioned on the point, Elkas said he would have asked for an hour or two to contact his colleague John Ciaccia about less drastic avenues that might have worked. There were no contingency plans for the raid, and the SQ's intelligence about the quantity of weapons and the number and state of mind of the people in the Pines was seriously inadequate. Tactical control was poor. The SQ made no attempt to evacuate or even warn neighbours who were in easy range of high-powered weapons. Even their ability to figure out which way the breeze would blow the tear gas was lacking.

DURING THE GILBERT inquiry, it was revealed that police planning went back to April 22, when a trifecta of events had added to the accumulated apprehensions of the St.-Eustache post of the SQ. Scheduled for that day were a demonstration by environmentalists against cutting the forest for the golf club expansion, the annual feast of the earth to be celebrated by the Mohawks in the Pines and a brunch at the golf clubhouse a few yards away to mark the opening of the season. The local SQ post prepared to keep order if needed. But even after Mayor Ouellette's May 7 demand that Elkas send in the police, senior levels of government did not take the Oka confrontation all that seriously. Elkas had even given an interview in which he said "he had no intention of sending Sûreté policemen to play cowboys in the Pines."[28]

Despite the minister's sensible caution, on May 8 SQ Inspector Jean-Pierre Gariépy asked the St.-Eustache sergeant, Bernard Desnommée, to prepare a more thorough plan.[29] Police intelligence—there was a uniformed officer, Paul Despatis, on the file, as well as a plainclothes agent from the security information service of the SQ, Yves Jodoin—was picking up evidence of arms and new faces in the Pines. As well, the Regroupement des citoyens d'Oka was adding its own particular pressure to the kettle.

Between May 8 and July 10, despite a growing number of incidents involving gunshots, Warrior sightings, vandalism, arms smuggling, intimidation and social discord, the SQ did nothing to elaborate on or improve a plan drafted by a rural sergeant. The initial plan was put on the shelf as something to guide an "eventual" operation at Oka. The SQ were deeply reluctant to undertake an operation that might be dangerous and would have doubtful public support. Indeed, the police believed—and had told Longhouse member Minnie Garrow, when she asked at the SQ station at St.-Eustache on July 3—that the occupation itself was not illegal and thus not justification for an intervention. But all that changed on July 6, when Elkas, in a radio interview referring to the town's injunction, said of the Mohawks in the Pines, *"Ils ont jusqu'au 9 juillet, après cette date ça va descendre."*

Seeing trouble ahead, Inspector Gariépy called Lieutenant Réal Marcotte—whom the May 8 plan specified was to be the commander on the ground—to suggest a familiarization tour of the area. Marcotte said that would not be necessary. He had the plan in hand, and it would be nothing more than a crowd control situation as the Mohawks were removed.

For SQ Assistant Director-General Marc Lizotte, a watching brief had become active. Lizotte called a meeting of a dozen senior officers to review plans at SQ headquarters on July 9—not because he anticipated having to act by that date, he later testified, but because action might become necessary after the time allowed for compliance by the injunction expired. Counsel advised the meeting that though police had assured Minnie Garrow that there would be no arrests for one specific charge, there were numerous other criminal incidents that could justify an intervention. The injunction, set to expire that evening, was not definitive, the lawyer said, but it added weight to the idea of intervening. Discussion turned to options. The do-nothing option was rejected in view of the deteriorating social climate and the strong tensions between the two communities.[30] Noting that trying to arrest all demonstrators would only make things worse in what was, after all, a 270-year-old dispute, those at the meeting turned to the idea of a mild intervention with a minimum of arrests, followed by a modest increase in patrolling. Their objective would be simply to restore peace and social order. Others could settle the ancient grievances. Despite many sightings of arms and of camouflage-suited Warriors in the woods, and despite repeated warnings from John Ciaccia to Sam Elkas, the senior police simply could not imagine that the Mohawks would use their arms for any purpose other than making noise. As Lizotte later told the Gilbert inquiry, "I could not conceive that one would confect a plan for an attack by fifty armed persons who would fire on the police. That's a plan for war; that's not a plan for peace. There was no plan to that effect, that's for sure."[31]

In his findings, Commissioner Gilbert noted with astonishment that the SQ meeting concluded without any discussion of the risk posed by the presence of arms, and with no review of the operational plan by senior officers. Lizotte knew there was a plan, he had testified, but he did not know that it dated back to May 8. When he informed Robert Lavigne about the decision, Lavigne in turn asked no questions, pronounced himself satisfied—and failed to inform his minister.[32] Stimulated in part by Elkas's radio comment of July 6, on July 8 John Ciaccia had called Elkas, Bourassa's chief of staff John Parisella, and Mayor Ouellette. Accounts of these conversations differ in detail, but in the first and the third call Ciaccia pleaded for forbearance—from a raid, and from a call for a raid. We know what he got from the mayor. According to Ciaccia, he underlined to Elkas the inadvisability of sending the SQ to Oka, where there were well-armed Warriors, some with Vietnam experience. According to Elkas, the two men reached the conclusion that Elkas would get the authorities to hold off, to give Ciaccia's negotiations time to succeed. Probably both thoughts were actually expressed. The two men, if not close friends, were colleagues, part of the same team. Ciaccia's call to Parisella was to keep the premier informed, no more. Had Ciaccia had a strong disagreement with Elkas, he could have requested a meeting of the cabinet. In any event, Elkas relayed the message to his political office—where, unaccountably, it stopped.

IN THE AFTERMATH of the shooting, amid the confusion and the precipitate retreat of the SQ, Warriors seized the abandoned payloader and used it to overturn several SQ squad cars, creating a well-televised barricade across Highway 344. One Warrior, Richard Nicholas, stood on top of the wrecked cars and waved his rifle derisively at the humbled SQ. Later, the cars would be stripped of radios and other useful gear and taunting messages would be painted on the wrecks.

The SQ slowly established a distant cordon around the Pines, staying for the most part a mile or so from where the shooting had occurred. They counter-barricaded Highway 344 both east and west of the Warrior blockade and set up other roadblocks in the area to the north and west of the Commons, thus greatly inconveniencing many uninvolved citizens, white and Mohawk, who found themselves inside the police lines and, especially if they were Indian, being harassed every time they tried to cross.

The Mohawks who had seized the Mercier Bridge at Kahnawake that morning were joined by Warriors from Kahnawake, in an apparent case of "I must hasten after them, for I am their leader." Mohawk and police blockades were soon erected across Highways 207 and 138, and workers driving to Montreal from Châteauguay and neighbouring suburbs were enraged at the thought of adding several hours to their commuting time. The next day, with police binoculars trained on them, a couple of Warriors with high-steel experience clambered around the bridge girders under the road-bed, conspicuously planting black packages with wires coming from them. They would turn out to be empty shoeboxes painted black. By now, though, the sq was taking even far-fetched contingencies seriously, and authorities would worry all summer about the possibility that this vital urban bridge might be dropped into the St. Lawrence Seaway. Or worse—dropped on a ship that was passing through the seaway. The Warriors knew a good deal about "asymmetrical warfare," and they enjoyed a joke besides.

So, by halfway through that soft summer day, the obduracy of the town of Oka, police fears of public opinion and the insouciance of the sq had brought about the death of an honourable man, the seizure of the Mercier Bridge, multiple highway blockades and a galvanizing of Kanienkehaka (and shortly most Indians in Canada) behind a band of suddenly respectable armed men. The government of Quebec could not count on the ability of their vaunted police force to maintain law and order, or even to figure out which way the wind was blowing. From mean and narrow purposes rose consequences that would shake the nation.

6

NEGOTIATIONS BEGIN

ROBERT BOURASSA, in the opinion of his chief of staff, John Parisella, was "the third casualty of Oka," after Lemay and an elderly Mohawk man, Joe Armstrong, who was struck on August 28 by a rock thrown by a white rioter at LaSalle and died in hospital the next day.[1] As Meech Lake was winding to its depressing end, Bourassa had felt unwell, but put off seeing his doctor until the last days of June. Diagnosed with melanoma, he was advised to get immediate treatment and arranged to go to the National Cancer Institute in Bethesda, Maryland. But Corporal Lemay was killed before the appointment, and Bourassa decided he had to stay at the helm of his sometimes fractious cabinet during the crisis. It was not until the end of the summer that he was able to get away, and even then—because he kept his diagnosis a secret—he was mocked in the press for taking a "holiday" in a time of crisis. The surgery at Bethesda was much more serious than Bourassa had let on, and he never really recovered his health. He died in 1996.

Robert Bourassa, a Rhodes scholar, was first elected premier in 1970. His second term, as had his first, would end in defeat by the Parti Québecois. A quiet and private man, he was a somewhat unlikely politician. The essence of the political problem at Oka, for Bourassa, was the popular impatience, even anger, felt by most francophone white Quebecers about the seizure of the Mercier Bridge. This impatience, manifest in the many voices who called for an immediate and if necessary forceful end to what was seen as an armed insurrection, was echoed by the members of his cabinet. Most were pretty hard-line about the affair, with two notable exceptions. One was Claude Ryan, older, austere, a thoughtful and observant Christian, a former editor of *Le Devoir* and a principal keeper of the flame of honour of old Quebec. Ryan commanded great respect in the Bourassa cabinet, and his centrist, conscience-driven approach to events supplied important ballast to hotter tempers.

The other minister who stood outside the general consensus of his colleagues was John Ciaccia, the minister of native affairs. Unlike most politicians in this portfolio, Ciaccia had long experience with Indian affairs and not a little sympathy for the people who were the subjects of public policy. Ciaccia had been not just an assistant deputy minister in the federal department of Indian Affairs but an advisor to Jean Chrétien back when the new young minister was clawing his way out from the wreckage of the infamous White Paper.[2] At the time, Ciaccia was the senior official responsible for Indian lands. He knew the file. Ciaccia saw himself as uniquely positioned to find a negotiated solution to the crisis at Oka, and he threw himself into the fray right from the beginning. His memoir of that summer is both passionate and sad.[3] Better than anyone else in his government, he knew the dangers, opportunities and protocols in the game, and he understood that unless immediate resolution of the land issues at Kanesatake could take place, the issue would swell way beyond what Quebec could do. Getting the federal government to promise to buy the land and persuading Tom Siddon to take a back seat were key tactics for Ciaccia, but in the end they were not enough. As the summer wore on, his efforts would become increasingly desperate, and increasingly distant from those of his colleagues in the Quebec cabinet.

John Parisella was also an important player for Quebec that summer. He knew Bourassa better than any of the premier's elected colleagues did, shared Bourassa's cautious, centrist, federalist views and often acted in his name. It was Parisella who would authorize Ciaccia to go behind the barricades to negotiate at Oka. For Parisella and Bourassa, managing the tension between Ciaccia and Sam Elkas was a constant effort through the summer—not made any easier by the fact that the maintenance of public order was a fundamental concern for the premier and his chief of staff.[4]

OTTAWA'S LANGEVIN BUILDING, across Wellington Street from Parliament, is a whimsical pastiche of every architectural style of the barely post-colonial period. Completed in 1873 as the first office building of the new Dominion and named after Sir John A. Macdonald's minister of public works, the building was erected under a contract that continued the fine tradition of corruption and scandal established by the colonial Board of Works. Once, it held most of Canada's civil service; today it houses the political and official offices of the prime minister. The Prime Minister's Office, not part of the civil service, is headed by the leader's chief of staff. At the beginning of the summer of 1990, that role was filled by Stanley Hartt, a lawyer from Montreal and an old friend of Brian Mulroney. The Privy Council Office, also housed in the Langevin Building, is the apex of the public service and the most central of central agencies. It is headed by an official with the grandly nineteenth-century title of Clerk of the Privy Council and Secretary to the Cabinet. In 1990, that official was Paul Tellier, a forceful and energetic lawyer from Quebec whose rapid ascent through the bureaucracy had included, helpfully, a stint as deputy minister of Indian Affairs. Tellier's associate clerk was Bevis Dewar—quiet, thoughtful and immensely experienced.

In the Westminster tradition, the Clerk, like all deputy ministers, is expected to be politically aware but non-partisan. A deputy minister's objectivity and expertise are at the service of whatever government the voters return, and his or her actions are entirely professional, not political. As a consequence, each serving minister also has a political staff to assist that minister with winning elections, managing intra-party relations and (putting it bluntly) mastering spin. The prime minister has the biggest of these staffs; PMO normally coordinates the actions of ministers and their staffs and deals with the prime minister's public and party leader roles. PCO, for its part, is the prime minister's device for managing the vast apparatus of the public service. Both offices speak with the authority of the prime minister, whose powers are not circumscribed by statute but, since they include appointing and specifying the duties of both ministers and their deputies, are decisive. However, on the day Corporal Lemay was shot, the Langevin Building was all but empty. Exhausted and disheartened by the failure of Meech, Mulroney and Hartt were nevertheless attending the G7 meetings in Houston. Tellier was on holiday, tearing up the back roads of Quebec on his powerful motorcycle. I was in Germany by then, touring the wreckage of the Cold War and getting briefed on current politics by Canadian diplomats in Bonn and Brussels. Many second- and third-tier officials were likewise on vacation. Bev Dewar was the only senior PCO person on duty. The senior officer on duty in PMO was Paul Heinbecker, a brilliant diplomat and wordsmith on loan from External Affairs as the prime minister's speechwriter. Most of the federal machinery was on standby, including the Department of Indian Affairs and Northern Development, whose minister was in British Columbia and whose deputy—me—was on holiday in East Germany. Fred Drummie, DIAND's associate deputy minister, was feeling a bit lonely.[5] In Quebec, Public Security Minister Sam Elkas and his deputy were both on vacation, as were their respective stand-ins.[6]

On the evening of July 11, as accelerating events threatened to engulf Ottawa, Drummie called Bev Dewar at home. Drummie was going to need decisions from the centre of government, and he would need resources. In the morning the two men began to build the team that would evolve, over the next two weeks, into a formal, day-to-day crisis management group.

July 12 was a busy day, as reaction to the events of the day before set in. The media were all over the story. DIAND communications staff worked frenziedly to prepare backgrounders, set up a hot (not "war") room, field media calls and explain that the minister was temporarily incommunicado in B.C. Quietly, in the background,

National Defence Headquarters ordered Mobile Command to prepare to provide vehicles, drivers, weapons and special equipment to the SQ. Some troops were moved to CFB Longue Pointe on the northwest tip of Montreal Island, and an intelligence officer was sent to Montreal to liaise with the SQ and the RCMP. With him were elements of the Second Electronic Warfare Squadron (2 EW SQ) and the First Intelligence Company (1 Int Coy). NDHQ also started comprehensive air photography of the rather rudimentary defensive positions at all three reserves, Kahnawake, Kanesatake and Akwesasne. Army commander Lieutenant General Kent Foster and Brigadier General Armand Roy, the commander of the Fifth Mechanized Brigade Group, met at St.-Hubert to discuss further contingencies.

In Ottawa, the initial federal strategic position was developed at a meeting on Thursday morning, July 12, at PCO. Paul Heinbecker and Tom Trbovich were there for PMO; Tellier, Dewar, Dan Goodleaf, Ron Bilodeau and Bill Rowat represented PCO; and Fred Drummie was the sole line departmental official. No one was present from the department of the Solicitor General, the RCMP or National Defence—oddly, given the emphasis on law and order. The position, as recorded in Drummie's notes, boiled down to six points:

1. Whatever is done, the primary objective is no more deaths. That is, all decisions are to be assessed as to their risk of a resumption in the shooting.
2. The law and order and police issues are within the province's jurisdiction and other than responding to requests from the provincial government or the Sûreté, the federal government should not insert itself into the situation.
3. The federal government is willing to address all matters associated with land and is prepared to purchase land to satisfy the needs at Kanesatake.
4. The federal government will not negotiate or address the land matters while the blockades are up and guns are present. "We will not negotiate with a gun to our head."
5. There are to be no negotiations behind the barricades for fear of a hostage taking.

6. Federal ministers and officials will support provincial ministers and officials in their efforts and will attempt to use influence rather than direct intervention.[7]

Points 2, 4 and 5 turned out to have short lives. And the land the
federal government was willing to discuss was that outlined in the
Pluritec report, not the sovereign seigneury that some Mohawks
wanted to talk about. Nevertheless, it was important that ministers
be informed about the events at Oka and that the draft objectives
have the support of the government. A conference call was arranged
for 3:00 that afternoon, with an ad hoc committee of cabinet, and
run from Drummie's office.

From the various parts of the country to which they had dis-
persed with the summer recess of Parliament came the voices of
Don Mazankowski, the deputy prime minister; Tom Siddon and
Shirley Martin, the senior and junior ministers of Indian Affairs;
Pierre Cadieux, Solicitor General; Bill McKnight, National Defence;
Kim Campbell, now in Justice; and Robert de Cotret, president of
the Treasury Board. The supporting cast of officials included Tom
Trbovich from PMO; Joe Stanford, the Deputy Solicitor General;
Robert Fowler, the deputy minister of National Defence; John
Tait, deputy minister of Justice; and, from PCO, Bev Dewar, Dan
Goodleaf and Rem Westland. Uniquely, all of the ministers except
Mazankowski and de Cotret were current or past ministers of
DIAND and understood the issues well. De Cotret, as a Quebec minister, nonetheless knew the ground, and Mazankowski, from Veg-
reville, Alberta, had grown up with aboriginal neighbours. From
the beginning, then, this was a file that ministers knew better than
central agency officials. The exceptions were Goodleaf, assistant
secretary to the cabinet for social policy and himself a Kahnawake
Mohawk, and Tait and Westland, who had served in DIAND earlier
in their careers.

To begin the discussion, Fred Drummie summarized the events
of July 11–12. He then spoke of John Ciaccia's efforts over the past
several months, noting that the Quebec minister had procured a
verbal promise of a moratorium on golf course construction from

Mayor Ouellette, had given an undertaking that the federal government would negotiate the purchase of the ninety-seven acres
in question and had agreed to the proposed establishment of a special review group composed of representatives of four governments,
including the Kanesatake band council, to examine all areas in dispute. Ciaccia, Drummie reported, did not have carte blanche and
could not offer the Mohawks immunity or the right to retain their
weapons. Federal participation to date had been the provision of
some equipment and some preparatory work on the purchase of an
initial twenty-three acres, should that be useful.

The ministers on the phone agreed that the general strategy as
outlined was appropriate and should guide officials. The federal
government was prepared to negotiate the purchase and transfer of the land in question, though not as a "land claim." Food and
medical supplies for the people of Kahnawake were a concern, and
provincial authorities, notably the SQ, were to be encouraged to
end the siege tactics that were not letting groceries through. Work
would proceed on the terms of reference, process, and membership
of the suggested special review group. Siddon would issue a statement in response to the Ciaccia proposal for the joint review group.
Frank Vieni, the DIAND regional director-general, was to be the
French-speaking spokesperson. The armed forces would continue
to respond to requests from Quebec for equipment. Finally, communications would be given increased attention.[8] Tom Siddon indicated he would be flying to Ottawa on Saturday, and the call came
to a close.

EARLY IN THE day on July 12, John Ciaccia arrived at Kanesatake to
try to negotiate. He had little credibility with the Indians, however,
as he clearly did not control the principal source of dissatisfaction,
the SQ. Siddon called him for an update from the front.[9] At Ciaccia's
request, they agreed that one minister was enough and that nothing would be served by Siddon's presence on the scene—indeed, the
effect could be negative, since the Indians wanted to discuss larger
land issues and both governments wanted to settle the immediate
situation first. Still, it was an odd move on the government's part.

Many Canadians expected federal leadership, and the Mohawks were publicly insistent on "nation-to-nation" talks. There was a political price for tactical deference, and Siddon was soon paying it. Lead editorials in the *Globe and Mail* and the Montreal *Gazette* pilloried him for his absence.[10] The Deputy Chief Commissioner of the Canadian Human Rights Commission wagged her finger.[11] Even the town manager of Oka said Siddon must have been dreaming when he offered to buy the Commons. A letter arrived from Kanesatake grand chief George Martin demanding that DIAND's Yves Desilets be fired and blaming the minister for the crisis.

As promised, Siddon flew to Ottawa on July 14 and spent the next day, Sunday, in his departmental offices in Hull. Minister of State Shirley Martin, a shrewd and empathetic M.P. from Niagara, also flew in, and she and Siddon were joined by Jack White, Siddon's outgoing chief of staff; Ray Castelli, White's replacement; Fred Drummie; and John Bray of DIAND's communications staff. Siddon was concerned about the growing public outcry for the federal government to become involved. The strategy of supporting Ciaccia was rational, but it was politically difficult. Siddon and Ciaccia again spoke by phone. Ciaccia reported that he had had an arduous session with the municipality of Oka from three to ten PM the previous day. He felt he had a degree of consensus. "There will never be a golf course," he said. He had the mayor on side and was expecting a written agreement from the town to give up the project.

Separately, Frank Vieni had been receiving signals from the municipality that they were interested not just in abandoning the planned expansion but also in selling the existing nine-hole course. The town preferred an outright immediate sale but would be satisfied if negotiations were to commence to acquire the land. Vieni confirmed he had told them the federal government was prepared to sit down to negotiate land issues.

Ciaccia had also come away from the barricade at the Pines with what he thought was an agreement for disengagement and an understanding there would be a process put in place for a "nation-to-nation" negotiation of the Kanesatake "land claim." The tentative agreement included the acquisition for Kanesatake of the disputed land, plans for a public inquiry into Lemay's death and a withdrawal of the SQ under the benign observation of a number of churchmen who had come forward to offer their help. After the police withdrawal, the Kanesatake people would dismantle all barricades. The Mohawks wanted a third party on hand for the police inquiry, either from the United Nations or from the Quebec Human Rights Commission. Officials considered the latter more likely, or at least less objectionable.

The problem was the weapons. This was a non-negotiable item for Ciaccia; the Mohawks would have to lay them down, and they were unwilling to do so. In any case, no negotiator on the Indian side could really commit on behalf of the Warriors in the woods or at the Mercier Bridge. Nevertheless, in just a few days, the Mohawks had what they wanted: an end to the expansion of the golf course and a transfer of land ownership into their hands, or at least into federal hands as their trustee. At that stage, the process of disengagement seemed eminently negotiable.

Siddon and Ciaccia then moved to the issue of a federal presence at the negotiations. A press report had Ciaccia saying he would "ask the federal government to assume its responsibilities." Ciaccia denied he had said that; instead he had made reference to the federal government carrying the responsibility for the negotiation of land matters. The provincial minister again stated, rather forcefully, that he didn't need Siddon on site and thought it would be counterproductive to have more than one minister present. He recognized the pressure that was coming to bear on Siddon, though, and said that on the next occasion he had to speak to the press, probably that afternoon, he would clarify that during his conversations with Siddon he had not asked for federal participation and had not made particular requests of Ottawa, other than a commitment to pursue discussions on land. It was understood the federal government would participate in any negotiations on that issue.

"Somehow we have to back up to March 6," Siddon told Ciaccia, referring to the time before the start of the occupation of the Pines, when land reunification was the main item on the table. "We are even willing to change our negotiator, not immediately, but soon, if we can restart the discussions. How? Whenever the parties are willing, we will be there."[12]

Ciaccia incisively noted that hostilities would have to cease before anything could proceed. There would have to be real commitment by the Indians and a clear statement of the changes they required. He summed up: "I can live with what you're saying. I repeat, I have not asked for a federal presence. I have spoken with you and have federal support."[13]

On Sunday, Ciaccia was expecting twenty people from Kahnawake to join in the discussions and had made arrangements for them to travel to Kanesatake. These were Longhouse people, including eleven clan mothers. Ciaccia hoped that the inclusion of the "decision makers" would enable him to bring the crisis to a conclusion. But the negotiating group by now included an increasing number of Warrior leaders and other hard-liners, with Kanesatake residents being slowly squeezed out. Stanley Cohen, a radical lawyer from New York and an associate of William Kunstler, had joined the group as an advisor. With fewer Kanesatake band members had come a shift in the issues, away from the concerns of the community about adding to their land base and toward larger concerns about Kanienkehaka sovereignty.

Ciaccia left a senior official, Georges Beauchemin, at Kanesatake to spend the night. In a shared tent, Beauchemin's fitful sleep was interrupted by cellular calls. By Monday morning, the world had changed. The Sûreté had not reduced its presence but expanded it. Disregarding the negotiations of their civilian masters, the police moved to tighten their lines and through multiple checkpoints began seriously to interdict supplies of food and medicine to citizens, Mohawk or not. People were harassed by officers without name or number badges. Jacques Parizeau, leader of the opposition Bloc Québecois, had openly called for the army to take over.[14] At Kahnawake, fears of an imminent attack by the army terrified residents, leading somewhat perversely to an escalation in demands. John Ciaccia's efforts were rejected, and negotiations collapsed. There was a pause as attention turned to the funeral of Corporal Lemay, which was carried out on July 16 with full police honours. Pierre Cadieux, the Solicitor General and chief federal law enforcement officer, represented Ottawa at the funeral, and he took the opportunity to speak with Sam Elkas, both to assure the public security minister of federal support for Quebec's position and also to express concerns regarding the police denial of food and medicine to the two communities.

Two days of relative quiet and calm followed—a calm before the storm, as it turned out. Tom Siddon was keeping the lines open. He spoke to Ciaccia, to his Anglo-Quebec colleague and National Caucus chairman Robert Layton, to the alarmingly racist Quebec Tory backbencher Ricardo López, who was fanning the fires at Châteauguay, and to the hard-pressed but sensible mayor of Châteauguay, Jean-Bosco Bourcier. Bourcier's town was in an uproar. Kahnawake residents shopped in Châteauguay, and kids from the two communities played hockey together. But the seizure of the Mercier Bridge exposed latent racism among the town's citizens. About four thousand people had rioted and attacked police lines. With the situation escalating, it was decided at a cabinet committee meeting chaired by Don Mazankowski that Tom Siddon should make a trip across Canada to meet with Indian leaders, explain the federal position and try to tamp down the possibility of violent sympathy protests. Janice Cochrane, DIAND's able director-general for B.C., was tasked with arranging for continuing situation reports and compiling lists of key names and venues for Siddon's meetings from her colleagues coast to coast.

At about the same time, the Kahnawake Longhouse sent an assistance wampum to the Oneidas of western New York and southern Ontario, resulting in about a hundred reinforcements for Kahnawake and Kanesatake. Individuals from tribes as far away as the Tahltan of northwestern B.C. and the Mi'kmaq of Nova Scotia arrived at Kanesatake. Military intelligence discovered that ten Mohawk U.S. Marines had taken leave and were at Akwesasne. Quietly, DIAND approached the U.S. consulate in Montreal with a view to having these men ordered to return to their units. Kahnawake chief Joe Norton, trying to straddle the several factions in his community, played host to an increasing number of chiefs from across

Canada—eventually about a fifth of the members of the Assembly of First Nations—and called for federal intervention to protect Indians against the depredations of the SQ and the province. In the middle of all this, apparently unscripted, a Canadian Forces spokesman said he expected the Canadian Armed Forces would be called in. Premier Bourassa denied this the next morning. Regardless, the comment spooked Kahnawake residents, many of whom began to evacuate the community.

Alarm was spreading through native communities all across the country. We had often said in the department, ruefully, that we were the only people who could unite Canada's Indians. Early on, the department had attempted to elicit a moderate voice from the Assembly of First Nations, but this was unrealistic. National Chief Georges Erasmus and his colleagues had constituents whose opinions ranged from strong support for the Warriors to eye-rolling contempt for Mohawk intransigence. In consequence, to Erasmus's frustration, there was very little he could say. A more moderate group of federally appointed community leaders, the National Aboriginal Economic Development Board, urged the federal government to give up the pretence that the situation in Quebec was a provincial law and order issue and get directly involved at senior political levels, including with the Grand Council Chiefs of the Haudenosaunee; to ensure unrestricted access of food and medicine; to stand down the police; to use the affair to put meat on the skeleton of land claims and self-government policy; and, for good measure, to establish a Royal Commission on Aboriginal Peoples (RCAP).[15] As Harold Calla, the long-time councillor and finance director from Squamish, recalls:

> Oka mobilized Indian activism all over the country. Squamish received several requests from Eastern tribes—don't remember whom—asking us to shut down both bridges [First and Second Narrows, in Vancouver] to bring attention to their plight. [Squamish Chief] Joe Mathias, after lengthy discussion in Council, said no, but did agree to leafleting on First Narrows (and maybe Second; can't remember). We decided we were not ready to put our

kids through the reaction that blockading two bridges would bring. The Council took an ad in the *North Shore News* inviting all citizens to come to the Longhouse for a discussion of Indian issues, and Squamish history and ambitions. The Capilano Longhouse was absolutely filled that night. We described our story; many were surprised, stunned even. Four to five hundred people attended; it was all very well received. The power of Oka was that it forced these exchanges.[16]

In Saskatchewan, Indians stopped traffic in Regina to hand out leaflets urging people to contact the government. In British Columbia, aggravated by Premier Bill Vander Zalm's delay in producing a promised land claims policy, no fewer than twelve demonstrations and blockades took place between July 17 and 24. At least thirty-four Indian organizations and chiefs issued statements variously condemning the government and calling for its involvement in withdrawing the police. There were demonstrations and blockades in New Brunswick, Nova Scotia and Manitoba. At one point, Don Goodwin, assistant deputy minister for Lands, Revenues and Trusts, was dispatched to northern Ontario to deal with a blockade on the Canadian National main line. Canadian Pacific, with a rail line through Kahnawake, had some cars imprisoned and had to reroute freight; they sent John Ciaccia a stiff lawyer's letter saying the incident was all his fault and he should be prepared to pay damages.[17] At the other extreme, the Mackenzie Delta (now Gwich'in) Tribal Council in the Northwest Territories—a Dene organization and as such part of the old power base of AFN national chief Georges Erasmus—issued a statement calling Mohawk Warriors thugs and criminals, saying they should not have taken up arms to settle their land dispute. DIAND's regional offices, and frequently its ministers, were occupied in explaining what was going on and in calming ardent spirits, all without much need for guidance from departmental headquarters beyond the backgrounders, fact sheets and press releases prepared by Ruth Cardinal's people.

Up until the time of the SQ raid during the Akwesasne disturbances of the spring and the early stages of the Oka affair, military assistance had taken the form of the loan of specialized equipment to the police. But now General John de Chastelain, chief of the defence staff, and his army commander, Lieutenant General Kent Foster, had begun to consider what to do in case of a provincial requisition.

Back in Ottawa, Fred Drummie met with Ward Elcock, the senior lawyer in PCO, to follow up on the possibility of a royal commission once things had returned to normal.

ON THE MORNING of Wednesday, July 18, one week after the abortive police action at Oka, a new set of Mohawk demands arrived in John Ciaccia's office by fax from the office of James O'Reilly, long-time legal counsel to various Indian groups. A new and different phase of the crisis had begun. It is worth quoting the whole text to show how the situation had escalated from a local land issue:

> Given the repeated disruption of the Mohawk nationhood by Canada and the United States; and given the desire of our three Nations to resolve the present conflicts in our territories with peace and fairness; and given the establishment of the World Court [*sic*] at the Hague to resolve conflicts among Nations as required under international law it is hereby agreed:
> 1. The extension of the golf course shall be immediately abandoned in Kanestake [*sic*] and the Kanienkehaka Rotinonhsionni title thereto restored and confirmed in perpetuity as well as title to the historical Commons.
> 2. At the time of the signing of this agreement all foreign armies/police shall be withdrawn from all Kanienkehaka territories which shall then be restored to their respective positions prior to March 9, 1989.
> 3. All barricades should be removed from Kanesatake and Kahnawake upon the signing of this agreement with free and ready access to and from all Kanienkehaka territories guaranteed.
> 4. For 48 hours after the signing of this agreement, all people shall be permitted to depart from Kanesatake and Kahnawake without a search of their persons, property and automobiles.

All persons so departing residing therein may do so without being detained, interrogated and [illegible] and without having to show identification documents to police and/or army personnel.

5. All other issues regarding the present events at Kanesatake and Kahnawake, both civil and potentially criminal, as well as disputes relating to Kanienkehaka sovereignty and land rights shall be referred to the World Court at the Hague with all parties hereto to be bound by that Court's determination following a full and fair presentation of all the respective positions.

6. Pending the resolution by the World Court of any disputes over other land rights at Kanesetake not specifically referred to above, there shall be a moratorium on any existing or future land development thereof.[18]

The communiqué caused considerable dismay in both federal and provincial camps. O'Reilly's fax was a long way from the initial Mohawk preconditions to the negotiation of barriers and land—access to food and medicine, the unrestricted passage of clan mothers and spiritual advisors, and the presence of neutral observers at the barricades. Although using the letterhead and symbols of the Haudenosaunee, the new demands were not authorized by the Iroquois Confederacy; they were the work of the Warrior Society, the Mohawk Nation Office and their advisors. The inclusion of a reference to the United States in the preamble seemed designed to widen the agenda by drawing in Akwesasne. Indeed, "all Kanienkehaka territories" would seem to include Tyendinaga, Wahta, Doncaster, Ganienkeh and Ohsweken, and perhaps all territories claimed by them—the old seigneury, the Grand River Valley—in addition to the three eastern communities.[19] More seriously, the references to the International Court of Justice at The Hague and the attempt to define "nation" as "state" implied that the Mohawk Nation was a sovereign state.

The first demand, in one sense, had already been met, in that the town of Oka had given up on the idea of extending the golf course and Siddon had committed to buy it. But the implied ceding of sovereignty and the document's preamble were non-starters for the government. Even were it to be argued that the sovereignty concept behind the word "Rotinonhsionni" (Confederacy) was the qualified "domestic, dependent nation" of Justice Marshall, Canada was unwilling to extend free trade with the Americans that far. The second demand, the withdrawal of all police forces, including "foreign" ones, from Akwesasne, Kahnawake and Kanesatake, combined with a demand for a forty-eight-hour period without search, interrogation or even identification, was a get-out-of-jail-free card that would enable the Warriors to leave with their weapons and to evade the laws of Canada.

The fifth numbered paragraph continued the theme of Mohawk national sovereignty by demanding immunity from charges under the Criminal Code of Canada and sending any disputes regarding sovereignty or land to the World Court. By agreeing to use the International Court of Justice, which deals only with disputes between sovereign states, the government would be recognizing the sovereignty of the Mohawks. By comparison, the final demand, for a moratorium on land development at Kanesatake while negotiations proceeded, was small beer, but it was still well beyond the statutory powers of Canada or Quebec.[20]

In summary, Canada and Quebec were being called on to recognize the Mohawks as a sovereign nation; to recognize the existence of Mohawk aboriginal title at Kanesatake and, by implication, over an undefined area of Quebec, Ontario, New York and Vermont; to withdraw the police from the three communities; and to allow all Indians and advisors who had broken the laws of Canada and the United States to go free. The only element missing was compensation.

7

ESCALATING DEMANDS

UNDERSTANDABLY THE new *démarche* led to confusion at a disintegrating negotiating table and
to public statements that underscored the widening gulf. At first,
John Ciaccia refused to return to the table, saying events had made
it clear that the Mohawks no longer trusted him. The federal side
concentrated on acquiring the disputed land at Kanesatake and
on trying to make it clear to the larger public what we were doing.
Tom Siddon, together with Shirley Martin and Pierre Cadieux,
gave a press conference in Ottawa, after talking with Ciaccia and
Sam Elkas, that focused on the land purchase. Longhouse voices at
Kanesatake denounced the idea of buying land that was theirs anyway, saying that Indian money in the hands of DIAND should not be
used. They knew that if the department bought the land, the cost
would come from our appropriations and in a sense be a small tax
on Indians across the country. At Kahnawake, about a hundred of
the chiefly membership of the Assembly of First Nations had met
for three days in July, producing a manifesto that demanded the
withdrawal of all police and military forces (there were no military
forces present at the time); the personal involvement of the prime
minister as the negotiator; the reconvening of Parliament; a complete amnesty; the appointment of a UN commission to investigate
violations of the rights of the Mohawks; and condemnation of Canada by other countries, to be followed by sanctions if Canada "fails

to act promptly on the chiefs' suggestions for a settlement."[1] Back in the department, Fred Drummie met Frank Vieni, Yves Desilets and others to review events and tactics. On Friday, July 20, Siddon, Martin and Cadieux met Ciaccia and Elkas at SQ headquarters in Montreal without much concrete result, though with increased understanding of one another's difficulties. That day, too, Bev Dewar from PCO called me home from Dresden.

On Monday, July 23, I arrived at the office to get caught up on events. Later that morning I got a call from Stanley Hartt. The Prime Minister's Office was having a hard time being heard in the media, with the waves crashing everywhere, and nobody from the press seemed to have any idea what the affairs at Oka and Kahnawake were all about. I should be prepared to give them a backgrounder that afternoon, Hartt said.

I was already familiar with the background, and meetings and phone calls filled me in on the rest. Late that afternoon, accompanied by Richard Van Loon, the senior assistant deputy minister for Indian Self-government, I went to the National Press Gallery and talked at some length about the 170 years of the land dispute, the recent provocations by the Oka town council and the several sources of governance in the Mohawk communities. The Warriors, who had recently begun to stiffen the occupation of the Pines, were young men, I said, often with weapons experience, who were also involved in smuggling cigarettes across the St. Lawrence.

My comments ignited a flood of questions. How did I know these things? What did I mean, Indian "criminal gangs"? I dug myself in deeper with some more factual information, then ended the session. I could see Rick Van Loon holding his head in his hands. Naive and tired, I had failed to follow the accepted media framing of events, which was all about brave Indian victims and intolerant white land thieves. But at least it was only a backgrounder, an Ottawa institution of some durability. All the media could report, I felt sure, was something about a "senior government official" charging that some Mohawks were involved in criminal activities. Besides, I had said nothing that wasn't already in the press.[2] Van Loon was just being histrionic.

I was wrong. Elly Alboim, Ottawa correspondent for the CBC, and his network bosses had decided that the news was too delicious for the rules to be followed, and that evening I was the lead item on the CBC national news. Once the dam had broken, I was headline news across the country. "Deputy Minister Calls Mohawks Criminals" was the tone of most of the headlines.[3]

On Wednesday morning, wondering if I still had a job, I tried calling my minister. He was unavailable—and furious, I was informed.[4] In public, Siddon's line was to the effect that he would not have used the words I had, but the facts spoke for themselves. Midday, the Privy Council Office called: there was a full cabinet meeting the next morning, and I was to be there.

I was at the Centre Block by ten the next morning. The smirks of junior PCO officials, bustling in and out of the cabinet room with their papers and messages, did nothing to improve my sense of doing something for the last time. Eventually the Oka item came up on the agenda, and one of the junior officials summoned me in through the carved double doors, into the gracious room with its large oval table and the carved frieze on the wall, *"Aimez-vous la sagesse, vous qui jugez la terre."* In the moment of relaxation between agenda items, ministers were chatting and laughing with a scatter of senior officials. No one met my eye. Convention has it that an official summoned to cabinet goes to sit beside his minister, speaking only when spoken to and then only on matters of fact or analysis. I paused, looking for the minister to whom I had been unable to speak for sixteen hours. All of a sudden, the prime minister spotted me standing there miserably.

"Well, look who's here," boomed Brian Mulroney, "the only guy in this room who could win a by-election today!" And off he went, kidding about "background" press conferences and how good it was that some of the true story was getting out.

Thus began the most strenuous summer of my life.

The next few days produced a wave of denunciations from people who did not understand, or would not accept, the intermingling of patriotic and criminal elements among the Kanienkehaka. These were followed by more thoughtful commentaries that recognized that the Warriors' interests in smuggling and gambling closely aligned pecuniary gain with Indian nationalism. As Tom Siddon's chief of staff Ray Castelli remembers:

> Relatively early in the process... it was an outpouring of emotion, and everyone was on the side of the Indians, and the government was bad. Then Harry went into this off the record briefing for journalists... and called them gangsters. And the Minister was immediately accosted by the media in the House, outside the House, saying, "Your deputy minister called these poor defenceless Indians, called them gangsters, thugs. Do you agree, Minister? Do you think they are gangsters?" He says, "Well, no, I don't agree." Then the whole thing was getting Harry to resign. Then we had, "Are you going to ask for Mr. Swain's resignation?"[5]

Naturally, the furor extended to the Prime Minister's Office. According to Stanley Hartt, then Mulroney's chief of staff,

> I was sitting in the opera one night with Beverly [Mrs. Hartt]... and the usher comes and taps me. "You are Mr. Hartt, aren't you?"
> "Yes."
> "Come with me"—in the middle of the opera. "Call from the Prime Minister."
> They take me to a phone and I say, "Yes."
> He says, "This guy Swain, he's a friend of yours?"
> I say, "Very much so."
> "Will you kindly get him to stop saying the Indians have more weapons than the Canadian Armed Forces?"
> I say, "I will, Prime Minister, because you are asking me, but the trouble is it happens to be true."[6]

The prime minister may have phoned Tom Siddon next. Ray Castelli recalls:

> I get called to a meeting over at the PMO [after Siddon's public statement]... I go in there all ready to say yeah, we should hang

Harry. What the hell is Harry thinking?... I walk in there and
I get the crap beaten out of me by Bev Dewar and Stanley Hartt
saying, "What is your minister thinking? What's he doing?" And
Bev Dewar, sitting at the edge of the table... says to me, "I'm
sorry, young man, but can't you control your minister?" I'm
thinking to myself, "Well, you don't know my Minister very
well," but I didn't say anything. Little did I know that Stanley
had put Harry up to this [press conference] and he was out there
on direction from PMO, but somehow nobody let the minister
in on the joke. So now we're now offside with the message. So
Siddon ends up getting beat up internally and externally, hangs
Harry a bit out to dry. But I think that it was the turning point
because, up until that point, the notion that these guys were
gangsters and the analysis by the media of, who exactly these
guys are, and their relationship to Akwesasne, and the gun running, cigarettes, smuggling, and the casino stuff... the media
hadn't picked up on that.[7]

Face-to-face talks with Kanesatake had broken off, but the
fax wires were busy. John Ciaccia offered to meet Mohawk leaders outside the barricades under conditions that would guarantee
their freedom of movement, including observation by neutral parties. The Red Cross would ensure that food and medicines crossed
the barricades while negotiations took place. The Mohawks said no,
not outside their barriers, and insisted on international observers.
The UN Working Group on Indigenous Populations (WGIP) began
sessions in Geneva, opening with a rather prejudicial anti-Canada
statement and an initial Canadian response.

Roger Gagnon, the department's ADM for self-government,
worked with External Affairs to prepare Canada's statements to
the WGIP, later travelling to Geneva to represent us. Once we got
over some false pride about being monitored by international do-
gooders, Gagnon also helped arrange for the international observation team. These conscientious people were all unpaid volunteers.
The department provided them with all the information they
wanted, as well as arranging for them to meet Mohawk spokespeople. Gagnon also helped us keep communications open inside the

department. As an example, working through the department's internal Council for Change, we met interested DIAND employees for an hour of briefing and answering questions. Recounting the story from the front lines was one thing; dealing with the wounded feelings of our diverse staff was another. Non-Mohawk native employees were divided in their views, and many Quebecers were upset at the Mohawks.

Abroad, Canada's distinguished trade ambassador Gerry Shannon, a top-level Finance official, was accredited to the GATT headquarters in Geneva, where he was a key player in preparing for the creation of the World Trade Organization. External being External, and always looking to save a penny, Shannon was also accredited to the UN Human Rights Commission, parent body of the WGIP. This was not his home turf. Daily, during that summer, the WGIP would hear Canadian Indian delegations and then demand to know what Shannon had to say about their evident truths. He found this style of discourse unnerving after the cool, rational, greed-dominated trade talks. More than once he called me before a meeting to ask what on earth we thought we were doing back there in Ottawa. This would typically be at 3:00 AM Ottawa time—and sometimes only an hour after Tom Siddon had called in high dudgeon from British Columbia, having just seen the CBC national news. In midsummer, this was two or three hours after distinguished members of the old Confederacy had left my house after a few hours of talk.

There were all sorts of these back-stairs conversations going on at the time, especially involving those not at the official tables; I for one did not want to see any avenue for a peaceable solution left unexplored because of Justice's strictures about which Mohawk group was legally in charge. There had been some threats against me, which resulted in the RCMP Protective Service parking a car and a Mountie in our driveway from the time I got home until 10:00 PM, which was shift change time. The Mountie departed, since in Ottawa all assaults happen by ten, and shortly afterward the Confederacy men, who had been waiting at the corner, came to call. And to smoke—they were the only people my wife, Julie, ever allowed to smoke in our home. Between the chiefs, Siddon and

Shannon, I often got very little sleep before our daily early-morning meetings at PCO.

Once the crisis was up and rolling, the federal government put in place a rudimentary crisis management group that consisted of the heads of all the relevant agencies, under the chairmanship first of Stanley Hartt and then of the cabinet secretary, Paul Tellier. The group met every morning at 8:00 AM in the Privy Council Office to share news and coordinate action. The policy framework in which we operated had evolved from the one Drummie and his colleagues had laid out for ministers in the hours after Lemay's death, since the attempt to keep Quebec in the headlights had been predictably unsuccessful. By and large, only principals, with the exception of PCO staff, attended the morning meetings. The deputy ministers of Indian Affairs, Justice, Federal-Provincial Relations and the Solicitor General's office were regulars, as were the heads of the RCMP and the Chief of the Defence Staff. (This arrangement worked well enough that it would be copied, with different players, for the subsequent command and control of Canada's participation in the Gulf War of 1990–91.)

For Paul Tellier, the meetings were an efficient way to fulfill his mandate from the prime minister—avoid further bloodshed—and be well briefed for his frequent conversations with Robert Bourassa and the Quebec cabinet secretary, Benoît Morin. Tellier's crisp, intense style was a contrast to the government's approach in the first days of the crisis, when most of the principals were still out of town. As the able Ray Castelli remembers, "I don't think people really appreciated... the value that Tellier brought to government, until he was not there... We were floundering around the first week, ten days." He continues:

Stanley Hartt... called these strategy sessions, and every day, for about three or four, five days thereafter, we would show up at PMO, at eight o'clock in the morning... These strategy sessions would go until two in the afternoon, they were like five to six hour affairs, and the entire meeting consisted of Stanley arguing with himself. Arguing both sides of the argument—oh you know, we could do this, we could do this, and then of course if we do that, they will be able to say, this, this, this and this— and he would go on and on and on. It would go around the table, and around the table, and around the table, work over issue after issue, and we'd literally be sitting there for hours wondering are we actually going to do anything?

Bev Dewar would sit there quietly and occasionally pipe in, and he was Tellier's right hand, and I'm sure at some point, Bev Dewar must have told the prime minister, this thing is spinning in circles, and Stanley is just having this conversation with himself, with witnesses around the table, and Tellier got called back from wherever he was on vacation... So Tellier came back, and took control of this meeting, and then from then on, it was like chop, chop, chop, it went very efficiently.[8]

At this early stage, the information available to the federal government was accurate in broad strokes but tended to be exaggerated in detail—a problem that was to plague us from time to time throughout the crisis. But since the exaggerations were usually related to the ferociousness and well-armed character of the insurgents, the effect was to underscore the wisdom of the prime minister's desire for caution and an end to bloodshed. In brief, we knew from both DIAND and police sources that Kanesatake had seen an infiltration of Warriors, mostly from Akwesasne, but in some cases from Kahnawake and Tyendinaga, after the shootings of Mathew Pyke and Junior Edwards at Akwesasne on May 1. The department also knew the history of the land dispute at Kanesatake, the fractiousness of the community, and its inability to make decisions, the nature of the several governance systems operating simultaneously in the community, and the key players. The RCMP was the principal source of intelligence about the arms, boats and communications gear of the Warriors. The identities of the masked and nicknamed warriors were initially unknown to us, but that did not last for long.

As for weapons, police and military intelligence claimed the Warriors had a wide variety of rifles, including fully automatic assault weapons, plus at least two .50 calibre heavy machine guns,

Barrett .50 cal sniping rifles and probably rocket-propelled grenades. After the Mercier Bridge was seized, both the police and
the army added remotely controlled explosives to the list, having watched Warriors climb among the steel supports under the
roadbed and attach black packages with wire. The latter, as noted,
turned out to be a clever hoax by the Warriors. No heavy machine
guns were ever found either, but the army nevertheless made a
video of a .50 cal machine gun destroying a well-built bunker. The
video was shown to officials at the PCO morning meeting, as well
as to ministers of both the federal and provincial governments and
eventually to the public, with appropriately sobering effect.[9]

At the international level, a tired Roger Gagnon briefed me on
July 31 about the WGIP in Geneva. The principal interest of its chair,
Miguel Alfonso Martinez of Cuba, in the crisis at Oka seemed to be
maximizing embarrassment to Canada. In a notable departure from
U.N. rules, Martinez had allowed a Warrior representative, Kenneth
Deer, to address the group. Deer complained of lack of access to food
at Kanesatake, despite the facts and Canada's guarantee. He quoted
selectively from the report of the Quebec Human Rights Commission and told the group that Canada was trying its best to break the
spirit of the Indian people. Deer had tried to pass out red lapel rib-
bons to the other Canadian Indians present, including Ted Moses, a
Cree from Northern Quebec, but they refused to wear them. After
hearing Gagnon's report, DIAND prepared an information package
about what was actually happening. Canada's general strategy was
based on remembering that the working group was not a court and
we were not the accused—and should not act like it—while flooding
the delegates with accurate information. Our case would later be
helped by a presentation to the WGIP by Judge Jean-Claude Fouque,
president of the International Federation for Human Rights. Fouque,
whose observers were on the ground from August 16 to August 27,
cited a few minor violations but said that, on the whole, things at
Oka were decent and getting better.

The department's attempt to buy the disputed land at Oka provoked not only a demonstration by the town's white citizens but
also a denunciation by Mohawks. Both the municipality and the

parish of Oka demanded to be observers at the negotiations but were ignored. Jacques Parizeau, the separatist leader of the Quebec opposition, jumped in with a demand that Bourassa personally lead the negotiations; he was likewise ignored. Native protests swelled around the country. DIAND's Saskatchewan office was occupied by Crees, and Algonquins set up camp on Victoria Island, in the middle of the Ottawa River between the department and Parliament Hill. The breakdown in talks led many Mohawks to fear another SQ attack, and their unease was amplified by a comment from Sam Elkas that any future raid would involve units of the Canadian Armed Forces. The SQ announced that they had opened "hundreds of files" in preparation for future criminal charges.

Judge Jean-Claude Fouque of the International Federation for Human Rights arrived in Montreal to prepare the way for his team of observers and was met by Fred Drummie and Dan Livermore from External. From our point of view, Fouque was a distraction that simply meant more work. The presence of his team would not change federal tactics or behaviour, which already met international standards of human rights. On the other hand, his presence was important to the Mohawks and their supporters, and to whites across the country who were suspicious of government motivations. But distraction was everywhere. The same day, Kanesatake band lawyer Eric Belhassen filed a class action lawsuit against the SQ for income losses to band members stuck behind the SQ barricades.

On July 27, Tom Siddon announced that DIAND had purchased the sixty housing lots that were to surround the expanded golf course from Maurice and Jean-Michel Rousseau for the not unreasonable price of $1.4 million. The federal government was ready to start negotiations on the golf course expansion land, land claims and economic development as soon as the barricades came down. John Ciaccia, in a letter to both Kanesatake and Kahnawake, warmly supported Siddon's announcement, saying that Quebec would withdraw most of the police and include the Mohawk groups in the negotiations if the Warriors would surrender their weapons and take down the barricades. The Mohawks complained that Ciaccia's proposal did not meet their preconditions regarding access

to food and medical supplies, advisors and international observers. They were not rejecting the offer, they said, but it would not be
considered until the preconditions had been met. All this was happening against a backdrop of fiery speeches. Kahnawake chief Joe
Norton, for example, told a crowd of two thousand, "We will fight
and die if we have to."

The Oka town council, recognizing that it was a seller's market,
announced on July 31 that it would not sell the land until the barriers came down. A few days later, Frank Vieni made a new offer
to acquire the land. The town council began to add costs for lost
development opportunities to their already high asking price. On
August 1, the Senate Standing Committee on Aboriginal Peoples
opened hearings in Ottawa. Walter David Sr., the respected elder
and spokesman for the more conservative of the Kanesatake Longhouses, called for the federal government to step in and take the
lead in nation-to-nation negotiations. David said the only reason
the Mohawks had talked with John Ciaccia was that Ciaccia claimed
to represent the federal government as well. Negotiations, said
David, should start with the premise that the Six Nations Iroquois
Confederacy was a separate nation, recognized in the 1784 Treaty
of Fort Stanwix between the Mohawk Nation and the United States,
and was the only legitimate government of the Mohawks. No senator thought to interject that these sounded more like conclusions
than preconditions to a negotiation. Billy Two Rivers and Davis
Rice, representing the Mohawk Council of Kahnawake, seconded
David's views.

On the second day of hearings, Rick Van Loon and Yves Desilets defended the government rather modestly.[10] They described
current policy and asked the senators for thoughts on how things
might be improved. Other voices were more critical. Georges Erasmus and Vice-Chief Ovide Mercredi of the AFN and Max Yalden of
the Canadian Human Rights Commission both called—the former
two presenters more vehemently than the latter—for a rework-
ing of the land claims process. The AFN's critique was hard-hitting
and so comprehensive it would have been hard to know where to
begin. Yalden focused on the multiple and conflicting roles of the

government—really, DIAND—as negotiator, adjudicator and funding source. All three agreed that the recent decision in the *Sparrow* case meant that extinguishment of aboriginal rights as the price of a treaty should no longer be a federal objective.[11] Kahntineta Horn, a Kahnawake Mohawk who had accompanied Walter David Sr. the previous day, testified that the Warriors, once the barricades came down, would require protection from the SQ. She spoke mainly of the Mohawk Nation's desire for complete sovereignty—separate nationhood from Canada, and nothing less. On this point the AFN did not wholly agree, saying only that the eventual solution had to come from Kanesatake.

Fred Drummie and I met with Confederacy chiefs at DIAND, a departure for a department hitherto adamant that the only legitimate leadership was the band council recognized under the *Indian Act*. Quebec, for its part, dropped its objections to international observers and announced it would compensate citizens who suffered financial losses stemming from the conflict. On the international front, Bishop Desmond Tutu, a hero of the resistance to apartheid in South Africa, announced he would be coming to see the situation for himself.

The Warriors had their share of distractions as well. On August 4 a passel of AFN lawyers and advisors arrived at Kanesatake but were rejected by the Mohawks as probable government spies. The AFN's constituency was too divided—and Erasmus's feelings too bitter— for the delegation to be effective. The AFN's muted pronouncements tended to focus on side issues, such as the desirability of having international observers around.

The federal and provincial governments reiterated that the preconditions regarding access to food, medicine and advisors, as well as the presence of international observers, had long been met. Could we please get back to the table? Our insistence produced only the release of a whole new set of preconditions, which Siddon denounced the next day, August 5. The Mohawks, using without permission the letterhead of the Haudenosaunee, were back to demanding recognition as a sovereign state in a territory extending over parts of Ontario, Quebec and New York State. It is hard to imagine what the substance of negotiations might have been about if these were but preconditions. Nonetheless, the Mohawk legal advisor, the egregious James O'Reilly, said on behalf of the Mohawk negotiating team that Ciaccia had not agreed to the three original preconditions "and was dragging his feet purposely." Bourassa, incensed, said that unless negotiations began within forty-eight hours, Quebec would take the steps it had to take to restore public order. Kanesatake made a rude riposte. Things were not simplified by a release from George Martin and the Traditional Hereditary Chiefs denouncing the Pines negotiating committee. The release called them a "select negotiating committee... controlled by a minority of external interests," and said that the Warriors' true objectives were "beyond territorial disputes and settlements, and concerned directly their lust for greed and power." In Châteauguay there was a further violent demonstration, once again requiring the SQ to act in the unaccustomed role of protector of Mohawks from the larger community.

It was in these circumstances that on August 6 Bourassa sent his famous requisition to the Chief of the Defence Staff for the use of the armed forces in aid of the civil power. National Defence Headquarters formally ordered Mobile Command to prepare to intervene. In Geneva, the WGIP's immediate parent body, the UN Sub-Commission on Prevention of Discrimination and Protection of Minorities convened, with the Mohawk issue raised the first morning. At Kahnawake, fears were running high. The community grapevine, always effective, was supplemented by the Kahnawake radio station CKRK. Some further evacuation of community members took place, and Mohawk defensive works were extended in the next few days.

Lawyers continued to be enriched by various parties affected by the blockades.[12] At Kanesatake, an orchardist sued, claiming the barricades prevented him from harvesting his ripe apples. The Club de golf d'Oka Inc. rather imaginatively claimed damages resulting from the cancellation of its insurance policy, as well as loss of enjoyment of the use of the course by its members. The club maintained that DIAND was responsible for the Mohawks and vicariously for all damages the Mohawks caused, an extension of fiduciary duty which we in the department thought remarkable. As a final bit of absurdity, the club claimed that the whole situation resulted from DIAND failing to meet its responsibility to the Mohawks. At Kahnawake, Canadian Pacific launched a new claim, saying it could not use a portion of its track on the reserve because the Indians had dumped gravel on the tracks. DIAND was at fault, the CPR alleged, for not finding a solution to the blockade. A local automobile company sued the department for business losses flowing from the blockade.[13] High drama brought farce in its wake.

IN THE SPRING of 1990, the greatest achievement of Brian Mulroney's premiership hung in the balance. Eight years before, Pierre Trudeau, Jean Chrétien and nine premiers had amended the Canadian constitution to include a Charter of Rights and Freedoms and to cut forever the old colonial ties to Britain. The nine premiers did not include René Lévesque of Quebec, and repairing this wound in the fabric of confederation was Mulroney's greatest ambition. For this Anglo-Catholic son of Quebec who had won two majority governments by forging an electoral alliance between his home province of Quebec and the West, bringing Quebec willingly into the new arrangement was fundamental.

The story of the Meech Lake bargain has been told in detail, not least in Mulroney's own memoirs. The story of how it impinged on the affair at Oka is less well known. Meech failed at the last moment, after the most strenuous efforts by the prime minister, sixteen days before the death of Corporal Lemay. Both Mulroney and Bourassa were distraught. "Mulroney was in tears in the Cabinet room. I've never seen him... under any circumstances of adversity break down."[14] Depression and exhaustion followed, a period in which neither man was paying much attention to a minor road blockage in some woods in exurban Montreal.

Mulroney loved focus. His style was to concentrate on one issue at a time, to the degree that is ever possible for a prime minister, all the more so if the issue was basic to his political agenda. So when the deadline for ratification of the Meech Lake Accord by the provinces came and went on June 23 with two legislatures outstanding, Mulroney retreated to his summer residence at Harrington Lake for a few days and then had to depart for Houston and the G7 summit. Corporal Lemay was killed just before the end of the concluding press conference in Houston, and the prime minister was briefed on the plane coming home.

Under the circumstances, it made a lot of sense to Mulroney to accept the approach being worked out by officials and ministers in his absence: play the situation as a Quebec law enforcement issue and avoid taking the lead. He had great confidence in Robert Bourassa, a colleague and a friend since at least the October Crisis of 1970. In the aftermath of political defeat in 1976—Bourassa losing to the Parti Québecois (and losing his chief of staff to suicide for advising a snap election) and Mulroney to Joe Clark in the Tory leadership race—the two would meet at a restaurant called Chez Son Père, drink too much and bemoan their fates.[15] Later, both back in power, their relations were strong, and the emotional intimacy of the Meech Lake negotiations had only deepened the trust.[16] "How did this affect Oka? Well, massively in terms of his motivation. His motivation was to help Bourassa," Stanley Hartt recalls.[17]

There was another aboriginal twist to the Meech Lake catastrophe. Manitoba's Gary Filmon had promised to put the deal to his legislature, but when the time came to deliver, he stalled. The pretext was procedural, but the real truth lay in Manitobans' angry response to Filmon's agreement to produce official documents in two languages. The tactical advantage of this bit of bigotry was seized upon by the leader of the Liberal opposition, Sharon Carstairs, an old ally of Trudeau's.[18] Unlike Newfoundland's rigid and imperious Clyde Wells,[19] who openly disdained the deal, Filmon ducked behind a Cree member of the Manitoba legislature, Elijah Harper.

Many aboriginal leaders across the country were unhappy that Meech was a single-purpose amendment, intended solely to bring Quebec into the fold. They did not trust promises that other demands for constitutional reform, including those coming from aboriginal Canadians, would be dealt with in a later round. The vice-chief of the Assembly of First Nations, Ovide Mercredi, and future national chief Phil Fontaine were both from Manitoba, and they had determined to use the annual meeting of the Assembly of Manitoba Chiefs to get the deal opened, or at least to get binding promises of a future they would favour. Their weapon was the supposed necessity of unanimous consent in the Manitoba legislature to bring the Meech Lake Accord to a vote. Harper, eagle feather in hand, was the soldier.

Everybody at DIAND saw this coming. I warned PCO and PMO in increasingly strident terms as the AMC meeting approached. With some force, I urged Stanley Hartt and Norman Spector in PMO to send someone very senior who could clearly speak for the prime minister to Winnipeg to make the necessary deal, but neither took me all that seriously. The two Montreal intellectuals knew a lot about federal-provincial relations but little about Indian politics. I should have appealed, through Tellier, to the prime minister, but to my continuing regret did not. As the hours passed and the news from Winnipeg got grimmer, it was suddenly decided that Hartt, Spector, Senator Lowell Murray and I would take a Challenger and go out to Winnipeg. Unhappily, by the time we got there it was late on the second day of the meeting, and the minds of the Manitoba chiefs were made up. By that point, they were prisoners of their own rhetoric. As Hartt recalls, "We just got frozen out."[20]

Meech Lake was not the only thing on Mulroney's agenda that summer. There were the G7 summit, a visit from the Queen and a war to mount, following the surprise invasion of Kuwait by Saddam Hussein on the night of August 1–2. It was in this overheated context that the prime minister made his first important public intervention in the events at Oka on August 8. As Mulroney recalls in his memoirs,

> I decided on a carrot-and-stick approach. As a carrot, I announced that the highly respected Alan Gold, chief justice of the Quebec Superior Court, would serve as a mediator to seek agreement on preconditions to full negotiations. The stick? I also said that the Canadian Armed Forces would be available to the

Quebec government... Bernard Roy agreed to serve as federal negotiator. All parties in the dispute knew he had my full and complete trust.[21]

Mulroney had of course arranged all of this beforehand with Gold and Bourassa. It remained to retrieve Judge Gold from his summer home in New England. While Fred Drummie and a Challenger went off to collect the judge and brief him, army commander General Kent Foster made one of those quiet statements that allow all parties to take a deep breath. It would be a week, he said, before the army took up positions. There were logistical issues, and besides, he wanted to give Judge Gold's negotiations time. The residents of Châteauguay continued to manifest their impatience, and Elkas, in an attempt to mollify them, promised a bypass highway around Kahnawake—an announcement that did not help a lot, as it would take several years to build the bypass and the traffic jams were immediate.

Judge Gold arrived fully briefed on the federal position, met the Quebec authorities and was driven to Kanesatake, where he went behind the Mohawk barricades. Drummie met Judge Fouque, along with the experienced diplomat Dan Livermore, for dinner on August 11. They reached conditional understandings about the obligations of governments and the International Federation of Human Rights, subject to whatever coals Gold might be pulling out of the fire. In short order, the immensely experienced Judge Gold had agreement on preconditions to the resumption of negotiations. They were straightforward:

> The governments of Canada and Quebec agree that there will be unimpeded access of food, clothing, medical supplies, health care, fuel and the basic necessities of life to and from Kanehsatake and Kahnawake.
>
> The governments of Canada and Quebec will ensure unrestricted access to and from the Mohawk communities of Kanehsatake and Kahnawake of spiritual leaders, clan mothers, chiefs, advisors and attorneys as designated by the Mohawk Nation.

> The parties to this agreement accept the presence of an international team of observers to ensure the implementation of this agreement and to observe the process among the parties during which negotiations will be carried out. This team will consist of 24 persons chosen by the International Federation for Human Rights who will act as observers at Kanehsatake and Kahnawake.[22]

Tom Siddon and John Ciaccia arrived at Kanesatake for a signing ceremony. The shirts and ties of the government officials contrasted with the informal and sometimes masked and camouflaged appearances of the Mohawks. Gracious speeches were made by Ellen Gabriel, John Ciaccia and Tom Siddon. No matter: it was the pictures that counted. They made every news broadcast and newspaper in the country.

There was, of course, hell to pay. After all the promises of not negotiating with armed and masked men, or at the point of a gun, or while the barricades were up, the governments had allowed their most senior representatives to be manipulated into a Mohawk photo op. Never mind that the document was an innocuous statement of bland principles and understandings long reached. The Quebec media went nuts. Châteauguay rioted. Former Kanesatake grand chief Clarence Simon belatedly denounced the agreement as "void and non-existent," objecting to a lack of Kanesatake representation on the committee that signed it and that Kanesatake did not care about amnesty (a matter not in the agreement). The Montreal *Gazette* quoted Chief Tom Porter of the Mohawk Nation Council at Akwesasne as saying that governments had signed an agreement with the Warrior Society.[23] The paper noted that one of the Mohawk signatories was masked. *La Presse*, the mass-circulation Montreal daily, went further, providing the English names of the Mohawk signatories, all of whom used only their Mohawk names. Only two of the five signatories, Walter David Sr. and Walter David Jr., lived at Kanesatake, with the others coming from Tyendinaga, Six Nations and the "radical Longhouse" at Kahnawake.[24] John Ciaccia lost hugely, both with the general public and with his cabinet colleagues. Siddon's loss was mitigated by the fact that he was present mostly to support the prime minister's man, Judge Gold, but this did not abate the frustration in the Langevin Building. The government's claim that what had been signed was merely procedural, a clearing of preconditions before real negotiations began, was neither heard nor understood. And that claim was vitiated by the revelation that a Mohawk document whose text was unrelated to the English and French, and which recited Mohawk sovereignty goals, had been inserted into the package in the guise of a Mohawk translation and been duly signed by ministers.

THUS IT WAS that an apparently successful agreement on preconditions led to another two weeks of negotiations. These were doomed from the start, for several reasons. First, two new senior negotiators named by the federal and Quebec governments were unfamiliar with both the issues and the personalities involved; their claim to office was the prestige of earlier jobs and the personal confidence reposed in them by the two first ministers. Second, the large machinery of the army was beginning to swing into action. Within a week of the requisition, the army had replaced the SQ; within two weeks they were squeezing the two sets of Mohawk barricades; and by the end of the third week they had lifted the barricades on the Mercier Bridge. Third, non-Indian public opinion was beginning to harden, and not just in Quebec: the sympathy that was the Mohawks' principal negotiating capital was eroding day by day. And fourth, on the Mohawk side, the radicals, including imports like the U.S. lawyer Stanley Cohen, were in the driver's seat. Their demands became more and more extravagant, less rooted in reality and increasingly impossible for governments to agree to.

On August 11, Bishop Tutu arrived in Canada and visited the remote and media-free Osnaburgh reserve in northwestern Ontario. From our point of view, he contributed little except a widely published admonition to pay more attention to the plight of Indians in Canadian society and the suggestion that the country was practising apartheid.

Three days later, Tom Siddon formally announced the appointment of Bernard Roy as the federal government's negotiator for the renewed talks. Roy had arrived in Ottawa in September 1984 as principal secretary to the prime minister with no experience and · one credential, a friendship with Brian Mulroney going back to their days as law students at Laval. Roy's considerable intelligence is narrow, linear and legalistic, and his sense of humour can be well hidden. He lectures rather than converses, is stubborn in pursuit of *idées fixes*, is unaware of the impact of his pedantic self-presentation and has no guile. He is a great litigator and would have been a wonderful prosecutor. As a negotiator, he is utterly transparent, going straight to his bottom line. He is then bewildered when the other side doesn't immediately meet him there. The Indians loved him.

Roy was matched for Quebec by Alex Paterson, a distinguished litigator from the Anglo-Quebec bar and at the time chairman of the board of governors of McGill University. Many of the government players that summer had to be recalled from holidays, and Paterson was no exception. It took calls from Ciaccia, Parisella and Quebec justice minister Gil Rémillard to persuade him that his duty lay back in Montreal late that summer.[25] Paterson has a more relaxed personality than Roy, but he suffered from poor briefing and an unclear mandate. Quebec's "strategy committee" was composed of the calm and widely respected Claude Ryan; John Ciaccia, who wished fervently for a negotiated solution and was willing to go some distance in policy terms to get it; Sam Elkas, whose pragmatic instincts were affected by his responsibilities as minister for the police; Yvon Picotte, minister of municipal affairs; and André Bourbeau, minister of manpower and a representative from the south shore whose constituents were feeling daily the inconvenience of long commutes. As Paterson recalled in his memoir, *My Life at the Bar and Beyond,* "I quickly learned that, once the committee had made a decision, Parisella and Chamberland [Rémillard's deputy minister] had the political authority to give instructions regarding this decision but that Ryan, as chair, had the moral authority to change the instructions themselves."[26]

Paterson's account of the negotiations is first-rate. He describes having to phone a woman at Kanesatake to learn that the negotiations would begin at the Dorval Hilton on Thursday, August 16.

There was a crowd of more than fifty Mohawks present that day, as well as a throng of media people. The Mohawk spokesman, Joe Deom, berated Paterson for guiding the press to the negotiating site, which Paterson had not done. Paterson agreed that negotiating in the middle of such a circus would not be productive, declined Deom's invitation to go behind the barricades and insisted that he would not negotiate with masked or armed people. Deom and Paterson agreed to meet the next day at a Montreal restaurant, where a smaller crowd of Mohawks and no press showed up. Loran Thompson opened the meeting with a "theatrical and impressive speech on the Great Law of Peace . . . and also recounted the story of the Two Row Wampum Treaty, which I had not heard about."[27] Canada had broken the treaty, said Thompson, by sending missionaries, taking most of the land and polluting the rest. Paterson realized that the issues at the heart of the Mohawk position went well beyond his mandate, which was limited to arms, barricades and the Mercier Bridge:

> Despite the sincerity and single-mindedness expressed by Chief Thompson, I found him to be an example of the confused state of affairs. He was a spiritual leader who nevertheless believed that the Akwesasne Longhouse should share in the profits made through the gambling casinos and the cigarette trade. He was obviously not alone in this view. Joe Deom represented another contradiction. A Kahnawake Mohawk who endorsed the Warrior Society, he claimed to follow the Great Law quite literally. Others in the room opposed the Warrior Society but seemed to have no problem joining the Warriors at the negotiating table.[28]

The next day, the negotiations moved to the Trappist monastery near Oka. Paterson reports in his memoir that Ellen Gabriel and Billy Two Rivers were helpful in keeping the process on track. Two Rivers, in particular, explained that frequent pauses would be necessary for the numerous Mohawks present to compose a single view.

By August 20, the deployment of the army was in full swing, leading to understandable accusations that the negotiators were not serious, not to be trusted, a stalling front for an invasion and the like. At this stage, Mohawk demands were clear: transfer land title to Kanesatake (which Roy could agree to); an inquiry into the sq raid of July 11 (quite possible); negotiate the short-term land needs at Kanesatake with the Longhouse (the federal government had already agreed to the objective, if not the legitimacy of the interlocutor, though that was bridgeable); and amnesty for all (vehemently denied by Quebec justice minister Gil Rémillard and his deputy Jacques Chamberland). There was no impossible gulf. But between August 18 and 23, recalls Paterson, "Whenever I thought that we were close to a plan to dismantle the barricades, I would find the next morning that the members of the Mohawk negotiating team had changed."[29] Things changed again on August 23. "That morning, Joe Deom arrived and began to read out a long list of frightening and heartbreaking incidents that had occurred during the standoff. The culminating story was of Annette Diabo, a pregnant woman from Kahnawake who went into labour on the reserve but then, part-way through delivery, began to haemorrhage. She needed to get to the hospital, and an ambulance was called."[30] The Châteauguay mob stopped the ambulance and stripped Ms. Diabo, supposedly to verify what her medical attendants were saying. After an hour, and with the arrival of a second ambulance, she was taken to hospital, where the baby arrived. Both mother and child were unharmed, but the incident underlined the inability, or worse, of the sq to protect the most vulnerable members of the community.

August 23 was also the day the army moved to shorten its lines. The atmosphere of the talks became so bad that Paterson concluded that "it was unlikely we would reach a settlement... By the next day I had accepted that the larger issues of land claims and recognizing Native people as a distinct society had to be dealt with... I concluded that our major achievement had been providing a delay that helped other negotiations—between the army and the Mohawk, between Ciaccia and another group of Mohawk, and between Elkas and a third group—take their course."[31] Two days later, the Mohawks escalated their demands, saying that the territory around Oka and Châteauguay should be ceded to them. Ciaccia, who had been negotiating with the Confederacy in Toronto, pleaded with his cabinet colleagues for more time, but by then Bourassa's mind was made up. On August 27, he announced the end of negotiations, saying his government "would not be held hostage by a bunch of hoodlums, many of whom are not even Canadians." Bourassa's cabinet, meeting that day, was united against John Ciaccia and in favour of bringing the affair to a quick end. The army would dismantle the barricades.

The escalating demands of the Mohawks, first the Pines and the golf course, then land unification for Kanesatake, then the whole of the seigneury of Lac des Deux-Montagnes and finally full-bore international sovereignty made a negotiated solution impossible. No federal government, especially one dedicated to fighting Quebec separatism, could possibly acquiesce in tearing hunks out of Canada for a new country called Kanienkehaka.

above Early days in the Pines at Kanesatake. In May and June 1990, masked Warriors began to supplant local Longhouse people.
© CP PHOTO/RYAN REMIORZ

top right Warrior Richard Nicholas ("Cancan") stands atop the barricade on Highway 344 built in the hours just after Corporal Lemay's death on July 11, 1990. © CP PHOTO/TOM HANSON

bottom right Piles of earth lie on the Châteauguay approach to the Mercier Bridge. They were added on July 17, 1990, to a concrete barrier set up immediately after the Sûreté du Québec raid at Kanesatake on July 11.
AP PHOTO/GEORGE WIDMAN

left A Warrior keeps watch on the SQ from behind the new barricade on Highway 344 on July 12, 1990, while two others check press reports.
© CP PHOTO/PAUL CHIASSON

above The SQ man their barricade at the Oka end of the Highway 344 hill running down from the Pines while Warriors maintain their position at the top, July 24, 1990. © CP PHOTO/RYAN REMIORZ

above Ellen Gabriel, *centre,* with supporters. Gabriel stood up to the
SQ on July 11 and was the principal spokesperson for one Kanesatake
Longhouse before the Warriors pushed her aside on July 18, 1990.
© CHRISTOPHER J. MORRIS/CORBIS

top right John Ciaccia, Quebec's minister of Native Affairs, *under umbrella
at right,* seen here in July 1990 with clerical observers, tried passionately
to prevent the SQ raid and to build bridges afterward, but he was overcome
by larger political forces on both the Quebec and Mohawk sides.
© CP PHOTO/RYAN REMIORZ

bottom right Newly elected Prime Minister Brian Mulroney and the co-
chair of the national economic conference, Stanley Hartt, in 1985. Hartt
became deputy minister of Finance and, in 1989, Mulroney's chief of staff.
© CP PHOTO/RON POLING

top left Behind the barricades at Oka, with the flags of Quebec and Canada framing those of the Mohawk Nation and the Haudenosaunee, Tom Siddon, John Ciaccia and Judge Alan Gold, *left to right*, sign an agreement to seek agreement on August 12, 1990. © THE GAZETTE (MONTREAL), 1990/ JOHN KENNEY

bottom left Norman Spector, Mulroney's new chief of staff, hands documents to the prime minister at a federal-provincial meeting on Meech Lake in June 1990. Senator Lowell Murray is at lower left, with Joe Clark, minister for Constitutional Affairs, looking prayerful at lower right. ANAND MAHARAJ/OTTAWA CITIZEN. REPRINTED WITH PERMISSION.

above Elected premier of Quebec for the third time, Robert Bourassa introduces his youthful chief of staff, John Parisella, in 1985. © THE GAZETTE (MONTREAL), 1985/GEORGE BIRD

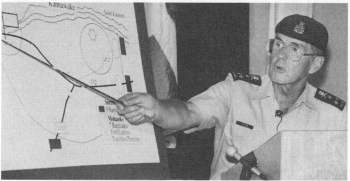

top left Senior officials deal easily with the disjointed questions of M.P.S. Clerk of the Privy Council Paul Tellier responds to a question during the parliamentary inquiry into the al-Mashat affair, June 1991. CHRIS MIKULA/ OTTAWA CITIZEN. REPRINTED WITH PERMISSION.

bottom left Talks lead to an agreement to hold more talks. *Left to right:* Assembly of First Nations regional vice-chief Lawrence Cantorelle, Kahnawake chief Joe Norton, Quebec Minister of Native Affairs John Ciaccia, Premier Robert Bourassa and the AFN's regional vice-chief for Quebec, Konrad Sioui, in July 1990. CP PHOTO/CLÉMENT ALLARD, © 1990

top Chief of the Defence Staff General John de Chastelain talks to the press on August 28, 1990. PAT MCGRATH/OTTAWA CITIZEN. REPRINTED WITH PERMISSION.

above Lieutenant General Kent R. Foster, head of Mobile Command (the Canadian army), at a press conference at CFB St.-Hubert.
© THE GAZETTE (MONTREAL), 1990/PETER MARTIN

top left Soldiers from the Third Battalion Royal Twenty-second Regiment (the Van Doos) load guns and equipment into their armoured personnel carriers as they prepare to go to Châteauguay to replace the badly rattled SQ on August 18, 1990. © CP PHOTO/TOM HANSON

bottom left Jenny Jack, a Tahltan woman from British Columbia, kept her head on September 2, the day the army squeezed the Warriors into the treatment centre. She saved at least one life that day.
© LINDA DAWN HAMMOND

above Warrior stares at soldier, September 2, 1990, saying (for the ever-present cameras), "You're going to die today." Neither man did.
© ROBERT GIROUX/AFP/GETTY IMAGES

above and right Sympathy protests exploded around the country—from tents on Victoria Island, a traditional camping place in the Ottawa River, just under Parliament Hill, to a Lil'wat blockade on the Duffey Lake Road in B.C.'s Pemberton Valley to drummers at a rally in downtown Vancouver.

top left Celebrities came to burnish their reputations for fearlessness in defence of human rights. The Reverend Jesse Jackson, however, was refused entry to the treatment centre and missed the hoped-for photo op.
© CP PHOTO/GAZETTE, PETER MARTIN

bottom left Warrior Gordon Lazore ("Noriega") protects Kahntineta Horn as they are arrested when the occupiers exit the treatment centre on September 26, 1990. © CP PHOTO/BILL GRIMSHAW

above The Mohawk cemetery in the Pines, its very existence denied by some in 1990, is peaceful today. © THE GAZETTE (MONTREAL), 1999/PHIL CARPENTER

8

THE ARMY
TAKES OVER

WHEN THE anticipated requisition for the use of the Canadian Armed Forces arrived from Quebec on August 6, Brian Mulroney's political conundrum crystallized. The prime minister might have pre-empted Bourassa by using federal powers under the *Emergencies Act;* that way the federal government would have remained the locus of political accountability for the armed forces. But intervening without a clear request from the province was impractical, as well as politically unthinkable, and when the request came, it arrived in a form that transferred accountability unequivocally to the Quebec government.[1] Popular demand for federal involvement was about to be satisfied, but in a manner that left Ottawa looking like it had complete political accountability for the behaviour and effectiveness of a great but long-starved national institution that it did not, in law or in fact, control. In Quebec, even the staunchly federalist provincial government wondered about an attack from the sovereigntists for using a federal institution to solve a Quebec problem. In the end, both concerns evaporated. The army carried out its duties with a degree of thoughtfulness that—given the budgets and respect that society at large is willing to accord its armed forces in peacetime— Canadians had little right to expect. Domestic internal security operations require strategic sensitivity, tactical brilliance and firm discipline where boots meet the ground. Canada was lucky on the first and well served on the rest.

The *National Defence Act* charges the Chief of the Defence Staff alone with deciding how to respond to a provincial requisition. Any level of effort, from a sergeant on a bicycle to the whole of the armed forces, any rules of engagement consistent with the Queen's Regulations and pretty much any kind of accountability to civilian authorities is up to the CDS to decide.

Canada's top military man in 1990 was General John de Chastelain. His unusual background endowed him with a breadth of thinking exceptional for a man who had taken up his profession as a teenager. He was born in Bucharest in 1937 of English parents, his father having been sent to Romania as a senior manager of British interests in the Romanian oil fields. The senior de Chastelains lived well and knew everyone who mattered in pre-war Bucharest. British intelligence, realizing the dangers posed by Hitler's plans for eastern Europe, recruited de Chastelain's father, Chas, to organize the sabotage of the Romanian oil fields to keep them out of the hands of the Germans. De Chastelain's mother, Marion, took John and his sister to England, where she later worked for William Stephenson, the Canadian chief of British and American counterespionage who was code-named Intrepid. Reunited after the war, the family moved to Calgary, where Chas continued his career in the oil business. It was from Calgary that young John joined the militia in 1956, transferring to the regular forces later that year. He was sent to the Royal Military College at Kingston, took a degree in history and settled down to an army career. It was a solid one, built in the context of the Manichean struggle between East and West in central Europe. His experience included Cold War regimental service in Europe, a peacekeeping assignment in Cyprus, a stint at the British staff college, command of an armoured brigade and headquarters staff work. In September 1989, Mulroney chose de Chastelain as Canada's seventeenth CDS, a position he would hold through the end of the Cold War, Oka and the first Gulf War.[2]

Like many other senior people in Ottawa, de Chastelain was out of town when the balloon went up on July 11. He was in Leningrad, as a guest of the Soviet chief of staff, General Mikhail Moiseyev, when he got word from Vice Admiral Chuck Thomas, back in Ottawa, that it looked as if Bourassa was on the verge of asking for aid to the civil power under the *National Defence Act*. The Russians arranged for de Chastelain's plane to pick him up, and he arrived home to not one but two crises—Oka, and after August 2 the dawning commitment of Canada to provide a naval squadron to the multinational force being assembled to wrest Kuwait back from Saddam Hussein.

The general's first formal act on getting Bourassa's requisition was to task Mobile Command at its headquarters in St.-Hubert, Quebec, to prepare to intervene. The order was not as content-free as that bald statement suggests, since de Chastelain had informally discussed what needed to be done with the army's commander, General Kent Foster, in the preceding days.

Foster came from a military family. His father, Ross, and two uncles had served in World War II; Ross Foster, a coal miner from the Alberta Rockies, fought as a private soldier through the desperate battles of Ortona and Monte Cassino and took part in the liberation of Holland. The army was in Kent's blood. He joined the cadets in high school, took time off for a degree in engineering and began his military career with the storied Princess Patricia's Canadian Light Infantry. Over the years, he rose to command First Battalion PPCLI, the Airborne Regiment, the First Special Service Force, and eventually, as lieutenant general, Mobile Command—the whole Canadian Army. Like de Chastelain, who was the best man at his wedding, Foster qualified as a paratrooper. Like all successful soldiers in the Cold War era, he had served with much larger formations in Europe than Canada's modest military could provide, and he had developed a strong sense of comradeship with soldiers of Canada's Western allies.

Foster is not a tall man, in an organization that prizes physical strength and endurance. Nor, as a chemical engineer coming from Coleman, Alberta, was French a natural for him. At the peak of his military career, he was called on to command, among others, the francophone troops of the Twenty-second Regiment, the Van Doos, and to answer to a francophone government in a province whose public opinion was markedly different from that in the rest of the country. Quite a challenge.

The forces had had a close-up whiff of violence in the Mohawk world through their assistance to the RCMP at Akwesasne that spring. From then on, they had kept an eye on Kanesatake, and from July 11 on they had been actively, though quietly, providing equipment to the SQ. By the time the formal requisition came from the Quebec government, a good deal of planning and forethought had already gone into the exercise, and de Chastelain and Foster had come to some basic conclusions. The most important was, as Foster later said, "There's nothing in a golf course—a *nine-hole* golf course, fer Chris' sake—worth a human life."[3] Foster and de Chastelain would, in other words, craft rules of engagement and operational orders that minimized the chance of injury to Indians, bystanders and soldiers. They also realized that, police forces having failed, the army was the last barrier before social breakdown. Displaying visibly overwhelming power, both men thought, would make it clear that there was little future in armed opposition, thus minimizing the chance of further shooting from the Warrior side. And while political accountability lay with the Quebec government, the politicians in Ottawa had a real need to know what was going on. From the beginning, the two men split the job. Foster, already stationed in Quebec, took on most of the conversations with the Bourassa government, while de Chastelain handled the day-to-day communications with the prime minister, the cabinet and official Ottawa.

They also decided to assist the Quebec government in specifying precisely what it was asking the forces to do. On the suggestion of Major General Gordon Reay, the chief of land operations, a simple letter was drafted in response to the requisition, specifying four objectives and asking for the premier's concurrence. The objectives were to (1) remove the barricades at Kanesatake and Kahnawake; (2) restore freedom of movement on all roads and bridges; (3) remove all strong points; and (4) restore normal conditions of public order and security. Capturing lawbreakers or retrieving weapons were not specified objectives. As de Chastelain recalls today, "Essentially what we didn't want, in the event of a problem, was the province coming back and saying, 'Well, we never asked you to do that.'"[4]

The civilian side of the Department of National Defence was headed by Deputy Minister Robert Fowler, a career diplomat who had been Mulroney's foreign and defence affairs advisor in PCO. Fowler was highly regarded by his peers in what was not always an easy job. Understanding and being duly guided by the proper spheres of command in this Janus-headed department had led to difficult relations and ill feelings between deputies and chiefs of the defence staff in the past. In the event, Fowler and de Chastelain managed the relationship exceptionally well.[5] Minister of National Defence Bill McKnight, never a headline-grabber, was more than usually invisible to the public on the Oka file in 1990, in part because he bent over backwards to avoid even the appearance of interfering in a colleague's business, and in part because the army in Quebec was not under his control anyway. Better, therefore, that communications come from the professional military or from the Quebec government.

Grumbling about headquarters micromanagement has bedevilled military (and diplomatic) field operations ever since the dawn of modern communications. The archetypical example is probably that of President Johnson and Secretary of Defense McNamara and their senior officials in Washington targeting air strikes in Vietnam. And it is true in this case that an activist deputy minister and a fully engaged political level in Ottawa suffered temptations that were not always firmly rejected. However, the formal command arrangements, which made the army commander the responsible authority for domestic operations and all assets assigned to Op SALON, were firmly on the side of good sense. They allowed Foster to build a fully integrated multi-disciplinary and multi-jurisdictional headquarters in the field. As a side benefit, Foster explained, "It allowed me to keep appropriate tabs on the SQ. I knew more about what they were doing than some of the ministers being given reports from them."

As noted, after the prime minister made his speech on August 8—Judge Gold or the army—General Foster announced publicly that it would be a week before the army took up positions. In a briefing at the time, Vice Admiral Chuck Thomas told the federal cabinet, "I am going to do this so deliberately that I might be accused of sloth. But I am going to create time for you politicians to use words before we have to use bullets."[6]

On Saturday, August 11, in the picturesque south shore resort town of St.-Jean Port Joli, Premier Bourassa met Canadian Forces and Sûreté du Québec commanders at a closed and unpublicized planning session. They agreed that soldiers of the Fifth Brigade would replace the SQ at the barricades but would rely on the Quebec police for all normal duties behind the lines: traffic and crowd control, regular policing and so on. Lines of communications, billeting and transport of troops, vehicles and weapons would involve both groups. The army made Bourassa and his staff aware that they could shut things down very fast—in "a couple of hours"[7]—but at an intolerable cost. Two days later, the Fifth Brigade deployed units involving 2,500 troops from CFB Valcartier to assembly areas near Kanesatake and Kahnawake. These movements were announced by the CDS just before they happened.

While all this was going on, things turned decidedly worse at Châteauguay. There were three nights of rioting: August 12, 13 and 14. Angry commuters and others threw rocks, bottles and Molotov cocktails at the SQ, who were stationed between the Mohawks and the mob. Because of past overzealousness, the SQ had been ordered not to charge rioters but simply to hold the line and absorb the abuse. Tempers were short all around, and the SQ was becoming seriously overstressed. Rumours of an offer of amnesty angered police further, and through their union they demanded an unqualified statement of support from the government and threatened to strike if their members had to endure more assaults by the crowds.

On August 15, the RCMP were asked to assist the SQ, and Superintendent Lowell Thomas was sent from Ottawa to take tactical control of 240 Mounties drawn from various units who had been sent to the site. Rather than parcelling out the reinforcements in penny packets, Thomas arranged for the RCMP to take full responsibility for one particular sector, while he worked with SQ regional headquarters in Delson to keep actions coordinated.[8] Having the RCMP present relieved some of the pressure on the SQ and seemed to have, for a while at least, a moderating effect on the mobs that gathered each afternoon. Kahnawake residents, now behind police lines, were becoming somewhat ambivalent about their own actions and the way the police should be viewed. Partly in preparation for possible evacuation, the community appointed an emergency planning coordinator, whom DIAND assisted in connecting with the province's emergency preparedness people.[9] As a practical matter, the Mohawks were shut off from their normal shopping venues in Châteauguay, and over the contrary views of some SQ officers, one of the first tasks of the RCMP (and of the army, when they arrived on scene a day or so later) was to arrange deliveries of food, clothing and medicine to the community.

Oka-inspired blockades continued to arise sporadically across the country. On August 13, DIAND was informed by CN that the Long Lake #58 Indian Band, in northern Ontario, had erected a tent reinforced with railway ties on the main line where it passed through the reserve.[10] The people there questioned CN's legal claim to the right-of-way and disputed that they had been a party to the Robinson-Superior Treaty of 1850, so that aboriginal rights persisted on unceded land. Their chief disappeared, and a strong sympathizer, Professor Tony Hall from the University of Lethbridge, appeared as negotiator.[11] Again, DIAND's Don Goodwin handled the issue, settling matters without giving the appearance of acquiescing to the sort of blackmail that could engender dozens of copycat actions. A key part of the resolution was getting Ontario to pay its share of the cost for a highway right-of-way that had been expropriated years before.

British Columbia was also the scene of many protests. During the second week of August, there were road blockades by the Penticton, Okanagan, Mount Currie, Kispiox, Boothroyd, Gitksan-Wet'suwet'en and Skeetchestn bands; one or two charged tolls.[12] Under pressure, Premier Vander Zalm called for the province to join treaty negotiations, while denying the existence of aboriginal title and refusing any responsibility for the costs. He managed to both insult the Indians and look weak at the same time.

On August 17, again with the idea of causing no unpleasant surprises, the Canadian Army announced it would be replacing the
SQ at Kanesatake and Kahnawake under aid of the civil power. On
the following Monday, 400 troops moved into Kahnawake and 385
into Kanesatake. The loose cordon that had been set up by the SQ
at Kanesatake was moved up by 400 metres. Angered Mohawks
initially refused to resume negotiations at the Trappist monastery.
By the end of the day, the army had fully taken over from the SQ
at both locations. Not that the SQ could go back to ordinary duties,
especially at Châteauguay, where they were still needed to keep the
white mobs at bay. On Tuesday, August 21, white commuters barricaded the Mercier Bridge, angered that it was open to Mohawks
only. There was some jostling over one of the Mohawk positions, but
by 6:35 PM all posts were occupied and all checkpoints functioning.

The next day, after a briefing for DIAND employees with Fred
Drummie and Roger Gagnon, I went to St.-Hubert to meet and
brief the army leadership. That day, a bunch of white vigilantes
had tried to stop Kahnawake residents from bringing in supplies by
small boat from Dorval. Comprehensive air photography revealed
there had been many improvements to the Mohawk positions over
the previous week. There were many more infantry trenches, anti-
armour traps and route denial obstacles designed to force infantry
to dismount from armoured vehicles and thereby increase their
vulnerability to hidden Warriors. As a result, three Leopard tanks
with bulldozer attachments were quietly ordered up from CFB Gagetown. It was not their cannons that might be needed but rather
their ability to reduce barricades while under fire. With the agreement of the armed forces, the RCMP and the SQ began monitoring
traffic on Lac St.-Louis.

On August 23, the army moved forward again, to the north of
the Pines at Kanesatake. The northern barricade on Chemin du
Mille was not being manned, and the army simply moved into the
vacated positions. This produced the first serious nose-to-nose
confrontation. Although they had announced their intentions,
the army's move seemed to surprise the Warriors, some of whom
became extremely upset. One man, shrieking and brandishing his

gun, caused a soldier to drop to his knees, load and cock his weapon. Jenny Jack, a Tahltan woman from northern B.C., herded the angry Warrior away, yelling, "Get back," and pushing him. Having seen footage of this incident, I have no doubt Jack saved at least one life that day.

On Saturday, August 25, as negotiations were breaking down again, the Mohawks accused the army of not letting food and medicine cross the barricades. This was either a misunderstanding or deliberate disinformation for the media. The story was quickly dispelled, but tensions were climbing. In one incident, a Warrior and a soldier yelled at each other until the soldier was ordered back. Late that evening, a shot was fired by a Warrior when air force parachute flares lit up Kanesatake; the flares had been sent up because of vehicle noise and Warrior movements. The next morning, the feds turned the screw by releasing a communiqué from the Confederacy, which stated, "The Warriors represent no one. They represent themselves." General Foster attended a federal-provincial meeting of officials at which the political decision to end negotiations in the face of escalating rather than converging demands was relayed, with all recognizing that it was now up to the forces to complete their mission.

August 27 began as a hard day for the Mohawks, and it was soon to get worse. The Quebec cabinet confirmed that there would be no further negotiations and that the army would proceed to remove the barricades; Bourassa said all this and more in public. Siddon, in parallel, expressed regret to the media that this must be so and released the latest Mohawk position papers with their extravagant demands for land, sovereignty and amnesty. These were widely published, and they had the expected effect on Canadian public opinion. In response to worries expressed publicly by Finn Lynghjem, one of the international observers, Monique Landry responded vigorously that Canada had been, and would continue to be, completely cooperative with the international observer team. General de Chastelain said he hoped no one would be hurt but announced that the army would fire if fired upon. Less publicly, the general warned Canadian Forces bases across the country that local demonstrations might be stirred up by impending moves at the barricades. By this time, however, secret communications between the army and the Kahnawake leadership were also well established. The Kahnawake leaders began to bargain for float planes to be allowed access to their community—not to bring more *matériel* in, but the other way around.

Early the next morning, Warriors at the Oka barricades were replaced by elderly men, women and children. The move was slightly unnerving, since it was the tactic that had been used before the SQ raid on July 11. However, whether there were armed Warriors in the woods behind the non-combatants mattered little, since the army was not about to storm the encampment. General Foster announced that the three Leopards had been summoned, but only for the safe removal of barricades, if it came to that. Meanwhile, unpublicized talks across the wire at Kahnawake were going well, despite a horrible incident at the north end of the Mercier Bridge. In a disgraceful exhibition of racism, mob violence and SQ non-interference, a convoy of seventy cars trying to leave Kahnawake on August 28 was stoned on the LaSalle (Montreal Island) side of the bridge. An elderly Mohawk man, Joe Armstrong, was hit in the chest. He died in hospital the next day. The Kahnawake Warriors, however, seemed to make the distinction between a mob of bigots and the disciplined behaviour of the military. In the talks, Loran Thompson and Chief Joe Norton were the principal spokesmen for the Mohawks, while Brigadier General Armand Roy, and from time to time Sam Elkas, spoke for the authorities. Bit by bit, an understanding grew on both sides about the role of the Van Doos and army engineers in clearing the Mercier Bridge, and about the use of small aircraft when the magic moment came.

There has been a degree of controversy over these flights, which were alleged to have taken place on the night of August 28. After the fact, the army told civilians and police assembled in the Langevin Building for our regular PCO meeting that a number of flights—up to twelve—had landed and taken off during the night, presumably carrying high-value weapons and personnel. The DND War Diary records these flights as having been observed by 3R22eR (the Van

Doos on the spot), by the ADATS[13] radars at St.-Hubert and by U.S. Customs on the New York State line as they flew back and forth between Kahnawake, Ganienkeh and Akwesasne.[14] For some time, I thought these "flights" might be fictitious, a fabrication to explain why no one had found weapons that matched the more lurid lists provided by police and military intelligence. I recall asking at the time what kind of aircraft, flown by whom, and destined for where, and getting very vague answers: "We don't know. Down the St. Lawrence?" Even today, people's memories are spotty. Kent Foster recalls:

The day it was to have happened was one of foul weather and very limited flying conditions. Reports of aircraft sounds were made and noted. Our surveillance assets could not confirm conclusively the nature of the reported sounds nor any activity. The stories ranged from huge amounts of weapons and malcontents to failed attempts to achieve anything. What I know is the key personnel were there at the end and in custody and the weapons burned at the site are in the photographs.[15]

Even de Chastelain is vague on the subject:

I recall hearing about it, but I don't recall ever getting any evidence that it actually took place... And it would have to have been a light aircraft to be able to get in, and therefore the amount of weaponry they would be able to take out would be small. But why by plane? Why not by just packing them in a truck and driving down the road?[16]

On balance, I am now inclined to believe that these flights actually did take place, and that they moved some heavy weaponry to places of hiding in preparation for the next insurrection. Otherwise, the army would have had to fake entries in a document, the War Diary, that it considers holy. Moreover, the instructions to the CDS under the requisition were written by three experienced generals, and those instructions deliberately did not include objectives any police officer would have put at the top of the list—the apprehension of the bad guys and the seizure of their weapons. Under the circumstances, I believe what probably happened is that General Roy and his men saw a way of opening the bridge early if they let some Warriors and guns escape. Since the troops were officially peace officers under Quebec legislation, a little studied ambiguity after the fact could well have been constructive.

August 29 was the breakthrough day. All day long, the army and the Warriors struggled to find a way to take down the barriers at the Mercier Bridge without bloodshed. Today, General de Chastelain credits Joe Norton and Loran Thompson as realists who slowly brought most elements of the community onside.[17] Early in the day, General Roy announced that he had a simple mission: to clear the barricades. Later, Foster announced that the Mercier would be open "soon." Late in the day, as more troops were on the way from CFB Farnham, a group of Warriors emerged from behind their barricade bearing a peace pipe. Ceremoniously, with military courtesy, the two sides smoked the sacred tobacco.[18] The army announced that Indians and soldiers would work side by side to dismantle the barricades at the Mercier Bridge, starting that evening and continuing the next day.

At Oka, the military left a back door open. The road to the north was studiously uncovered, and the people in the Pines were so informed. They did not believe what they were told by the army officers on the ground, however, suspecting a trap. The army, though perhaps not the Quebec government, and certainly not the SQ, would have been quite happy if Warriors and weapons had quietly stolen away in the night. The fact that they did not raised in my mind even more insistently the idea that the situation was less a fight to the death and more a fight for headlines. Back in Ottawa, planning was going on for a post-Oka world. Joe Stanford, the Deputy Solicitor General, convened a meeting to discuss the elements of post-operational policing: good arrest procedures (that is, procedures that would not jeopardize successful prosecutions); ensuring proper behaviour by police and dealing with the inevitable accusations of police brutality, real or otherwise; and long-term policing arrangements at Oka and in other parts of Indian country.

By this point there were about thirty-five Warriors left at Kanesatake, twelve of whom were actually from the community. In addition, a number of women, children, elders, white advisors and journalists remained. The news from Kahnawake had made some of the Warriors at Kanesatake really angry. Some had a few drinks and began vandalizing properties, white and Mohawk, inside their perimeter. Two Warriors, Lasagna and Noriega, trashed a house belonging to a white veterinarian, then invaded another and beat up the Mohawk inhabitants, Ronnie Bonspille and Francis Jacobs, who had had the temerity to suggest that such behaviour did not match the high ideals of the Warrior Society.

On September 1, the army began a pre-announced squeeze of the Oka perimeter. They reduced the remnant Mohawk "territory" to a space about 100 by 200 metres, surrounding the alcohol and drug treatment centre between Highway 344 and the river. About ten of the Warriors took the occasion to melt away. Again, the Mohawks feared a final assault; again, the army said they would not shoot first. By the end of the day, all residences in the area were once more available to their owners, though many were in bad shape. All roads except 344 where it passed the treatment centre were open, and the last barricade across the highway was inspected for explosives and then demolished the next day, clearing the highway. The woods were full of soldiers camping, and the country motels and hotels were full of SQ officers, but things were otherwise close to normal. One aspect of that normalcy was some low-level grumbling among the troops, who compared their army pay with the overtime paid to the SQ, and their tents and sleeping bags to the motels and freshly laundered sheets enjoyed by the police.

Over the weekend, the army and the SQ did a detailed search of the area that had been retaken from the Mohawks. They also ensured the resupply of food to the group at the treatment centre. On Sunday, September 2, they moved the razor wire a few metres farther forward, including around the entrance to the treatment centre, where they stuffed the driveway with wire. My feeling that this was a media war, not a real one, was reinforced when Jenny Jack circulated a list of a dozen reporters chosen by the Mohawks to be there for their "last stand." The Montreal *Gazette*, whose reporting was relatively thorough and balanced, was not among the favoured. The army, always looking forward, discussed surrender modalities with Mark Davis, a lawyer for the Mohawks in the treatment centre.

Toward the end of August, an odd problem had arisen in DIAND. Kahntineta Horn, a Mohawk activist who had been on educational leave from the department, was overdue to return to work. It turned out that she was "behind the wire" at Oka. I sent Horn three increasingly peremptory letters demanding that she return to her post, under penalty of the disciplines specified in the *Public Service Employment Act*. When she refused the third letter, I fired her. I think this was a surprise to Ms. Horn. It was certainly a surprise to DIAND's human resources people, who blanched, obeyed and told me what Horn's severance pay and continuing health and other benefits would be. I said there would be no severance for abandonment of position, nor would there be continuing benefits.[19]

At Kahnawake, the road barricades and approaches to the Mercier Bridge were cleared by the end of the day on Saturday, with detailed inspection of the bridge itself scheduled for first thing Sunday morning by Quebec department of transport engineers. Shortly after midnight a company of soldiers walked and inspected the bridge, looking principally for explosives, and found none.

Not everyone was onside with the Kahnawake leadership, however. On Monday, September 3, a group of about fifteen Warriors attempted to re-seize the Mercier Bridge, putting a small sandbag barricade in place. The army responded with armoured personnel carriers and troops, and the Warriors retreated. Later that day, on the basis of RCMP intelligence, soldiers backed by SQ surrounded the Kahnawake Longhouse and seized dozens of weapons, including a .50 cal heavy machine gun and three AK-47s. Retaliation took place at the International Bridge at Cornwall, near Akwesasne, which three Warriors tried to occupy. They were foiled after ninety minutes, but two squad cars were overturned, and there was gunfire as well as a demonstration. The Quebec Transport people, spooked by the sandbag barricade, would not inspect the Mercier Bridge until that afternoon.

On Tuesday, the army displayed the seized weapons for the media. Chief Joe Norton said the weapons had been planted by the authorities, but he was not widely believed. The Mercier Bridge was declared safe, but five Ontario Hydro towers were brought down by explosives near the reserve of the Oneidas of the Thames, near London. Mohawk occupiers at Oka were increasingly stressed, not least by the night-time harassment of the armed forces, who shone spotlights into the area of the treatment centre, played rock music at high volume and occasionally flew wailing CF-5s at low altitude to take pictures illuminated by parachute flares. Edgy Warriors manhandled some troops, who, well-disciplined, did not respond. Again, the Warriors were told they could leave freely, as long as they abandoned their weapons, but their lack of trust and fear of the SQ meant there was no take-up. The Confederacy asked Tom Siddon to have the army stop their "constant night games," not understanding that the army was under the control of the Quebec government and in any case in charge of its own tactics. The army kept up the pressure, returning the bulldozer-equipped tanks, two Chinook helicopters and a battery of 105mm guns to Gagetown and the CF-5s to Cold Lake, but also doubling the line of concertina wire around the treatment centre and, with the SQ, setting up a log boom in the river to prevent small-boat access.

At 10:00 AM on September 6, the Mercier Bridge reopened for traffic, but relations between Kahnawake and Châteauguay remained poor. General de Chastelain urged the Warriors at Kanesatake to lay down their arms and place themselves under military control and custody, an important distinction for people who feared and despised the SQ. It had taken some artfulness on the part of lawyers to have Farnham, a military base, construed as an ordinary civilian jail under military control, which allowed the offer to be made, and it had taken de Chastelain and Foster a degree of studied impatience with government lawyers, who were good at finding reasons why things could not happen. The offer was spurned by the Warriors, but remained open. Late in the day, an accidental discharge of a weapon injured a soldier, resulting in half a dozen shots from the Mohawk side that hit nothing. At dawn the next morning,

Warriors breached the two rows of wire. Tempers flared, insults and rocks were thrown, but when the local commanding officer ordered bayonets fixed, things subsided. Oneida chief Terry Doxtator issued an unusually threatening statement, possibly related to the bombing of the power pylons near his home reserve two days earlier:

> This statement is the first of our warnings to the Governments of Canada and Quebec that our patience runs short, that we are now setting in motion plans for the liberation of our defenders of the Nation of Kanesatake. We only deliver three warnings, and the fourth time we speak it is behind the action we have set into motion.[20]

By September 8, the little patrol boat HMCS *Acadian* had finished her surveillance work after two weeks on station and was ordered home. General Roy agreed to the return of the displaced citizens of Oka and Kanesatake. A surveillance report gave the number of people inside the treatment centre as 78: 24 Warriors, 23 journalists, 11 children, 9 women, 6 negotiators and 5 treatment centre patients.

September 8 also saw one of the few incidents of indiscipline by the army. At about 5:00 AM, a reconnaissance patrol inside the wire stumbled on a snoozing Mohawk Warrior, Spudwrench—Randy Horne—and beat him up. His battered face was in all the papers, and he had to be taken to hospital. This was not only bad publicity; it was entirely unnecessary. A junior officer, "an adventurous spirit from one of the battalions,"[21] according to de Chastelain, had ordered the soldiers to have a look at Mohawk defences under cover of darkness, so it was the officer, not the soldiers, who got a rocket from General Foster. "It was the feeling of the person on the ground that he could do his job a bit better if he knew a bit more about what was going on behind the barricades. My reaction was we didn't need to know that,"[22] recalls de Chastelain.

The transformation of a serious armed insurrection into a continuing photo op for the media was becoming ever more apparent. At our morning PCO meetings we seriously debated cutting off communications between the treatment centre and the media and making the Warriors focus on a single channel: the hotline to the local commander. I argued strenuously that this was a media circus that would deflate quickly if punctured, a viewpoint increasingly supported by the military. The other view—that cutting off outside communications would be an infringement of the human rights of the people behind the barricades—was championed by John Tait, the deputy minister of Justice. The larger infringement, I argued, was that of the insurrection itself. In the end that view carried the day, and the Department of National Defence applied for warrants in a Montreal court. Bell Canada was instructed to inactivate the phones it could, and the army would jam the rest. One journalist had somewhat amusingly asked the army for supplies beyond food and medicine. De Chastelain recalls:

> A journalist from... the *Globe and Mail*... inserted himself behind the wire at Kanesatake—which was a police line... so what the reporter did in this case is illegal...—his batteries ran out on his cell phone, which he was using to file his stories, and he demanded that we replace them, and we said no... Later his newspaper took us to court over the fact that we would not provide him with the ability to carry out his livelihood. The judge who heard the case made his ruling the day the Warriors burnt their weapons and came out. As I recall it, he told the newspaper something along the lines: "I've made my ruling, but the situation is no longer extant... Do you still wish to hear the ruling?" And the *Globe* said, "We do." The newspaper did and was told (again, something along the lines): "I find against you. In the first place your reporter was breaking the law in going behind the line. In the second place it was his voluntary decision to go behind the line, and DND had no obligation to provide him with anything. In the third place, if anybody had an obligation to provide him with supplies, it was the Mohawks... So I find against you, and with costs." I never saw the papers publish an account of his ruling, and certainly not the newspaper concerned.[23]

Attempts to broker a solution continued sporadically. On September 8, Tom Siddon met with Manitoba MLA Elijah Harper, who had sent in a peace proposal from the Six Nations Confederacy. It was a non-starter, Siddon said after the meeting: "The proposal presumes that individuals involved in the dispute who may face charges will not be dealt with under the same system of law that applies to every resident of Canada. This is unacceptable."[24] A day later, the department issued a clarifying statement: "There is only one set of negotiations currently—between the armed forces and the Warriors via the 'hot-line' [a dedicated land line] into the treatment centre."[25] Then, just to keep the pot boiling, the Six Nations Confederacy chief, Oren Lyons, denounced Elijah Harper, saying the materials that purported to come from the Confederacy and through the Mohawk Nation Office at Kahnawake were unauthorized.

At the treatment centre, there was a small breakthrough. Oneida chief Bob Antone, an advisor who, along with Bruce Elijah and Terry Doxtator, had been allowed in on the grounds that they might calm troubled spirits, proposed that the Warriors surrender to the army and be held at a military base outside Quebec.[26] CFB Farnham, which was prepared both legally and logistically to receive detainees, was a base in Quebec, and the army had no police powers in any other province. Still, it was a step forward. On September 9, the army announced that Spudwrench was out of hospital and that he and his wife had agreed to be placed under military custody at Farnham. The wary respect among military professionals on both sides, which had helped get agreement on opening the Mercier Bridge, was beginning to sprout to a smaller degree at Oka. Meanwhile, ordinary military routines continued. Second Company of the Van Doos was replaced, First Commando went back on forty-eight-hours' notice and other troops were preparing to return to base. A plan to search an area near St.-Alexis where intelligence suggested there was a weapons cache was finalized. Countermeasures to a possible Mohawk "helicopter insertion" into the barricaded area were planned. At Kahnawake, the SQ, protected by a cordon of soldiers, performed a search and seized more weapons and ammunition. The siege continued.

Also on September 9, Tom Siddon met with more than a hundred AFN chiefs at St. Joseph's parish hall in the quiet Ottawa neighbourhood of Sandy Hill. Ovide Mercredi was presiding, and the mood in the room was genuine anger. Siddon's two young assistants, Susan Yurkovich and Jacquie Prokopanko, were frankly terrified.[27] After a period of venting in the hot and airless hall by the assembled chiefs, Siddon—who had been taking notes—rolled up his sleeves, stood up, threw away his prepared text and delivered the speech of a lifetime. All the passion and eloquence he could muster was laid before the chiefs. And of all things, at the end, they stood and applauded. Carol Goar gave Siddon the best coverage he ever enjoyed in the *Toronto Star* the next day.[28] His speech was a turning point in the conflict, and it made the eventual resumption of normal relations between the government and the First Nations considerably smoother.

Behind the lines in the treatment centre, U.S. lawyer Stanley Cohen was busy working on a new proposal. This "nine-point peace proposal" was passed across the line to the military, who forwarded it to the government of Quebec. When both governments rejected it outright, on the basis that it was illegitimate to treat Mohawks differently under the law from any other citizens of Canada, Cohen saw his influence inside the camp begin to decline. In Ottawa, seething at the rejection, Georges Erasmus threatened to "bring Canada to its knees," one of the few occasions on which the straitjacket of his constituents' disunity failed to restrain his rhetoric. Three days later, brought to heel by the chiefs, Erasmus was constrained to say, "We have blatantly [sic] ruled out the use of violence. Anyone who picks up a gun in this country and is involved in a political cause is threatening his cause."[29] In contrast, one of the strict constructionist members of Bourassa's cabinet, Justice Minister Gil Rémillard, said that the Mohawks were a great people and that Quebec was willing to recognize at least some degree of autonomy for them, even though the Cohen proposal was constitutionally impossible.

On Saturday, September 13, following the grant of a warrant, the army cut the civilian land line into the treatment centre, leaving only the military hotline and either killed or jammed cell phones. Besides cutting off access to the media, the end of the ordinary land line meant that the army no longer had to deal with the SQ listening in.[30] That day, there were two incidents of the Warriors firing blanks at troops. The next day, when the Priorities and Planning Committee of Cabinet met, Oka and Iraq were the principal issues. In a now-familiar pattern, the Second Battalion of the Royal Canadian Regiment assisted the SQ in two separate raids at Kahnawake, looking for arms. The soldiers formed a cordon around the police while police did the search and seizures. At Oka, commanding officer Lieutenant Colonel Pierre Daigle announced that journalists could no longer transfer film, video or audio recordings across the wire and indicated they should leave the treatment centre. The Canadian Association of Journalists protested, but to no avail. An announced demonstration by 3,000 native Americans at Oka failed to materialize: only 250 showed up. Water and electricity to the treatment centre were briefly shut off.

On Sunday, claiming they were out of food, Warriors started to raid nearby evacuated white-owned houses. Kahnawake delivered a formal eviction notice to the army, a letter alleging soldiers were drinking on duty and a complaint of harassment, all of which were ignored. The army told journalists that if they left the treatment centre to get legal advice they would not be allowed back. Negotiations of a sort continued over the hotline to the army. The only thing the army was willing to talk about were the modalities of the inevitable surrender, but the demands from those inside the wire became ever more strident. By the Monday morning, September 17, a complete impasse had been reached. Chief Bob Antone said that any agreement had to include provisions for future negotiations on sovereignty. The army's response was that it had no mandate to discuss such issues. Antone's second letter of the day backed away from grand politics and asked three simple questions: Who did the military and the government see as the legitimate representatives of the Mohawks? What assurances would the military offer if the Warriors turned in their weapons? Were any such assurances binding on the government?

At 2:30 in the afternoon on September 18, again in response to intelligence about weapons, the army descended in force on

Tekakwitha Island at Kahnawake. Troops arrived by helicopter and went toward the eastern end of the island, where a causeway joined it to the main part of the community. A large number of men and a few women from the community had come running when they heard the helicopters and crossed the causeway before the soldiers could seize it. A serious melee started, with about two hundred Mohawks confronting a platoon of soldiers. Fists and rocks were thrown, and the lieutenant in command was wrestled to the ground and semi-strangled with his binocular strap. Several soldiers were injured, four of whom later required hospitalization. Two C7 rifles were taken by Mohawks. The sergeant brought troops to the aim, and finally the platoon commander had his soldiers fire their rifles into the air and release CS, a really nasty sort of tear gas. Slowly the outnumbered (and ill-equipped, for crowd control) soldiers stabilized the line and performed their search for weapons. Five caches with a total of forty-seven weapons were uncovered.

In retrospect, the army recognized it should have sent troops equipped with riot shields, face masks and batons rather than with high-powered automatic rifles. Nonetheless, discipline carried the day. In a telling example of both honour among combatants and factionalism in the community, the two C7's were returned to the army the next day by Mohawk peacekeepers.

At Kanesatake, the Warriors and the army had agreed that there was nothing left to discuss. On September 20, General Foster announced, "The Army's task is near completion." His words caused a frisson of panic to run through the treatment centre, where people thought he was uttering an ultimatum. At his press conference, Foster made it clear that the offer of military rather than SQ custody still stood, that the flow of food, medicine and children's clothing would continue unimpeded, that the military footprint would be gradually reduced in preparation for the SQ to take over normal policing and, finally, that search operations would continue unannounced.

The last weekend of the occupation contained the usual mixture of farce and high drama. The *Ottawa Citizen* and the Montreal *Gazette* both said they would be going to court to get a reversal of the injunction that had authorized the cutting of cell phone communication. This met with an oblique response from Mobile Command, who told the *Citizen* that their reporter was free to leave any time he wished; the military would lay no criminal charges, but of course they did not speak for the SQ in the matter. The army, still worried about the possibility of a U.S.-based Mohawk helicopter extraction from the treatment centre, practised their planned counter-measures. Joe Norton announced that the Rev. Jesse Jackson and a television crew would be coming to Kahnawake and Oka on September 27. Reluctantly, Norton's colleagues on Kahnawake's emergency measures committee agreed to allow a police force of twenty native officers to be stationed in the community, fearing those officers would be traitors who would report back to the SQ. Earlier, Joe Clark, as minister of External Affairs, had replied to a critical letter from Barón Enrique Crespo, the president of the European Parliament, telling Crespo in the usual polite terms to get stuffed. Searches for arms continued. In the early hours of Sunday morning, a Warrior threw a smoke grenade at soldiers and warned that the next one would be real. Later, some of the journalists behind the wire expressed a wish to leave the treatment centre. The military agreed, under three conditions: (1) the journalists would be searched for weapons; (2) they would be taken to company headquarters, so that they could call lawyers if they wished to do so; and (3) they would be interviewed by the SQ. If they were accredited journalists, they would be free to leave; if not, they would be escorted to Farnham. No more Mr. Nice Guy, at least for journalists who had chosen to break the law.

On Monday, September 24, three days early, the Rev. Jesse Jackson, Joe Norton and a U.S. television crew appeared at the army lines at Kanesatake and were told to go away. Jackson had to settle for an interview with John Ciaccia, who was at least as sympathetic to the surrounded Mohawks as the Rev. Jackson was. It all made for poor TV. In a further sign that times were returning to normal, the Kanesatake negotiating team requested funding from DIAND for their operations. Without a continual cell phone feed from the treatment centre, media attention was drying up. On Tuesday, the

Warriors requested a special prosecutor; Bourassa said no. Chief Antone said the Mohawks were fed up and would disengage by the end of the week. Stanley Cohen walked out of the treatment centre, his credibility with the Warriors at an end. Offered army custody, he declined and surrendered to the Sûreté du Québec, who informed him he would be arraigned in court the next day. At that point Cohen reconsidered the virtues of military custody, but it was too late. His arraignment specified obstruction of justice and carrying a firearm, and he was freed on bail. Alanis Obomsawin, a celebrated filmmaker with the National Film Board who had been behind the wire since early August, likewise departed. She was searched for weapons and allowed to leave. A last-gasp Haudenosaunee proposal—army custody, weapons to go to the Confederacy and a special prosecutor—was sent to the Quebec government and briskly rejected by Rémillard, who cited the last point in particular as unacceptable. A water fight broke out in the treatment centre.

On Wednesday September 26, around 7:00 PM, the Warriors made a bonfire of their weapons, papers, tapes and other possibly incriminating evidence, prayed and then around sundown made a breach through the concertina wire and began walking out toward Oka. They had earlier signalled they would be coming out around noon, and the army had ordered buses to take them to Farnham. But it was an emotional time behind the wire. One or two Warriors, notably Lasagna (Ronald Cross), had not wanted to give up, and hours had passed in persuading him to join the consensus. Mad Jap (Robert Skidders), who had played a moderating role as one of the principal leaders in the treatment centre, helped Elijah, Antone and Doxtator convince people that there was nothing to be gained by carrying on. People shared hugs and tears as they prepared to leave. Their initial attempt to cut the wire was accompanied by a scuffle with the army and a high-pressure water hose, so they chose another exit. The soldiers were confused by the change, and in the fading light they started to round up the refugees. Most—26 men, 16 women, 6 children and 10 journalists—surrendered and were taken to Farnham. A young Mohawk woman, Kahntineta Horn's daughter Waneek Horn-Miller, sustained a minor wound from a bayonet.

In the confusion, Loran Thompson walked quietly through the woods and got clean away. Eleven people, including six who had escaped the military cordon, were detained by the SQ; three were later released. Three women and five men remained in SQ custody; the men were later tried. At Kahnawake, according to DND's after-action report,

> An hour and a half later there were two separate confrontations at Kahnawake between troops and large groups of Mohawks armed with shields, baseball bats and gasmasks. In one particular incident a military platoon was bombarded with rocks which caused a soldier to go to the ground. The crowd then moved in and attacked the fallen soldier. Fisticuffs resulted when his section extracted him. The natives continued to advance which caused the platoon to fix bayonets and eventually fire six M38 Flightrite gas grenades into the crowd. Warning shots were fired in the air and the platoon was required to load and cock their weapons in the face of the advancing crowd. Reserves were brought in and the situation calmed down. Two natives were injured by the ricochet of the M38 grenades. The injured soldier was a Private Feldman who sustained a minor skull fracture.[31]

These clashes were probably a response to arms raids rather than a demonstration of sympathy with the people at the treatment centre, though there was copious media coverage of the surrender. The Mohawks, quick learners, had adapted their tactics since the Tekakwitha Island raid; the army apparently had not. Fearing escalation, the SQ occupied and closed the Mercier Bridge for an hour and a half, starting at 11:00 PM.

Arraignments began the next day, with eleven charged. On Friday, a lawyer from the U.S. consulate in Montreal visited the military custody area in Farnham, since a number of the detainees were, in American if not in Mohawk eyes, U.S. citizens. By Saturday, the Van Doos had withdrawn from Oka to St.-Benoît, leaving the Sûreté in charge. A phased return-to-barracks plan was set in motion. (The army's initial plan would be modified following a discussion between the CDS and Bourassa in mid-October, in which it was agreed that a 500-man "rapid reaction force" would stay in the Montreal area for some time. Quebec was worried that the abrupt departure of the troops might lead to a flare-up of violence. The transition to SQ control was essentially complete by the end of October, but since the government of Quebec did not formally withdraw their requisition until May 30, 1991, some units were kept on standby for considerable periods. All costs were borne by the federal government.)

Following the departure of the occupiers, the army's search of the treatment centre grounds turned up burned debris from 12 shotguns, 4 handguns, 10 rifles, 28 assault rifles and 114 magazines. There was enough food in storage to keep the group going for months, along with tobacco, beer, hard liquor and marijuana plants. The Kahnawake peacekeepers also turned in a few weapons, bringing the total for that community to 141 weapons of all types, 44 Molotov cocktails, large quantities of ammunition and, curiously, one crossbow.

Altogether, some 4,500 military personnel were involved in Op SALON, the army's name for its response to the Quebec requisition, with a maximum of 3,700 at any one time. Despite provocations, including assaults and colourful epithets, army discipline held. The only reported injuries to Indians during the siege were to Spudwrench, in an incident of overreach by a junior officer, and to Waneek Horn-Miller, who was cut, presumably accidentally, during the sudden dusk departure from the treatment centre. Likewise, Warriors and their supporters at both Kanesatake and Kahnawake had shown restraint. About a dozen soldiers got beaten up severely enough to require medical treatment, but no fire was aimed at the troops. This may have been the only rational approach to the CDS instruction that the army would not fire first but would respond if fired upon. It nonetheless required discipline in the heat of the moment. In the end, the only deaths directly due to the crisis were those of Marcel Lemay and Joe Armstrong.

9

AFTERMATH

"People really learned something about First Nations."
ALANIS OBOMSAWIN,
in *Kanehsatake: 270 Years of Resistance*

JURY TRIALS eventually acquitted most people of all charges: there was clearly no stomach on the part of the courts for vindictiveness. Five people up on more serious charges, including assault and theft, were sentenced to jail for periods of up to six years, though Ronald Cross (Lasagna) was the only one to do time. Loran Thompson, who had managed to walk away through the woods unnoticed, had gone back to St. Regis, and a week later he gave himself up to the RCMP to face charges of assaulting a peace officer and breaking parole. Jean Ouellette was re-elected mayor of Oka. A year after the shootout in the Pines, the Indians staged a parade through the town; Elijah Harper was a prominent guest.

Some of the participants in the events at Oka died young. Tom "General" Paul, a Mi'kmaq from Nova Scotia and veteran of a number of actions including Wounded Knee in 1973, died in 1992 at forty-nine. Lasagna, half Italian, half Mohawk and all Warrior, was severely beaten in custody by the SQ, then convicted in 1992 of aggravated assault, uttering death threats, damaging two ambulances and possession of weapons, all stemming from Oka. After appeals, he served a sentence, then died of a heart attack in 1999, aged forty-one, defiant to the end. Eerily, Tom Hanson, the Canadian Press photographer who took the famous picture of the soldier and the Warrior standing nose to nose, died of a heart attack on the same day in 2009 as the photo's subject, Richard Nicholas, who was killed in a crash on Highway 344. Both men were forty-one.

Not all died young. New York lawyer Stanley Cohen declined to cross the border to provide testimony to coroner Guy Gilbert. In 1991, Cohen was busy in the New York courts defending Akwesasne Warriors. By 2006, his clients were plain drug smugglers.[1] Between the SQ and Cohen, the extremes of the obstructionist spectrum, Gilbert had his problems.[2] Ellen Gabriel, now the president of the Quebec Native Women's Association, is an eloquent spokesperson for social inclusiveness who reminds governments and aboriginal Canadians alike of their responsibilities. Kahntineta (now Kahentientha) Horn, a writer and the proprietor of Mohawk Nation News at Kahnawake, is as fierce as ever in her separatist views and her imputation of evil to the colonial settler governments. Her daughter Waneek Horn-Miller became an Olympic-level water polo player and is now coordinator of the First Peoples' House at McGill University. Loran Thompson continued to smuggle tobacco and liquor, though a judge dismissed one set of charges against him in 1998. His first witness at trial was Francis Boots, once war chief at Akwesasne, who told the jury that he believes "the Mohawks are a nation, a free people whose ability to adhere to their beliefs is compromised by the borders and laws of other nations."[3]

As noted, Robert Bourassa died in 1996 of the cancer whose treatment he had postponed during the summer of 1990. Judge Gold died in 2008. Claude Ryan retired in 1994 and died ten years later, respected and honoured by all. John Parisella is today an advisor to both Concordia University and Premier Jean Charest. All of the key federal government players are still around, with the exception of Robert de Cotret, who died in 1999. John de Chastelain went on to become a pillar of the ending of another much nastier insurrection, the war between the Protestants and the Catholics in

Northern Ireland. Kent Foster retired from the army and became the Health Canada ADM in charge of disease control as well as food and drug safety—still a guardian. Today, like retired Vice Admiral Chuck Thomas, he lives in Victoria. Brian Mulroney has been a highly successful corporate director—he had a strong hand in saving the U.S. agricultural company Archer Daniels Midland—but he has had health problems and has been the subject of a judicial inquiry into his dealings with a German businessman of ill repute.[4] Fred Drummie has retired to St. Stephen, New Brunswick, the province that kindled his interest in public policy. Richard Van Loon became the president who turned around a seriously troubled Carleton University. Ruth Cardinal and John Graham are associated with the Institute on Governance in Ottawa. Paul Tellier was successful in turning Canadian National from a sleepy, money-losing east-west railway into the most efficient of the six principal North American railroads, with service today all the way to New Orleans. Stanley Hartt became an investment banker. Tom Siddon retired to Kaleden, B.C., where he continues to contribute to public policy through his involvement in local government.

SOME DAYS AFTER the collapse of Mohawk resistance at the treatment centre, senior ministers of the federal government met at Willson House, an old mansion situated in the Gatineau Hills—on Meech Lake, in fact. On the agenda was an update on Oka. I was present to support my minister for what I'd been told would be a twenty-minute item. Twenty minutes became an hour and a half, as Brian Mulroney led his ministers through the most searching examination of aboriginal issues since Trudeau reversed course on his White Paper.

On being called into the room, I was again struck by the experience of the participants. Siddon, Crombie, McKnight and Campbell had been DIAND ministers. John Crosbie had wrestled with fisheries allocations for native people, as well as the recognition of an Indian band in his home province of Newfoundland.[5] Clark had negotiated extensively with Indian leaders during the Meech Lake constitutional fiasco. Mazankowski, McKnight and others had close personal experience of Indian communities dating to well before their parliamentary service. I can't think of a Canadian cabinet, before or since, with greater experience related to the issues at play.

Tom Siddon made a few remarks, then turned to me for a short factual update on the events of the past week. Following that, Mulroney opened a *tour-de-table*, asking each of his colleagues for their reflections. Each minister added a layer of depth to a discussion that began with old and familiar problems—the poor results and high cost of reserve housing programs—and continued to the darkest corners of our national existence. Personal stories from cabinet members elbowed out the special pleadings from staff in their briefing books. It was a remarkable discussion. At the end, Mulroney turned to me and said, "All right, Harry. Now I want you to pretend that you're the prime minister—and moreover, that you don't have to worry about re-election. What would you do?"

Seldom do bureaucrats get an opening like that. Three years' worth of everything I'd learned from travelling, talking to Indian people, reading, listening to and arguing with others in the department took wing. All that summer, John Rayner, ADM Policy pro tem, and his staff had been testing and refining ideas for what might fairly have been called the departmental agenda and discussing them with DIAND ministers. In twenty minutes, I presented the following arguments:

1. No progress on a new agenda could be made without dealing honourably with old obligations.[6] The government had to radically step up the pace of dealing with specific claims, and we needed new and less one-sided machinery for dealing with them. The biggest case going was treaty land entitlement on the Prairies, with Saskatchewan in the lead. That case should be pressed.

2. The present government had made huge strides in supporting self-government through modern treaties dealing with aboriginal rights. Nunavut was the brightest star in a cluster that extended across the Arctic and Subarctic, and the effort should be extended to British Columbia, the sole holdout.

3. Policy should focus on developing choices and options for Indian people. In that sense, the most important thing we did on reserves

was to support education, and it was fortuitous that funding for post-secondary education applied to all Indians, on reserve and off. These programs ought to carry high priority, and the government should avoid fiascos like the previous year's unthinking cutbacks to the post-secondary education program, one of our few unalloyed successes.

4. Self-government was unrealizable under the *Indian Act* and had certain practical limits if the polities concerned were limited to hundreds or a few thousand people at a time. Secondary institutions beyond the band council—either of a general political nature, like tribal councils, or sectorally focused ones, like tribal or province-wide school boards—needed support.

5. Finally, and crucially, the statutory base for Indian people needed radical overhaul. There were limits in how far the dominant society ought to go in consulting and accommodating the existing Indian political structure, itself a creature of the *Indian Act*. At stake was the honour of Euro-Canadians, who had invented this mess. But our goal should be to create options for aboriginal people, not take them away. Parliament should enact modern statutes to cover the subject matter of the *Indian Act*, as well as those areas that were usually in provincial domain but were constitutionally assigned to the feds, and make the choice of whether or when to move from the old *Indian Act* to a new one a matter of community choice. Over a period of decades, the old act would be hollowed out, relevant to fewer and fewer people, and could eventually be consigned to history's dust-heap.[7]

All of this was well received. We had been talking up Rayner's agenda all summer with the central agencies, and the prime minister had been briefed on the discussions. Mulroney had encouraged us with a statement in the House on September 25, the day before the end of the siege at Oka:

> The *Indian Act* is largely unchanged since the Victorian age. It fosters Indian dependency on the state, frustrates Indian self-sufficiency and undermines Indian self-respect. It diminishes Indians and non-Indians alike. In the new year, building on

work that is going on now with Indian leadership, we will bring in the first of many changes to the *Indian Act*. Consultation, and respect for the fiduciary responsibilities of the Crown toward aboriginal peoples, will be built into the process from the start. But we intend to go far beyond the status quo.[8]

Someone at the cabinet meeting that day asked what it would all cost. "Oh, perhaps $10 billion over 15 or 20 years," I said, suggesting a down payment of a billion for the next fiscal year. Moreover, some of that would be offset by lower social assistance payments as Indians repossessed productive lands and gained education that would better fit them for modern labour markets.

AN EVENT LIKE the Mohawk rebellion of 1990 would normally have called forth a judicial inquiry, a full-bore royal commission, a specific inquiry into an unlawful death, reviews by the several police forces and the armed forces and their oversight bodies, and reviews by Parliament and the Quebec legislature. Under the circumstances, the silence was astounding. As noted, the coroner's inquest that was held was delayed for five years by the legal manoeuvres of the SQ. Under trying circumstances, the distinguished lawyer Guy Gilbert finally managed to conclude as thorough an inquiry into the death of Corporal Lemay and the events that led up to it as any judge could have done.[9] Though the file remains open, it is unlikely that enough evidence will ever be found to charge anyone with Lemay's shooting. Gilbert was especially scathing about the nonchalance, prejudice and command failures of the SQ. His report did lead, however, to far-reaching changes in SQ management and practices in the latter half of the 1990s.

Quebec did not hold a broader inquiry and refused to participate in the Hughes Committee hearings, the only review undertaken by the federal government.[10] The province's rationale was that the Lemay inquest would cover everything in the provincial domain—it did not—and as for Hughes, a sovereign Quebec could not take part in a federal review that would necessarily touch on provincial responsibilities; indeed, a federal judicial inquiry would be improper, Quebec said, because of its invasion of provincial turf. In fact, neither government had much interest in the kind of searching review and recommendations that could have resulted from a properly constituted judicial inquiry. The sordid history of disregard for their own laws would alone embarrass any government not eager to pursue redress, and neither was. The Quebec National Assembly held no hearings. The feds, not eager to provoke the Quebec government in the aftermath of Meech and Oka, opted instead for a royal commission with the grandest possible mandate and a time frame ensuring it would report to the next government. The after-action reports of the army and police forces generally focused on the tactical and the local, drawing lessons for command and control but avoiding history and policy.

The Quebec Human Rights Commission published a report in April 1991 that detailed much outrageous behaviour by the SQ in particular.[11] After the conflict, four complaints about police brutality were filed with the Police Ethics Commissioner but were declared inadmissible. A new *Police Act* came into force on September 1, 1990. Any allegations from before that time had to have been filed by then, regardless of the difficulty of the circumstances. The Ethics Commissioner offered to have the director-general of the SQ take up the matter. In the face of the glaring conflict of interest, the Human Rights Commission asked that the investigation be undertaken by another police force. Claude Ryan had the last word: no.[12]

There was never a judicial inquiry with the powers to compel testimony, to examine and cross-examine witnesses in depth or to take testimony under oath. Instead, the procedures of a parliamentary committee would have to do: witnesses were invited to make brief presentations to the Hughes Committee and to answer questions from sitting members, each of whom were limited to ten minutes, with a possible second round of five minutes should the witness run out of words early. Such a committee's powers of subpoena are largely theoretical, and are certainly so in respect of the main players in a provincial government. One Mohawk group came to make brief, insulting and not fully factual presentations but would not stay for questions.[13] Some committee members could not resist the opportunity to land partisan barbs rather than focus diligently on sorting out the truth. Given the procedural disabilities that Parliament foists on itself—it makes its own rules, and fails miserably in enforcing them—the fact that the chair and the staff of the standing committee managed to procure so much useful testimony is quite remarkable.[14]

The committee's final report was brief, a mere forty-seven pages in English including all the tombstone procedural matters, and it made seven recommendations.[15] The report's call for a royal commission on First Nations in Canada would soon be answered. The committee spent some time in the report setting out their reasons for alarm about Part XI of the *National Defence Act,* which put in the hands of an overwhelmed provincial government the full powers of a modern military force fettered only by the good sense of its tactical commanders, and called for that part to be reviewed, with the goal of inserting more accountability into it. The committee also called for better machinery to govern land claims, though the details of their proposal were not notably workable. They wrung their hands about Mohawk governance and vaguely suggested involving the old Confederacy in discussions, called for some means of resolving land use conflicts at Kanesatake, urged healing and compensation, and—recognizing how much more work there was to do—called for a judicial inquiry.

The committee's heart was in the right place, but it would be 2008 before there was even a semi-independent Indian Specific Claims Commission. Today, the Mohawks still haven't resolved their governance issues, and a judicial inquiry was never held. Nonetheless, the testimony from the hearings, held from January to March 1991, is worth reading. It includes vivid stories of what it was like to live through that summer: police and soldiers ordering people around, in some cases abusing ordinary human rights; relentless noise from traffic, helicopters and blaring loudspeakers; uppity media everywhere; houses and property vandalized; crops unharvested; the local economy stood on its ear; great difficulties in moving around or getting to work; the closing down of supplies into the various communities and of ordinary services like mail and schools—and on, and on, and on.

Tom Siddon made a lengthy and spirited defence to the committee of the federal government's actions. He frankly admitted government failures, as well as to frustration in trying to negotiate across such deep divisions in the Mohawk community. He put on the record the elements of the "Native agenda" DIAND had proposed to cabinet the previous fall and reviewed the surprising number of claims settlements the department had arrived at in recent months, as well as others on the verge of signature.

Chief Oren Lyons of the old Confederacy set the events of the summer and what he saw as the unfortunate behaviour of all parties in the context of the long history of the Haudenosaunee. His tone was cool and lucid: a voice from well above the fray. Don Worme, David Nahwegahbow and Darlene Johnston, for the Indigenous Bar Association, argued that the fiduciary relationship made many of Siddon's (and by extension the department's) actions during the crisis unlawful, and strongly deplored the agreement reached by Judge Gold and the two ministers in the Pines. Mayor Jean Ouellette and his colleagues, the only Quebec officials to appear before this federal body, were stubborn and forthright in defence of the positions they had taken throughout the affair. They accepted no responsibility for what the SQ had chosen to do as a result of their request of July 9—and properly so, as the town council was not consulted in advance, they said, nor did they approve of the SQ's attempt to use overwhelming force in a poorly understood situation.

IN THE SHORT run, the department decided to press on that fall with the assembly of more land at Kanesatake. During the crisis, we had managed to get control of the Pines, and one or two other pieces were purchased, but the air went out of the effort once the barricades were down. Sellers, who had developed a sense of entitlement and a conviction that government agents were suckers, demanded unrealistic amounts, and the Kanesatake community could not decide who should be the legitimate owners. On the prime minister's recommendation, Tom Siddon appointed Bernard Roy, the distinguished lawyer from Ogilvy Renault, to carry on from where he had left off.

Roy's mandate had three parts, each more difficult than the preceding. First, he was to arrange for a contiguous piece of land for Mohawks in the Oka area instead of the patchwork quilt of Crown lands then held for them—the reunification project. Then he was to negotiate a self-government agreement. Finally, he was to explore the parameters of an overall settlement of the ancient grievance of the Kanesatake Mohawks.

West of Oka, Quebec's Highway 344 is separated from the shore by a strip, a few hundred feet deep, of woods and high-value exurban residences. Most of the Mohawk lands are north of the highway, though in several places farther west the Crown plots cross the highway and go right to the shore. Since the white-owned properties south of 344, within municipal boundaries, were some of the most expensive pieces of real estate in the area, the department's intention had been to concentrate on initial purchases in the interstices between Indian plots north of the highway.

Alas, the rational bureaucratic mind had once again failed to appreciate local reality. The baker's dozen of properties south of 344 had suffered exceptional drops in value due to the events of 1990. The wooded area where the confrontation had begun was just across the road, and the strip of properties had in its midst the treatment centre that was the focus of the siege. One or two of the properties had been trashed by Mohawk occupiers and left to rot by despairing owners, whose insurance companies had refused their claims on the grounds of rebellion. These wealthy, well-connected whites had an exceptionally active Tory M.P., Lise Bourgault, on their side; a sympathetic regional minister in Monique Landry (who was also, as minister of state for Indian Affairs, one of my many masters); and a francophone press, which likes to blame Ottawa for neglecting aggrieved Quebecers—among their numbers the senior partner of Ogilvy Renault, Julian Chipman, who owned the grandest and most expensive of the properties. It was the department's ignorance of this last connection—or more precisely, Bernard Roy's failure to disclose the fact—that led to our quandary.

When the government decided that fairness required offers to purchase the properties south of 344, the local media made headlines of the fact that the government's chief negotiator would be dealing with his own senior partner. Roy and departmental headquarters immediately moved to scotch the story, saying that the decision to make those offers was cabinet's and that the details would be handled not by Bernard Roy but by Public Works. Roy went farther, however, telling the press that he had disclosed this potential conflict of interest at the beginning of his assignment.

When questioned later by Dan Goodleaf, who had become DIAND's other associate deputy minister, Roy was unable to remember to whom disclosure had been made. The people he mentioned as possibilities had no memory of receiving such arresting news, and there was no letter or memo on file. The first any of us had heard of Roy's relation to Chipman was at a midday meeting of ministers on January 28, 1992, when Roy capped ten months of advice about the south-of-344 properties with the plaint that ministers ought to decide one way or another, since his senior partner was becoming impatient with the continuing delay.

That was a bombshell not just for me but for several of the ministers present, who exchanged startled glances before continuing the discussion. Roy had been late getting to the meeting, as he had dropped in at the office of his Right Honourable Friend, just down the hall from the cabinet chamber. His access to Mulroney was better than that of any ministers, so none felt like belling the cat. I had already raised the matter of Roy's conflict of interest with Glen Shortliffe, the associate secretary to the cabinet, who wanted to discuss the matter with Hugh Segal, chief of staff to the prime minister. Shortliffe was running day-to-day matters at PCO in the absence of Paul Tellier, who was by then fully occupied with the Charlottetown constitutional file. Shortliffe's job carried with it the senior oversight role on ethical matters; he was, for instance, the man to whom the conflict of interest commissar really reported. A tough-minded graduate of External, Shortliffe shared with Tellier, Barbara McDougall, Raymond Chrétien and Bernard Valcourt the blame for the spectacular mishandling of the al-Mashat affair in the spring of 1991, a situation in which civil servants fast-tracked the entry to Canada as a defector of Mohammed al-Mashat, the Iraqi ambassador to the U.S., without telling their ministers. Suffice to say that PCO broke most of the rules of crisis management in their handling of this affair. Shortliffe, who had drafted an apology for two of the principal players to sign in an effort to low-bridge things, saw the apology spurned by the intended signers and wound up looking like one of those fiendish communist brainwashers who extort signatures on bogus confessions. The press had a field day.[16] Nevertheless, Shortliffe was a good example of the really senior mandarin: experienced, wary, intelligent, privately passionate about public policy and possessed of a lot of stamina, a good sense of humour and a strong sense of loyalty.

More urgent matters than Roy's apparent conflict of interest soon occupied the press and the opposition, however, and since pricing for the land to be purchased was up to Public Works rather than Roy, the issue blew over. He continued as our negotiator until he was replaced by the Liberal government of 1993. In the end, the government purchased a number of pieces of property, including some of the expensive waterfront lands, where there were willing sellers at reasonable prices. The overall pattern still looks like a gerrymandered congressional district, but contiguity is better than it was before 1990. The transfer of the Crown lands at Kanesatake to the band remains stalled to this day, impaled on the inability of the Mohawks, elected or otherwise, to put forward a government able to speak for the people. The lands are still held in trust by the federal government pending a community decision on what it wants and how to treat existing tenures.

As for the rest of the agenda, talks sputtered on without substantial progress. The feds have from time to time been willing to consider a large *ex gratia* payment, if they could only figure out to whom it should go, but the one point on which the community seems firm is that land, not money, is the issue. Neither the federal nor the provincial government has the legal power to expropriate lands in these circumstances, and the possibility of getting enabling legislation through either legislature is, realistically, zero.

Of course, neither government will contemplate for a moment the cession of territory to a new nation.

WHILE LAND DISCUSSIONS dragged on fruitlessly, punctuated by occasional minor purchases by DIAND, a grander enterprise was taking shape. By the late summer of 1990, it was in the air that the government should establish a Royal Commission on Aboriginal Peoples—not a narrow or backward-looking inquest into the particular circumstances of Oka, or even of the Mohawks, but something that would take the broadest possible view in hopes of both reconciliation and setting a new path for a new century.

I was of two minds about this at the time. On the one hand, royal commissions can be wonderful tools for exploring complex questions and educating people about alternatives. Donald Macdonald's royal commission on Canada's economic prospects in the early 1980s was a classic example. The commission worked hard, held hearings all over the country, and through a brilliant staff published background papers still relevant today. The commission's report paved the way for a new openness in Canadian economic policy, and for the eventual negotiation of the Canada-U.S. Free Trade Agreement in 1987 and its NAFTA successor. Equally, there were commissions that ran amok. The later Somalia Inquiry under Mr. Justice Gilles Letourneau lost its way entirely and had to be closed down by a subsequent government. Much depended on the commissioners appointed and the terms of reference drawn up by the Privy Council Office.[17]

In this case, Mulroney asked the former chief justice of the Supreme Court, Brian Dickson, to consult widely and recommend terms. Dickson took a year to do so, meeting aboriginal groups across the country. No plea for inclusion was rejected. The result was terms of reference so broad as to be unmeetable:

The Commission of Inquiry should investigate the evolution of the relationship among aboriginal peoples (Indian, Inuit and Métis), the Canadian government, and Canadian society as a whole. It should propose specific solutions, rooted in domestic and international experience, to the problems which have plagued those relationships and which confront aboriginal peoples today. The Commission should examine all issues which it deems relevant to any or all of the aboriginal peoples of Canada.[18]

There then followed no fewer than sixteen specific subjects the commission was empowered to investigate, each of which would require a huge study by itself. On August 26, 1991, the government appointed as co-chairs Georges Erasmus, the recently retired national chief of the Assembly of First Nations, and René Dussault, a judge of the Quebec Court of Appeal. They were joined by five others—Viola Robinson, a Mi'kmaq activist; Mary Sillett, a founding member and later president of Pauktuutit, the national Inuit women's association; Paul Chartrand, a Métis scholar specializing in aboriginal law; Bertha Wilson, a former Supreme Court judge who, with Chief Justice Brian Dickson, had authored some of the more trenchant judgements on native affairs in the decade since the Charter; and Allan Blakeney, a former NDP premier of Saskatchewan. Blakeney soon resigned and was replaced by Peter Meekison, the former top civil servant of Alberta.

Astoundingly, once established, the commission felt that its terms were still too narrow, or were poorly specified, and so made up some more of its own, as set out in the commission's final report. "[T]he problems that plague the relationship cannot be addressed exclusively or primarily as Aboriginal issues [but as] the premises on which Canadian law and government institutions are founded and the human values that Canadians see as the core of their identity."[19]

Not much was to be left out of the commission's scope—and in the ensuing five immense volumes, not much was. Unfortunately, the commissioners became intellectually hostage to a potent combination of idealists, one-issue people short on context and what Widdowson and Howard call "the Aboriginal industry."[20] The commission dragged on for five years, eventually reporting in 1996 after spending more than $50 million. Its extravagant recommendations arrived just as the Liberal government's program review, made necessary by two decades of deficit and debt, was slashing government expenditures. Dead on arrival.

The government gave lip service to the commission's recommendations. Jane Stewart, the Indian Affairs minister of the day, put together a wan subset of the more practical recommendations combined with actions already underway, called the result "Gathering Strength" and attempted to overcome the synthetic contempt of the opposition and that of the Indian political organizations. Ovide Mercredi, by now National Chief of the Assembly of First Nations, called it "Gathering Dust." Later, some of the RCAP recommendations were echoed in Prime Minister Paul Martin's Kelowna Accord, a plan to spend $5 billion on nothing very precise that was subsequently shelved by Martin's successor, Conservative prime minister Stephen Harper.

RCAP left all participants with a sour taste. Aboriginal Canadians had been encouraged to place great faith in the commission and its outcomes; indeed its chairman, Georges Erasmus, was full of dire warnings about "the fire next time" if the entire package of recommendations was not put in play forthwith. But aboriginal people were badly let down, as much by their own leaders as by an ill-designed commission. Progressive white Canada saw the ignoring of the recommendations, and more particularly, the dashing of the Kelowna Accord, as further evidence of the dumbheadedness of Canadian governments. Mainstream Canada tuned out early, put off by the triumph of emotional rhetoric over practical solutions. In many minds, RCAP represents little more than another set of broken promises. But however impractical, the studies and the recommendations represent a lot of thought and debate, and the texts will be mined for some years to come.

OKA HAD MORE concrete outcomes than a vaporous royal commission, however. It profoundly changed the way ordinary Canadians thought about their fellow citizens. First, there was the flood of information. Forgotten people were at the forefront of national consciousness for several months, and the smoke from that blaze has not yet disappeared. Press coverage of aboriginal issues in the intervening decades has gone from sparse to relatively moderate. Moreover, its tone has become much more empirical; writers do not automatically assume that the Indian plight is an irreducibly bad consequence of colonial oppression. Today, there are as many articles in the press about on-reserve governance and mismanagement, environmental sins and illicit activities as there are about housing conditions, health and incomes. Books that focus on the uncomfortable realities that get in the way of official goals like self-government in very small communities, or the diversion of government payments to lawyers, consultants or chiefs and councillors, would have had a hard time finding a publisher before Oka. Authors Tom Flanagan, Frances Widdowson and Albert Howard, and Gordon Gibson offer views sympathetic to individual aboriginal people, but not to their governments, white or Indian. They supplement the more traditional—since the Hawthorn Report of 1966–67, at any rate[21]—exposés that focus on grief, guilt and anger. Alanis Obomsawin's film *Kanehsatake: 270 Years of Resistance* is a passionate story brilliantly told from one side, which among its other sins of omission did not mention that the reason the situation was not solved by negotiation was the Mohawk insistence on national sovereign independence being the issue, not just the lands of an old seigneury. The film's lack of objectivity caused some controversy, and it was not until it won an Academy Award that the CBC stretched its internal guidelines and televised it.[22]

Aboriginal people are beginning to tell their own stories in other ways, as well. There are many more aboriginal periodicals now than before Oka, though they are not widely read outside aboriginal Canada. Aboriginal writers such as Doug Cuthand, Richard Wagamese and Thomas King have been successful in addressing a wider audience. A number of native scholars now adorn the Canadian academy, including David Newhouse at Trent University and Taiaiake Alfred at the University of Victoria. Alfred, a Mohawk from Kahnawake, has put the case for the rebirth of independent Indian nations in several books and articles.[23] Overall, the diversity and volume of published opinion on aboriginal people and by aboriginal people in Canada has considerably increased.

In the absence of parliamentary will to tackle the statutory framework for Indian affairs, the Supreme Court has been the principal maker—crystallizer?—of Indian law ever since *Calder*. Judgements in the 1980s, attempting to cope with the consequences of the new Charter of Rights and Freedoms, tended to be far-reaching, generous and imprecise in their guidance to governments and private citizens. After Oka, and in part reflecting the retirement of Chief Justice Brian Dickson and Justice Bertha Wilson, judgements have on the whole tended toward balance and reconciliation. *Guerin* erected the famous fiduciary relationship in 1984, and *Ermineskin* put some limits around that relationship in 2009; *Sioui* found treaty obligations in the darnedest places in 1990, but *Mitchell*, through the lower courts especially, put limits on an extravagant extension of treaty rights in 1997. A great expansion of the law in the aftermath of an earthquake like the Charter, followed by careful scholarship that puts limits around earlier judgements, is perhaps to be expected; maybe it is an accident of timing that this occurred in Canada before and after Oka. Personally, I do not favour mere coincidence as a plot device, though legal scholars would no doubt qualify or dispute this conclusion.

Public opinion has evolved in the face of new information. There is a great sense of unease, for instance, about the systematic deracination of Indian peoples through the residential schools program and religious proselytizing. There is national guilt about this period, though outside the context of sexual predators, the approach stemmed from intentions that seemed acceptable at the time. Payments to the afflicted and a solemn apology by the prime minister in the House of Commons have not been protested by non-Indian Canada. On-reserve social and economic conditions have come in for much attention. At the same time, the often poor governance in reserve communities, in part a result of the *Indian Act,* has been given a cooler assessment.

The repute of some of the other actors in the Oka crisis has also affected public policy. The Sûreté du Québec took the heaviest hit. The quality of police planning and leadership on July 11, the sq's sometimes vicious treatment of the Indian people who fell into their hands, the force's unwillingness to prevent mob actions at Châteauguay and LaSalle, the threats by their union to go on strike in the middle of the crisis, even the fact that SQ members were paid overtime and stayed in hotels all that summer while the army camped out on soldiers' wages—the steady reports of incompetence seriously lowered the esteem in which all but the most intransigent and racist segments of the public held the Sûreté. The shocking incident at LaSalle showed what police "restraint" could produce. In the words of John de Chastelain, "yobs with bricks were starting to lob them at native families in cars, justifying their actions with the thought, 'Well, they've got guns, and nobody is stopping them, so why shouldn't we?'"[24] The SQ's long fight against the coroner's inquest was self-defeating, as it only encouraged Guy Gilbert to lay out in excruciating detail the actions of the police in the period leading up to the shooting of Corporal Lemay. The RCMP handled themselves well, but their role was not nearly so public, and there was thus little impact on the general view of the force.

By contrast, the Canadian Armed Forces, specifically the army, emerged with their reputation burnished. Armed force is the last resort of Canadian governments for suppressing insurrection, but the army's power, competence, discipline and restraint were on view all that summer. The army's considerable efforts to provide public information contributed mightily to this outcome. "Yes, we used the press," Foster says today. "We flooded them with information!"[25] Army morale also got a boost from a job well done.

These new political perceptions have allowed successive federal governments to make progress in both public policy and expenditure terms. The following developments, for example, would have had difficulty gaining traction without the events at Oka:

> The Treaty Land Entitlement program, which started in Saskatchewan and has spread to Manitoba (though not Alberta). Making good on broken promises is an inescapable first step in reconciliation. The key here was getting the federal, provincial and municipal governments ready to act at the same time. That done, and with exceptional leadership from Chief Roland Crowe of the Federation of Saskatchewan Indian Nations, reasonable rules for operating the program were relatively easily agreed.

> Treaty negotiations in British Columbia. A highly imperfect process regarding which the definitive book has still to be written, but nevertheless a process required by the Royal Proclamation of 1763, a part of our constitution, and, indirectly, by a series of Supreme Court decisions.

> A growing respect for Indian land rights, manifesting itself in the court-imposed duties to consult and accommodate where traditional lands are concerned. Quebec has struggled with this, cancelling Grande-Baleine in 1994 on Cree objections and currently having difficulty with the development of north shore hydro projects. But where projects have gone ahead, there have been economic benefits for native people and protection of sacred sites.

> Water treatment. Since 1996, allocations for clean drinking water and wastewater treatment on reserves have more than doubled, in response to an indisputable failure to provide these services in a manner "similar to non-reserve communities in similar circumstances."[26] A bill to extend provincial water quality standards to Indian reserves, which are currently unregulated, died with the December 2009 prorogation of Parliament but will likely be resurrected.

> New statutes: New First Nations acts governing land management (1999), commercial and industrial development (2005), fiscal and statistical management (2005), educational jurisdiction in B.C. (2006) and the extension of the *Canadian Human Rights Act* (2006) have all received royal assent, usually after a lengthy period of working with Indian leadership. A more contentious First Nations Governance bill fell in the vendetta between Jean Chrétien and Paul Martin but is likely to be revisited.

The 2008 coming into force of the extension of the 1977 *Canadian Human Rights Act* to First Nations governments, which should have happened when the act was first passed, was opposed by many chiefs who had grown powerful by practising discrimination. At last it means that ordinary Canadian law with respect to, for example, the division of assets on matrimonial breakdown does not automatically leave the female partner out in the cold.[27] In 1985, as a direct result of the Charter, Bill C-31 amended the definition of "Indian" in a way that ended most gender discrimination. The remaining elements were struck down in *McIvor* (2009), a judge-ment of the B.C. Court of Appeal that has not been appealed and that will require Parliament to pass legislation in 2010, potentially expanding the number of status Indians by 5 to 10 per cent.

The controversy about water quality regulation on reserves has exposed a broader problem.[28] Section 88 of the *Indian Act* says that laws of general application, including provincial laws, apply to Indian people, not Indian lands. Section 91(24) of the *Constitution Act, 1982* says that "Indians and lands reserved for the Indians" are an exclusive federal jurisdiction. This means that if a provincial law is truly general and does not single out Indians or intrude on the essence of "Indianness," in the Supreme Court's exceedingly vague locution, and if there is no federal legislation in the field, then pro-vincial law applies. But the provinces may not legislate for Indian lands or for Indians qua Indians. The Supreme Court has ruled that band government and band-owned enterprises possess Indianness, but otherwise the field is wide open. Ancestral lands and waters are a good bet to fall within that ambit, at least if they are part of reserves or treaty settlements, as are a variety of cultural prac-tices, should the courts ever have to rule on them. This is a messy and haphazard way of establishing law, but in the absence of par-liamentary will to legislate comprehensively, lacunae will persist. The 2008 amendments to the *Canadian Human Rights Act*, which extend to Indians the rights all other Canadians have enjoyed since 1977, may in time be seen as a down payment on repairing a long-standing dereliction of Parliament.

Policy about aboriginal self-government has also evolved since Oka. By the time of the crisis, the government's insistence that the only legitimate form of community governance was a chief and a council elected by secret ballot every two years—an annoy-ance to Iroquois communities especially—had more or less given way to the enshrinement of "custom" elections, essentially any-thing the band wanted so long as it was written down. That has been replaced by a slightly more rigorous view: the system in place has to conform to the Charter of Rights and Freedoms. Within that context, First Nations are now said to possess an "inherent" right to self-government. This grand statement gives little practical guidance and does nothing to address the difficulties of very small governments burdened with a breadth of duties that exist nowhere else in the civilized world, but slowly some of the practical questions are being hammered out in treaty and other negotiations. There are ineluctable economies of scale in the provision of local services, and few aboriginal communities can afford to match the services provided by non-reserve towns and cities, which are fast becoming the comparators. Nevertheless, the upshot for the Iroquois world is a greater willingness on the part of federal and provincial governments to recognize that the Confederacy has a role at present, and perhaps a more important one in the future. The government no longer sees the Longhouse as illegitimate, just different.

Another factor has affected the speed of progress. As noted, the Meech Lake Accord was crafted with a single purpose in mind—bringing Quebec back into the constitutional ambit, by making just those modifications to the Charter that would allow Quebec to become a signatory. The cost of that single-mindedness was leaving aside, for the time being, various other groups who sought to better their prospects through constitutional entrenchment via a special new law. Pro-lifers, people who believed property should be constitutionally protected, western believers in Senate reform, aboriginal groups—the list was lengthy, and the government had promised to address all of their concerns and more in a second round. With the failure of Meech Lake, the agenda for a second round became impossibly long, since the Quebec issue also had to be faced all over again. Thus began, in the fall of 1990, the Charlottetown round of constitutional negotiations. Charlottetown is a story on its own. It is enough to say here that for two years the holy grail of constitutional entrenchment of Indian governments as a third order of government in Canada mesmerized Indian leadership to the exclusion of all else. Ovide Mercredi, as national chief of the Assembly of First Nations, led the fight. He demanded to be seated as a premier at federal-provincial meetings, demanded that the issues important to on-reserve populations be added to meeting agendas and demanded that he be treated by the media and the public with the respect due to the head of one of the three founding peoples of the nation. Quebec in particular resisted dilution.

This was a case of perfection driving out the merely good. It was not possible in that charged atmosphere for the government to find Indian political partners willing to work on improving housing or education or land, so focused was the leadership on the constitutional goal. And to a degree, ministers indulged that goal, focused as they were on "completing Confederation." Emulating the Reagan-Gorbachev "walk in the woods" of a year earlier, for instance, Joe Clark famously strolled the shores of Ghost Lake at Morley, Alberta, with Ovide Mercredi, showing the media how comfortable he was with aboriginal leadership and allowing Mercredi to demonstrate his status to audiences through the miracle of television. Negotiations went on for two years, until Canadians from coast to coast, including a majority of Indian voters, decisively rejected in a referendum the dog's breakfast that Charlottetown had become. Since then, despite the Cassandra cries of constitutional doomsayers—and one horrifyingly close brush with a losing referendum in Quebec—the constitutional file has been rightly regarded by Canadian politicians as a sort of third rail, never to be touched. For people interested in practical reform, the file has been a hugely unrewarding and unnecessary sink for political and policy resources.

IN KANESATAKE and Kahnawake the old sense of apartness, of being a pre-existing and continuing sovereignty, is still present today, manifested most obviously in the lack of ordinary law enforcement. Kanesatake remains a community riven with factions. After the barricades came down, lawlessness became the rule. The Mohawk police unit was forced to disband, and a new police station has weeds growing around its shuttered doors. In 2008, the Ontario Provincial Police arrested four men from the Kanesatake Mohawk community after their car was found to be carrying a stash of guns and drugs. The OPP had stopped the car for speeding on Highway 17 at Dryden, about 220 miles northwest of Thunder Bay. The men were charged with possession of illegal drugs and several counts of carrying illegal weapons.[29] External policing was imposed with federal cash through the agency of a disputed local government. In May 2008, the federal public safety minister, Stockwell Day, expressed unhappiness about the fate of much of the $34 million. An audit had shown that a substantial part of $9 million earmarked for the Kanesatake force was missing or misspent.[30] A year later, a raid by three hundred RCMP, SQ and Kanesatake police resulted in sixteen arrests and the closing of eight marijuana grow-ops.[31] When I asked a Mohawk friend in the community whether anything had changed since Oka, he replied that things had changed for the better for Indians all across the country—except at Kanesatake, where smoke shops provide the only obvious evidence of economic activity. Aside from social services, most employment income comes from outside the community, sometimes a goodly distance away.

The SQ do not routinely patrol the streets of Kahnawake, only the main highways leading to the Mercier Bridge. Relations with neighbouring Châteauguay took a decade or more to simmer down, with a consequent loss of business for Châteauguay merchants. By 2000, though, Châteauguay peewee hockey teams were once again visiting Kahnawake. Smuggling and gambling are the biggest employers in the community, and as before, the Montreal Mafia have been major investors. At a trial in 2008, reported the *Globe and Mail,* "Another major revenue source, according to the affidavits, was an online sports bookmaking outlet, with computer servers first based in Belize, then in the Mohawk community of Kahnawake. Between October 2004, and mid-March, 2006, the gambling operation raked in $26.9 million, police said."[32] One firm, Mohawk Internet Technologies, cheekily abbreviated as MIT, is said to house the server farm that supports 60 per cent of the world's internet gambling.[33] Employing two hundred in a well-secured building, MIT was said by *Maclean's* magazine to have profits of $30 million in 2008.[34] A person can also play high-stakes poker in Kahnawake, in a casino that offers live dealers and is unburdened by either taxes or No Smoking signs.

Naturally, these unregulated enterprises attract the anger of licensed casinos. The CEO of Great Canadian Gaming calls them poachers and "parasites on the butt of Canada." According to a

National Post story, Chuck Barnett, a member of the board of MIT, "sees Ottawa as a foreign government that has no business regulating activity on Mohawk territory. 'However, if I were a Canadian, I might instead be more interested in how explicit legislation could serve as the catalyst for a potential source of economic development, employment and revenues through taxation,' he said."[35] The federal justice minister, Rob Nicholson, criticized by his constituents for not enforcing the law on Indian lands, and downright cautious about trying to do so, predictably said that the problem of gaming was provincial and that he was discussing the matter with stakeholders.[36] In the United States, official approval of reservation gaming has advocates at the most senior levels. Senator John McCain, a lifelong gambler and Republican presidential candidate in 2008, has long ties to the Las Vegas casino industry and sponsored the *Indian Gaming Regulatory Act* of 1988.[37]

Smuggling is much more sophisticated and widespread now than it was in the late 1980s. Kenneth Deer, the editor of the Kahnawake newspaper the *Eastern Door,* had a tricky time arguing that "Kahnawake is not a haven for criminals" following a 1997 Canadian Press story about the spectacular enterprise of Matthew "Watio" Lazare and Bryan Jacobs in the counterfeit booze trade. Lazare had a warehouse through which passed, according to police, "811 cases of brand name alcohol from the hijacking of a SAQ tractor trailer... 1600 cases of French wine stolen from the Montreal harbour, 560 cases of Grants Whiskey... 300 cases from a container of cigarettes from an armed hijacking by masked men... at Dorval," among many other high value transborder goods.[38] Anchored in Akwesasne, smuggling has gone national. A multi-location raid on reserves by the RCMP in New Brunswick in December 2008 netted drugs, firearms and tobacco.[39] The tobacco game has evolved from the circular trade of the 1980s to one where loose, second-quality tobacco comes by trailer truck from the Carolinas to factories at St. Regis, on the U.S. side of Akwesasne, where it is made into cigarettes and taken across the non-existent on-reserve border line into Canada and trucked from there. A plastic bag of two hundred cigarettes retails for anything from $6 to $20 in Canada, against $65 to $85 for taxed and quality-controlled brand name cigarettes. Apparently

Canadians prefer their voluntary taxation to be in the form of drink and gambling. Police intercept some small fraction of the cigarettes as they are trucked around the country, but they rarely raid the Mohawk reserves, even when intelligence is solid. Two of the tobacco companies have been brought to bar, however, and fined. (As a footnote, anti-tobacco campaigners are remonstrating with Canada for not living up to its international obligations under the World Health Organization's Framework Convention on Tobacco Control. According to Cynthia Callard of Physicians for a Smoke-Free Canada, "On first nations territories, there is virtually no protection from secondhand smoke, there is virtually no monitoring of sales to youths or advertising or promotion at retail... What I don't accept is that we should let... people die of tobacco-caused disease because we don't want to have a confrontation.")[40]

At Akwesasne, relatives of Mathew Pyke and others commenced an action against Governor Mario Cuomo, New York State Police superintendent Tom Constantine and others for breach of their constitutional right to equal protection under the law. Summarizing three feet of documents into a few paragraphs, the learned Judge McGurn observed,

> The plaintiffs declare that the Warriors are a criminal organization. However, the descriptions and assessments of the Warriors in the record run the full gamut: young Mohawks who didn't know what they were getting into; traditional Mohawks whose main focus was maintaining the sovereignty of the Mohawk nation; pro-gambling enforcers hired by the operators of illegal casinos; terrorists who wouldn't allow the NYSP to enter the Reservation without the permission of the warrior leaders; and/ or a self-appointed law enforcement entity that protected the vast smuggling operation that was allegedly taking place on the international border, to name a few.[41]

In awarding summary judgement in favour of the defendants in 2006, the judge called attention to the great expenditure of state and law enforcement resources that had gone into trying to find a solution to the dispute, saying,

In negotiating, the defendants were trying to avoid the possibility of outright warfare and the bloodshed that likely would
have occurred had the New York National Guard or the [Mobile
Response Team] been sent onto the reservation to quell the violence ... [A]voiding the potential for significant loss of human
life is a compelling government interest.[42]

Twenty years after Oka, the bottom line about what has changed
and what has not might be summarized as follows. First, and most
important, the dialogue in Canada has shifted. The sheer quantity
of attention paid to the all-but-failed relationship between Canada and aboriginal peoples has increased, and with it the variety
of voices and opinions. This is an unalloyed good thing. Second,
despite improvements in most social indicators, Indian incomes and
health still lag those of non-Indian Canadians. This is much less the
case in the Iroquois communities, which are in highly urbanized
regions and which, moreover, benefit from a privileged position
in relation to commercial activities forbidden to most Canadians. Third, ever so slowly and uncertainly, Parliament is moving
in the right direction, with respect to both statutory reform and
experiments with self-government. Fourth, factionalism continues unabated in Iroquois communities, moderating the pace toward
the achievement of communities' own goals. The ancient yearn-
ing for unfettered sovereignty persists as a major strain in Mohawk
thought, though it does not command such loyalty among any
other Indian group in the country. But the Mohawks have learned
that the dominant power will shy away from enforcing its laws, tol-
erating a minor affront to its own sovereignty to avoid using force
against a minority that has suffered over the years at that power's
hands. Indians across the country have learned that they can get
away with a lot, especially if they pick up a gun while doing it. A
modern Canadian version of Jared Diamond's book might be called
Guns, Guilt and Waffle.[43]

10

DID WE LEARN ANYTHING?

Oka changed everybody's approach in the non-aboriginal world: address these [land] issues, or there will be many Okas. Oka said we're all at risk. Think about the militancy in the upper Fraser Valley, Pemberton and Lillooet. From Oka onward, there has been a more measured approach by non-Indians. Then the courts have been helpful: Delgamuukw, for example, was hugely important.[1]
HAROLD CALLA

KEEPING OUR PROMISES

FLASHPOINTS LIKE Oka occur when Indian people believe that governments have violated treaties or their own laws, when a long struggle to right the wrong has been unavailing, and when a government crystallizes matters by licensing a further insult or alienation. Land is always at the heart of the broken promises, even though its connection to satisfactory living standards in the twenty-first century is becoming more and more indirect.

Peter Russell, the constitutional scholar, argued forcefully in 2008 that the only way forward for Canada and aboriginal people is through a legal process that is fair and expeditious.[2] Russell cited with hope the announcement by Jim Prentice, minister of Indian Affairs and Northern Development in 2007, that a new Specific Claims Commission would be soon put in place. Russell based his argument partly on the disgraceful story of Ipperwash, Ontario. There, the Kettle and Stoney Point Ojibway bands were granted large reserves on the sandy shores of Lake Huron in an 1827 treaty, only to have the federal and provincial governments a hundred years later connive in fraudulently taking back, without consent and for derisory payments, the best shore-front lands for cottage development. In 1936, the province paid a developer three times what the Indians had been paid so that the shoreline could be turned into Ipperwash Provincial Park. Band members protested, but at that time it was illegal to hire a lawyer to press a land claim. In 1942, the army seized the whole of the remaining Stoney Point reserve for (supposedly temporary) wartime military purposes. DND subsequently made grudging payments to the Stoney Pointers but never satisfied their fundamental demand, which was to get their land back, as promised.

In 1989, I approached my colleague Robert Fowler, then deputy minister of National Defence, to see if we could not get some resolution of this matter, which was a continuing source of unhappiness. I could see no reason for DND to keep the land. It was used for about six weeks in summer as a training ground for cadets, and otherwise principally as a place for armed forces members to store their recreational vehicles and boats. Fowler, however, had been briefed by the military to the effect that the land was vital to the defence of the realm, there were no acceptable substitutes, and clearing it of unexploded ordnance would be fearfully costly. He fought his patch briskly, and we were not able to reach an agreement, even when I promised some cost-sharing. Only much later did Fowler discover, to his fury, that the information his people had provided was unreliable.[3]

Stoney Point members, tired of endless tergiversations, began "living on their reserve" in 1995. But, in the words of Peter Russell, "a racist premier [Mike Harris] let it be known that he wanted 'the f—ing Indians out of the park,'"[4] and the police raided their barbecue on the evening of September 6. An aboriginal named Dudley

George was shot and killed. It took eight years, a criminal trial for the OPP shooter, two elections and the demise of the Harris government before a public inquiry under Justice Sidney Linden was appointed to look into the affair. Linden concluded that the federal government's languor over the seized land, and its acquiescence in the underhanded way the province acquired its part for a provincial park, was at the heart of the tragedy. But provincial government impatience, bungled police tactics, a lack of communication between police and the aboriginal occupiers and no small degree of racism on the part of the police were also involved.[5] The OPP officer who fired the fatal shot was convicted of criminal negligence causing death. None of his superiors in the police or government were called to account. Premier Harris lost the next election. The federal government is belatedly cleaning the military land in preparation for its return to the Kettle and Stoney Point bands.

The RCMP had the task of handling a situation at Gustafsen Lake that same year, when a group of Indians refused to vacate lands owned by a B.C. rancher. Despite many angry words and much gunfire, only one person was hurt, and the occupation was brought to an end. Charges were laid against eighteen people, four of them non-native. Fifteen were convicted of assault and firearms charges and sentenced to jail terms of six months to eight years. The B.C. Court of Appeal refused to hear appeals based on an alleged lack of jurisdiction by Canadian courts. An interesting footnote concerns James Pitawanakwat, a convicted man who, once on parole, fled to the U.S., becoming the only Canadian ever to be granted political asylum in that country. The RCMP's tactics contained echoes of Oka: overwhelming force—more than four hundred officers—lots of patience and strong media relations.

An even closer analogue of Oka is the small town of Caledonia, a few miles south of Hamilton in southern Ontario. In 1784, a vast tract of mostly empty land, about 8.5 million acres, was granted to the Iroquois allies of His Majesty George III; among the losers in the U.S. War of Independence, the Iroquois had to flee their ancestral lands in what had become northern New York State. The new lands, known as the Haldimand Grant after the British governor of the day, were whittled away over the years, often through chicanery or outright fraud, until all that was left was the Six Nations reserve near Brantford. Protests during the years when Indians could not hire lawyers went nowhere. After the establishment of the original Specific Claims Commission in the 1970s, Six Nations registered no fewer than twenty-eight formal claims, but only one has been settled—for cash, not land—and that not until 2008.

In February 2006, an armed aboriginal occupation of a plot called the Douglas Creek Estates began. The flashpoint was the province's approval of a subdivision on land the Mohawks claimed but which provincial law said was unequivocally private, with the subsequent start of construction by the developer. More than two years of roadblocks, arson, intimidation, harassment, fistfights and beatings followed. The Ontario Provincial Police refused to enforce the law, leading to allegations of race-based policing. The province bought the Douglas Creek Estates and made small compensation payments to affected Caledonia businesses, but this was a pittance against the real economic damages. According to Haldimand councillor Craig Grice, by 2009 about $600 million in ordinary development had failed to occur, along with its expected consequences for local employment and taxes, and hundreds of homeowners in Caledonia and along the north shore of the Grand River, opposite Six Nations, were unable to sell their properties at any price.[6] During the severe recession of 2008–10, those homeowners were precluded from using home equity to see them through.

The failure of the province and the OPP to enforce the law in what they labelled a law-and-order crisis was especially galling. In the fall and winter of 2009–10, columnist Christie Blatchford wrote a series of articles in the *Globe and Mail*, including one about a family who had been driven to distraction by the events, and to a lawsuit, and another about the criminal charges brought against Commissioner Julian Fantino of the OPP for trying to intimidate the mayor of Caledonia,[7] who had expressed dissatisfaction with the quality of policing that Caledonia was receiving.

Caledonia differs from Oka in one important respect: Prime Minister Stephen Harper and Premier Dalton McGuinty are not on good terms. Federal-provincial cooperation in resolving the dispute has been largely symbolic, with the good work of negotiators and officials often stymied by partisan politics. But in other ways, it is the same old pattern: a long-simmering dispute of deep importance to the Iroquois but ignored by the larger society; a triggering incident involving white development on disputed lands; occupation and violent resistance; ineffectual response by the provincial police and the emergence of territories where Canadian law is not enforced and on which illegal enterprises flourish; and deep divisions in the native community about how to govern themselves and how to manage relations with the larger community. At least the army had not been employed. After all, in the absence of a decent attempt, it can hardly be said that enforcing the law is beyond the police.

The Mohawks do not have a classic comprehensive claim to lands north of the St. Lawrence. They have not lived continuously in these warred-over frontier lands "since time immemorial," and their claims are disputed by the Algonquins, among others. This is the normal state of affairs for mobile tribal societies, which usually have core areas and less well-defined peripheries, and it is not a reason to avoid settling the issue. Miscarriages of justice in the colonial period resulted in the radical diminution of Indian land rights at Kanesatake, starting with the Sulpician-sponsored move away from an unconditional grant of land to the Indians, followed by a conditional grant to the Sulpicians and finally to fee simple ownership by the order. A better post-capitulation decision by the British authorities would have been along the lines of what happened to Jesuit lands, as at Kahnawake, where the lands were vested in the Indians rather than in the surviving remnants of the French regime.

The Lower Canada ordinance of 1839 was probably inconsistent in law with the Royal Proclamation of 1763, and it is certainly inconsistent with a modern interpretation of the fiduciary obligations of the federal government. Old laws inconsistent with modern views on the constitution should not be allowed to stand. The Department of Justice needs to rethink the deep legal basis of some of the strictures it places on line departments trying to negotiate a reconciliation. The idea that there are only two kinds of legitimate land claims, specific and comprehensive, manifestly does not work in all cases, and even the Law Lords thought that the ordinance of 1839 had a peculiar odour.

For more than two centuries, until they finally washed their hands of the Kanesatake lands, the Sulpicians did not behave with anything like a present-day sense of responsibility to their charges. Hindsight is often unfair, but it took sustained wilful blindness for the order to behave as it did. The conscience of the federal government was properly pricked into seeking a resolution through *Corinthe,* but the suggestion of the Law Lords that something along the lines of a charitable trust be established was not followed up, and it should have been.

The successive intrusions by the Canadian government, starting with the *Indian Act* of 1876, into tribal government, religion and education exacerbated divisions within an exhausted and deracinated Iroquois population. To blame subsequent events on Mohawk factionalism is partly justified, but that view ignores the role of the federal government in creating and encouraging the many parties. We do not expect unanimous or one-party views in Canadian society generally, and it is strange to insist on it in these circumstances. On the other hand, for all the splendidly democratic features of traditional Iroquois government, it would be helpful if Mohawk communities could rise above our shared, sordid colonial history and find ways of composing reasonably durable views on serious matters.

Clearly there is much that we as a society have yet to learn. DIAND has known for decades that there is no future of reconciliation and working together until broken promises are addressed. This lay behind our interest in modern treaty negotiations, in treaty land settlements on the Prairies and in the recommendations the department put forward to the federal cabinet in 1990. A great deal of progress has been made on those projects, particularly in the Arctic and to a lesser degree in British Columbia. Yet it took until June 2008 for Parliament to create the new Specific Claims Commission. On the plus side, the tribunal was developed through extensive discussion with Indian leaders, and it was accompanied by political understandings to refine the terms under which lands acquired through settlements may be added to reserves and to deal with the special arrangements necessary regarding very large claims.

THE ARMY AND THE POLICE

Modern armies scrupulously examine their actions to make sure they learn everything they can, and the Canadian Armed Forces are no exception.[8] In a comprehensive document, DND reviewed everything about the military operations at Oka, from command and force structure to policy and doctrine regarding internal security, intelligence, operations and tactics, administration, training and equipment. The formal report, however, does not emphasize some points remembered long after by the most senior commanders. For one example, the importance of forthright, even blunt, public information: General de Chastelain characterizes the first statement that was prepared for him as weak-kneed, and he substituted an uncompromising statement that there was no need for the situation to go any further.[9] For another, the raid at Tekakwitha Island brought home forcefully that crowd control gear should include shields and batons, not C7's. Lieutenant General Foster, in the unpublished series of slides that accompanies his lecture "The Oka Story," gives special attention to media management, and to the importance of handling media as close as possible to operations, away from ditherers and political trimmers at headquarters. Credible spokespeople, available when the press needs them, are critical. The tactic of announcing movements in advance whenever possible, so as to minimize surprise and panicky reactions, was brilliantly done at Oka: the major tightening of the lines around the treatment centre when the army took over from the SQ was an early test for both sides. Despite agonistic behaviour by those whose perimeter was being shortened, no shots were fired. It is doubtful this could have been achieved by surprise.

The specification of rules of engagement at Oka—the specific meaning of "minimum force" in the circumstances—also got careful attention. Repeating over and over again that the army would not shoot first had a critical effect on the front line. Jenny Jack believed the generals and saved at least one life as a result. The Warriors did not succumb to the temptation they must have felt, either, to shoot at the machines that were driving them nuts at the treatment centre: the night-time helicopters with their glaring spotlights and incessant noise, the speakers playing rock music, the ground-based spotlights.

Commenting in 1991, the distinguished historian Desmond Morton was cautious about the practice of aid of the civil power. Civilians accept it only grudgingly, he felt, and to different degrees in English and French Canada. "The October Crisis damaged Trudeau's standing and Oka did not help Brian Mulroney's already tarnished image...," Morton wrote in an article in *Canadian Defence Quarterly.* "There are no victors in civil disorder." Further, "A nation's troops should be used sparingly, if at all, in tasks which have nothing to do with their role as defenders of national sovereignty."[10] But isn't that precisely what was at issue at Oka? What started as a civil dispute about land became an armed challenge to the sovereignty of Canada. The insurrection, palpably beyond the power (or willingness) of the police to subdue, was capably handled by the Canadian Forces. Not that this was a duty sought or celebrated: there was no glory in winning the skirmish at Oka, only the ever-present possibility of a disaster that would blacken the military's name for decades.

Morton was not alone in criticizing the use of the army for internal purposes. The House Standing Committee on Aboriginal Affairs was surprised and horrified by the way the law worked. In their final report on the Oka crisis, they recommended a review of Part XI of the *National Defence Act* "in light of concerns about the need for stronger review mechanisms and additional reporting requirements respecting the use of the armed forces as an aid to a civil power."[11] They raised no fewer than sixteen issues, including the lack of choice for the federal government given a provincial request, the unfettered discretion of the Chief of the Defence Staff, financial responsibility and the need for parliamentary involvement and review. Committee members appear to have been even more shocked by the use of Part XI than were ministers and senior officials, and they were unaware of the constitutional history of the provision. Their recommendation for review has not been followed up. In a thesis for the National Defence College, Superintendent E.P. Craig of the RCMP argued more narrowly that the federal government ought at least to have the power to override a province if the province is doing something contrary to the national interest.[12] The political practicality of such a power is dubious, however.

The use of the army at Oka was in a large sense regrettable, but I believe it was made necessary by the racist and incompetent leadership of the SQ, and by the failure of police forces and their civilian masters to calmly and steadily enforce Canadian laws about smuggling and arms over a period of many years. If, as the federal government maintained, the issue at Oka was one of law and order, a reasonable step before calling in the army might have been the reinforcement of the SQ by the RCMP: with 22,000 uniformed members across the country, a substantial contingent could have been made available. After all, 4,500 RCMP—coincidentally, the same number of troops sent to Oka—were detailed to the Vancouver Winter Olympics in 2010. The army's role could have been limited to provision of special technical assistance. Why the government allowed, through inaction, the use of Part XI of the *National Defence Act* over the much more accountable Part II of the *Emergencies Act* is still unclear, but it was a conscious choice, made at the highest political level. The NDA has serious deficiencies and reforming it is unfinished business. Finally, there was an apparent conflict in the use of the Canadian Armed Forces to assist a province in putting down an Indian insurrection when the Supreme Court had made it clear that the federal government had a duty to act in a fiduciary capacity with respect to Indians.

John Keegan, the eminent military historian, makes useful distinctions between operational intelligence, espionage and subversion.[13] The last has been confused with the first two through novels and popular culture, but there is a key difference between operational intelligence and a broader, less time-sensitive appreciation of an enemy's intent and capabilities, though of course Keegan is writing about large-scale warfare, not the kind of insurrectionist skirmish that Oka represents. Operational intelligence involves the timely delivery of tactical information, such as decrypted signals intelligence from yesterday that tells an admiral where his opponent's fleet will be tomorrow morning. That kind of intelligence is often a necessary resource for winning battles, but it is rarely sufficient. A broader appreciation of an enemy's strategic purposes, order of battle, history and cultural predilections that may affect tactics is built up over time. In the context of Oka, almost the only source of this background was inside DIAND, the exception being John Ciaccia—and he was strongly influenced by his time in the department as a young man. Such features of Mohawk behaviour as deep internal factionalism, strong guidance by non-European spiritual tradition, the absence of much in the way of hierarchical leadership, the necessity to bring many minds to agreement on negotiating positions and the many roles of women were mystifying to police and army players, at least at the beginning.[14] (One instance of the latter was the frustration of the SQ commander in the Pines on July 11 on being told by women that there was no Mohawk leader and he would need to wait until the dawn ceremonies were complete.) On the other hand, the police and armed forces had a good grasp of how many Warriors there were and what kinds of weapons they had. Only as the summer wore on did these representatives of the larger society begin to develop a limited kind of cultural appreciation that allowed some understanding, even prediction, of likely reactions to specific tactical moves.

The government's negotiators never really did achieve that kind of understanding, at least not those who were parachuted in to take over from the department. Neither Bernard Roy nor Alex Paterson was equipped by education or experience to understand the other side, and they were frequently taken aback by what in their Euro-Canadian lights were irrational positions taken by the Mohawks. This, plus Mohawk escalation of demands to include national sovereignty, was a fundamental reason why negotiations failed, and why the army had to resolve the issue. The most basic Mohawk position was the unqualified sovereignty of their people and their claim to a territory that would become the basis of a national state. This could never have been agreed to by the governments involved, and to that extent the talks were doomed from the start. But a frank declaration that demonstrated the Canadian side understood the Mohawk demands, coupled with a strong setting of limits and the threat of military action, might have helped. In a strange way, the Mohawk insistence that they had never ceded land nor been militarily defeated could have been turned against them. The argument would have been that persistence in an armed insurrection positively guaranteed a military solution adverse to their long-term interests. As it turned out, it is now plausible for the Canadian government to argue that in fact the Mohawks have been defeated militarily, since the affair ended with the surrender to the military, not to the police, and with the burning of arms.

The Sûreté du Québec did not learn much from Oka in the short run. Their failures of command were defended long past the point of public credibility, and the police did nothing to lower the level of fear and loathing with which they were regarded by Indians. Obduracy had its price, however. In the mid-1990s the force's structure was changed and new commanders appointed. The SQ are by most accounts a more professional force now.

Human rights abuses occurred during the Oka crisis at the hands of all parties. Some were inexcusable under any circumstances, as when the SQ and the RCMP stood aside while Mohawk evacuees were stoned by the LaSalle mob. Yet some human rights violations were justified by the urgency of bringing a dangerous confrontation, one that could have exploded into deadly gunfire at any moment, under control as quickly as possible.

Canada's police forces have generally shown a preference for cautious engagement. On the one hand they can be criticized for not upholding the law, but on the other, they are accustomed to being society's front line in cases of ambiguous justice. Interposing themselves between angry and riotous citizens is neither fun nor safe, yet police are asked to do this somewhere every month. In the cases of Indian lands, they have learned that a strict constructionist approach to law enforcement is a recipe for danger and public obloquy. As Peter Russell puts it,

> Canadian police forces have learned, over the years, that when they intervene in these flashpoint events, they do so primarily as peacekeepers rather than law enforcers. Their job is to prevent violence, calm people down on both sides of the barricades, keep lines of communication open and ensure that all concerned know what is being done at the political level to resolve the issue.[15]

For the army and especially the police, figuring out the proper means of accountability to the public and to political authorities is still a work in progress.

INFORMATION, PROPAGANDA AND THE MEDIA

As spring became summer at Oka, it became apparent to the Mohawks that the issue was not simple resistance to the expansion of a golf course. After all, they had won that battle definitively by late July. Rather, their purpose became telling a broader story of independence to Canadians and to many Americans, native and non-native alike. A more stern view was put forward by Joe Scanlon in one of the several symposia on the role of the media that occurred after the fact. Scanlon, a former journalist turned professor, had been studying terrorist incidents and hostage taking. In his view, terrorism was simply "violence as communications... what we saw [at Oka] were violent publicity stunts designed to attract media attention... That's why terrorists do what they do, and there's some evidence that they continue to do it as long as the media go along and in this case the media went along almost beyond credibility." He further argued that "an object may be a hostage... the seizure of a major bridge and the blockage of access and subsequent disruption is a pretty good example of a hostage taking." The best way for authorities to deal with a "brutal publicity stunt," Scanlon said, is isolation. Starve the media manipulators of access to the media, and very soon the air goes out of the protest.[16]

Of course, those whose bread was buttered by the retailing of such incidents had a much different analysis. Charles Bury, president at the time of the Canadian Association of Journalists, used strong language in his denunciation of the army's successively stronger measures to isolate those in the treatment centre.[17] The military provided too much information to the media, Bury complained, a veritable Niagara Falls of it, and ignorant or ill-informed journalists drank too freely from the fire hose. Sacred rights of freedom of the press were invoked. When the army would not provide services or even food to journalists behind the wire, they had to beg those from the Mohawks. But not all of those in the media were so ready to wrap themselves in the cloth of high principle. According to an article in *Between the Lines,* "*La Presse* columnist Lysiane Gagnon, speaking in Montreal, said she was not convinced the press even had a right to stay inside the treatment centre with the warriors. She said the situation was comparable to a fire scene, where firefighters routinely cordon off the premises for safety reasons."[18]

In truth, there were incidents the military would have been just as happy not to see on the news. The abusive catcalls in both directions, the beating of Spudwrench, the fiasco at Tekakwitha Island— none of these showed the calm, deliberate, disciplined face the army wanted to project. But a peaceful protest had morphed into an armed insurrection, and the army lines had the same force in law as police lines. No one had legal cause to be behind those lines, Warriors or journalists. General de Chastelain was surely right in refusing to provide Geoffrey York with fresh batteries for his cell phone. By August, most senior federal officials had come to a view rather like the one Scanlon would later espouse: cut off media access, and this affair would quickly deflate. We were correct.

Throughout the process, both DND and DIAND communications staff worked hard to tell the story as best they knew it. For our department, the job was not much tainted by tactical considerations. We supported our several ministers and Defence with factual background briefs, most of which were promptly made public. DIAND's job, and that of its ministers, was to tell the government's side of the story all across the country; DND's job was to fulfill the terms of its instructions from the government of Quebec without bloodshed. These were quite different tasks. The policy line of the government was clear and simple: negotiations will follow the laying down of arms and the lifting of barricades. There is one law for all Canadians. For DND, the release of information had more utilitarian ends and was a key part of the overall military effort. When the defence department wanted to move the better part of a mechanized brigade through the streets of Montreal, they announced it well in advance—partly to clear the streets, and partly so nervous people behind the barricades would not be surprised. For both departments, there was a constraint not operating on the Warrior side: the need to stick to the truth—at least more or less. Countering misinformation, indeed disinformation—"Lemay was killed by his own side," for example—was a constant issue.

The army's communications effort, like that of the Warriors, included a degree of psychological operations—psyops, in the jargon. Anything that messes with the opponent's head, makes him fearful or overcautious or fakes him into a wrong move, is a good thing in military doctrine. The Warriors and their highly visible planting of empty shoeboxes with wires attached in the girders of the Mercier Bridge were as one with the military people who prepared the video of a .50 cal heavy machine gun chewing up a bunker in seconds.

Oka was about as public a crisis as one could imagine, though it got little coverage during the period from March 10 to July 10. Once the disastrous SQ raid had splashed across the country and Mohawk demands had escalated toward full-bore sovereignty, the affair became a battle for media attention. All sides were trying to tell their stories in ways that would garner public support. One narrative was about poor natives, freedom fighters against cruel colonial oppressors, romantically resisting the mass forces of white society. One difficulty for the Mohawks with managing this story was that the sovereignty issue had to rise to the surface in negotiations with governments and in communications with Indian people without getting a lot of attention in the mass media. There was little patience in English Canada for another separation story, after fifteen years of constitutional drama over Quebec. In Quebec, there was no patience whatsoever for the idea that an oppressed minority, a nation, an intra-provincial distinct society, might demand for itself what Quebec was demanding from Canada. Managing the delivery of such a powerful idea to some but not all parties was a strategic difficulty for the Mohawk side.

Visual images are even more important than words in the battle for media attention. In that context, I have never understood why the costumes picked by the Warriors echoed those of the Palestinian Intifada rather than evoking well-understood North American images. It seems to me that war paint, feathers, buckskin and Iroquois topknots would have served their cause better. Put the Oka affair in the frame of a Canadian population that does not like guns and masks, and it becomes clear that the Mohawks had an uphill battle, despite reflexive popular sympathy for underdogs. Their masks certainly had nothing to do with concealing identity. We knew who the Warriors were within hours of their first appearance.

Some people believe that the Mohawks had a sophisticated communications planning apparatus behind the sympathetic faces of Ellen Gabriel and others. I don't think so. Tactically staging good communications relies on the repetition of basic messages—on having a consistent policy, in other words. This is impossible without tight leadership, which the insurgents never attained, though the confrontation hardened opinions in their camp behind the idea of sovereignty. In the end, these debilities meant that the Mohawks' communications achievements over that summer were ambiguous. Yes, they sensitized Canadians and their governments to a long saga of injustice and paved the way for renewed attention to reforms in public policy. Yes, there was a somewhat halting movement toward resolving the Kanesatake-specific issue. But the fundamental goal of Iroquois sovereignty was, if anything, set back. The more people knew about it, the less sympathetic they were.

From the government side, though with only partial success, there came a narrative that attempted to define the problem as one of law and order. Premier Bourassa, the prime minister and all their respective ministers—notably the fierce Kim Campbell,

Mulroney's brief successor in office—united in pursuit of this line. From this basic stance flowed corollaries: land issues would be addressed once the arms and barricades disappeared; there was one law for all Canadians; the army was there at the request of the province to assist in maintaining order; there would be no negotiations with masked and armed rebels; and so forth. It was only when Gold, Siddon and Ciaccia fell into the trap of signing the preconditions agreement in the Pines that we produced the sort of massive contradiction that the press loves. That error made room for a third narrative, namely that this confrontation was really about land and Indians, two subjects reserved for the federal government in the *Constitution Act, 1982,* and that the current derelict federal government ought to wade in and assume its responsibilities. Siddon had to struggle with that for the rest of the summer and in the parliamentary debates that followed.

The government of Quebec had a more difficult task. Its ailing leader did not enjoy the kind of cabinet consensus that Ottawa did, and in a climate of increasing *indépendentisme* had to admit the province's vaunted police force was incompetent and call in the Canadian Armed Forces. Quebec's utterances throughout the crisis were often muted: Ciaccia, trying ever more desperately to find a stance from which to negotiate a resolution, was undercut by Rémillard and other ministers, and the SQ retreated into sullen silence. Only when the premier himself spoke out on the law-and-order line did Quebec seem firm in its view, and he was reluctant to do that too early, since he had a minister trying valiantly to find another route. It was not until the final breakdown in negotiations at the end of August that Bourassa became adamant and un-nuanced.

The army was the most organized communicator of the summer. From the beginning and from the top, the military recognized that this was a media affair and governed itself accordingly. The doctrine of minimum force and their global experience with peacekeeping meant that the army had to substitute patience for arms, and that a variety of audiences had to understand what was going on. Only if the Mohawks really believed that the army would never fire first would it be possible for even the most ardent spirits among them to restrain themselves. At the same time, the hawks in the Quebec government had to understand that saving lives meant considerable local disruption as well as an ability to withstand the daily clamour on the parts of the press and the public.

The generals helped their communicators by defining a simple four-point task. Not for them the existential debates over sovereignty, land and fiduciary relationships; they were simply there as the last barrier before anarchy, helping the provincial authorities to remove barricades, restore circulation and turn matters back to the civil authorities as fast as possible.[19] The military began to flood the media with information—not on the background to the confrontation, but on the people on the ground, the arms they were facing and the tactical movements that would take place in the next day or so. The army's movements were deliberate. They did not fully take over the SQ positions until August 20, wanting to give time and space for the negotiations to succeed. They didn't, and so the army squeezed the perimeter. They provided so much information that journalists complained—then went ahead and used the videos and visuals the army provided anyway.

The relations between the army and the press got trickier in the later stages at Kanesatake, when access and facilities for journalists were successively restricted. The final military blow was shutting down cell phone communication from inside the treatment centre.

Naturally, the press went through an orgy of self-examination after the fact. DND held a seminar for journalists in Ottawa and got thoroughly beaten up for its efforts. Many newspaper articles and papers in learned journals addressed the performance of the press during the summer, and one can find every possible shade of opinion in the discourse.[20] There were, however, some frequently repeated themes. One was that the press were ill-prepared. They did not understand the history behind the confrontation and had to spend a lot of time catching up. A second was that, in general, there was too much deference to the underdog as romantic hero, at the expense of a hard look at what that underdog was seeking. And a third was the insatiable demand of television, especially the new CBC Newsworld, for arresting visuals and sound bites.

THE WARRIORS

John Thompson of the Mackenzie Institute has a model of the life cycle of insurgencies. Insurgencies start, he says, when idealistic young people coalesce around a cause. Their behaviour escalates from protest to violence. Once they are outside the law, finding a source of revenue becomes urgent, and they turn to illegal activities. Smuggling, counterfeiting, drugs and kidnapping for ransom are typical activities. According to Thompson,

> It should be noted that the Warriors were by no means alone in allowing their insurgent ambitions to be completely overtaken by organized criminal behaviours. In Ulster, the IRA and their Protestant Ulster Volunteer Force counterparts pay for their activities with bootlegging and smuggling. The Tamil Tigers of Sri Lanka have become notorious heroin smugglers and counterfeiters, while Colombian Marxists and Peruvian Maoist guerrillas are now [1996] deeply involved in the cocaine trade. It is also worth noting that two of the most deeply rooted organized criminal societies in the world, the Sicilian Mafia and the Chinese Triads, began as secretive rebels against the Kingdom of the Two Sicilies and the Manchu Dynasty, respectively. Criminality long outlasts the original grievances.[21]

Thompson's view of the Mohawk Warrior Society is bleak. "In less than twenty-five years, the Society emerged, armed itself, grew corrupt, and collapsed." In all the cases Thompson discusses, the period of corruption includes aggressive and intimidating behaviour toward the group the organization was set up to protect.

Time and again during the events of 1989 and 1990, there was a tendency for the Mohawk side to escalate their demands when they got pushed into a box. As they were losing the gunfights at Akwesasne and Oka, their requirements for disarming and for taking down the barricades grew more extravagant and less well connected to external reality. Why was this? My guess is it was partly due to distillation: as conditions became more exiguous, there was a tendency for the less militant to quietly leave, meaning the remaining protestors were progressively more hawkish. Part of it, too, was the escalation among the Kanienkehaka: if they were risking so much, even death, then surely their stand could not be about only a few acres around Kanesatake, it had to stem from a larger cause. And part of the explanation lay in the Warriors, as a faction, asserting control, dictatorial if necessary, over the whole community and suppressing voices of doubt and reconciliation.

It might seem easy to argue that the factiousness and indecision that plagued Kanienkehaka behaviour was equally manifested in the response of governments. There were, after all, many arguments within the federal system alone: for example, over whether or not to cut off cell phone communication from the treatment centre. And the Quebec cabinet was certainly divided, with John Ciaccia alone on one wing, Bourassa and Ryan in the centre, and the rest interested in a much more muscular approach, especially to the Mercier Bridge blockade. But each government knew what it wanted—a peaceful end to the barricades. Where they disagreed internally was on tactics. And where they had an advantage over the Indians was in a hierarchical institutional structure with a first minister at the top who could either bless a consensus bubbling up from below or impose a decision.

THE MACHINERY OF GOVERNMENT

To our faint surprise and great relief, the machinery of government proved robust under the circumstances. The strongly hierarchical nature of a Westminster government, in which power and authority flow predictably downward from a prime minister and his cabinet, produced decisions quickly, and those decisions were communicated efficiently to all who had to carry them out. The ad hoc grouping of senior officials set up by Fred Drummie with assistance from the Privy Council Office quickly became a daily meeting of the principal officials involved, with the chair of the group reporting several times a day to the prime minister. An ad hoc committee of cabinet was struck to oversee the work of officials and to either take or recommend to the full cabinet and the prime minister any necessary policy decisions.

We were lucky also in the personal chemistry of Bourassa and Mulroney. These old friends, deeply rooted in Quebec politics and bearing many scars from past battles, had a deep trust for each other. One hesitates to think what might have happened if their relationship had been like that of, say, Prime Minister Stephen Harper and Newfoundland Premier Danny Williams today, or merely had exhibited the ordinary distaste that flavours so much federal-provincial discourse at the level of first ministers, as in the case of Caledonia. The five top military officers involved—de Chastelain, Thomas, Foster, Reay and Roy, as well as the frontline battalion commanders Pierre Daigle, Greg Mitchell and Robin Gagnon—proved to be unflustered and professional throughout, again not something one can always take for granted. Bourassa was fortunate too in having John Ciaccia in his cabinet. Even if Ciaccia did not carry the day, throwing his passion and experience on the side of talking rather than warring allowed Bourassa and wise old Claude Ryan to balance what might otherwise have been an impatient and somewhat populist group of offended francophone ministers acting in ill-tempered fashion.

As ever, personalities mattered. Without good people, no design for management or arrangement of statutes will produce a good outcome.

HISTORY MATTERS

Charles Bury was perhaps right to complain that the media covering Oka were too ignorant of Mohawk history to tell a good story from a duff one. There is no question that reporters were on a steep learning curve that summer and that their collective performance since then has been markedly better. From a public policy point of view, historically deep understanding is critical. Canada has as permanent conditions of its existence some great and irresolvable problems. One is the regional nature of the country and its polities, nowhere more intense than in French-English relations. Another is living next door to Leviathan. Another is nordicity, though it is easy to forget this in the cities of the south. On the short list must also be inscribed the relations between the settler peoples and the original inhabitants. This half-millennium collision is not over, and never will be. Even within that diversity, the Iroquois, and especially their leading nation, the Mohawks, stand out for their uncompromising attachment to national sovereignty and to the illegitimacy of Canadian and U.S. operations on their traditional territory. One fact not widely appreciated in white Canada is that the Indian nations of this country have greater cultural, linguistic and economic differences among themselves than do the people who came here in recent centuries. There are more original language families in British Columbia alone than there are in all of Europe, for instance.

In this context, the growth of a syncretic or composite Indian identity across North America is interesting. Iconic symbols like the feathered war bonnets of the Plains Indians, the intricate carvings of the west coast tribes or the silver jewellery of the Pueblo groups are increasingly used by all Indian peoples. In part this supports, and is in turn furthered by, the politics of identity, but it goes deeper than that. The ways in which Indian people conceive of themselves as individuals and as part of historic collectivities is changing. There has been a revival of pride, of comfort in an aboriginal identity that the larger society tried to stamp out. If Indian attachment to the idea of Canada is weak, it should come as no surprise. It is not widely appreciated, for instance, that it was not until 1962, courtesy of the crusty old Yukon M.P. Erik Nielsen, that Indians could vote in federal elections.

There are two specific lessons from history that Canadians seem to have to learn over and over again. One is that land really matters; it is fundamental to Indian identities. Even if we are generations away from Head-Smashed-In Buffalo Jump, the memory of free-ranging peoples on the Great Plains helps to define what the Lakota and the Blood peoples think about themselves, as do, for other groups, memories of great canoe journeys up and down the west coast, of hunting and respectfully taking the lives of animals to sustain whole sharing communities, or of prayer at sacred places where the spirit world lives especially close to the beauty of nature. When the awkward bargains of the nineteenth century are unilaterally abrogated in the twentieth or twenty-first, trouble is guaranteed. In this context, as a relatively minor matter, an Indian Specific Claims Commission without teeth—without genuine independence and the ability to order meaningful compensation and in some cases land restoration—is doomed. Thankfully, the federal government is moving, if slowly, in the right direction, through a renewed commission and through the Treaty Land Entitlement process in Saskatchewan and Manitoba.

The other specific lesson is that in a crisis the U.S. will offer Canada all help short of actual aid. A nation that sees the right to bear arms as constitutionally guaranteed is unlikely to get exercised about Canadians arming themselves with weapons bought legally in the United States.[22] If something smokeable or fireable is smuggled out of the U.S., the onus lies on the recipient nation to do whatever it will; it is of no concern to the country of origin beyond a few calming words in the name of international comity. On the other hand, the U.S. has periodically become concerned about the southbound flow of marijuana and illegal immigrants, facilitated by the same Indian gangs that move tobacco and firearms north. The concern about illegal immigrants has become sharper in the wake of 9/11. At the core of U.S. policy is the old adage that a country has no friends, only interests.

SOVEREIGNTY

At the root of the issues is the persistent claim by the Iroquois that they are a sovereign state. It is hard to see anything ahead but capitulation or bloodshed if the issue is forced. In the long run, perhaps the best outcome is for neither side, public government nor Haudenosaunee, to give up their claims—in other words, to let the constitution and practical reality prevail without forgetting the ancient ideal. In time it may be that Justice Binnie's 2001 view of the constitution replaces the studied non-interference of the two-row wampum: all of us together in the same ship, which is made of the historic elements of wood and canvas and iron, all distinctive, all proud of our contribution, all dependent on each other, sailing off together. On the other hand, if Mohawk or Confederacy insistence on being a pre-existing and continuing principality takes other than rhetorical forms, perhaps the government should declare the taking down of barricades at Kanesatake and Kahnawake a military defeat.

What turned Oka from a local, if longstanding, issue of land rights into an event that seared the nation was its escalation into an issue of national sovereignty and its amplification by the Warrior Society. Understanding where the Warriors were coming from, and the ambiguity of their actions and motives, is thus at the heart of the story. A group of people with mixed motives, few economic opportunities as attractive as smuggling and gambling, and time on their hands, responded in patriotic fashion from their homes on both sides of the border at Akwesasne and at Kahnawake and Oneida territory to Kanesatake's call for help.

An interesting question is what, if anything, the Warriors learned from that summer. On the evidence of subsequent activity on Mohawk reserves and at Caledonia, it appears they learned that de facto sovereignty and the protection of economic activities judged illicit (at least if those activities are unlicensed or untaxed) can be achieved with sufficient belligerence. Intimidation, arms and barricades manifestly work. No leader of white society wants to be remembered as the Butcher of Oka or Caledonia. So long as the Warriors can convince the authorities that the consequence of enforcing the law will be widespread bloodshed, they win—even in the more severe climate of public opinion in the post-9/11 era.

The solution, if there is one, lies not in testing the will of Mohawks to resist but in so arranging matters that their appeal to their own Indian constituency is continually narrowed by honourable behaviour on the part of the government aimed at reconciliation. This is a long, tough game. It cannot be divorced from land rights. It must be a positive invitation to belong voluntarily to Canada, without giving up a distinctive identity.

WHERE TO NOW?

Many issues remain. Education suffers.[23] Life expectancies lag. The health, social and economic indicators attaching to aboriginal Canadians, and to reserve residents especially, are shameful, but there is no appetite for applying modern rules of microeconomics to this scattered archipelago. Illegal activities flourish, and gangs of disaffected youth plague prisons and prairie cities.[24] Better choices regarding diet, smoking, substance abuse, education, work and parenting need to be offered—and taken up. These are uncomfortable topics, but better futures cannot be bestowed. They must be taken.

The "Indian industry" of lawyers, consultants, bureaucrats and native political organizations created by the *Indian Act* is a well-funded national disgrace. B.C., as one tiny example, had by 2008 burned through $22 million in fees and expenses for that industry as it cogitated on a child welfare system that was scrapped before it started.[25] Modern critics such as Flanagan, Gibson and Widdowson are right to focus on the dysfunctional aspects of current Indian country: poor governance, poor incentives and the rest. Gibson argues brilliantly in favour of redressing the balance of collective and individual rights. Parliament's occasional stabs at mending holes in an increasingly obsolete legislative framework, such as the current work on water safety, are well-meaning and not harmful, but they are not transformative, either. In the meantime, the dream of sovereignty and the romance of resistance, in the sense of Taiaiake Alfred, seem to me essentially negative: one's identity is framed by others. Realism means that there will not soon be a new national sovereignty in North America, and that a life in the bush, or as a Warrior, cannot be expected to yield a high income and good health. On the other hand, it costs little to offer communal autonomy, and land, to those who want it.

But changing the laws that reinforce bad outcomes is hard. No budding Member of Parliament or political party campaigning for office pays much more than lip service to statutory reform. Spending is easier. Indian political leadership complains about the *Indian Act* but has offered few alternatives, with distinguished exceptions, starting with Chief Manny Jules's amendment of 1986 that allows bands to tax non-Indian lease-holders on reserve lands so as to provide needed services. Worse, from the point of view of reform, is that the combination of the *Indian Act* and Section

91(24) of the *Constitution Act, 1982* effectively pre-empts one of the great advantages of the federation: in other circumstances, we might have ten provinces and three territories experimenting to see what works best instead of reserving the legislative task to a single, national government. And to ice the cake, putting aboriginal and treaty rights into the Charter in 1982—into, in other words, a constitution that for all practical purposes cannot be changed—has upped the ante too far. Now every treaty is a constitutionally protected document. So is the Royal Proclamation of 1763. So is General Murray's *laisser-passer* of 1760. What a straitjacket we have invented! Even the simplest of agreements now has to be looked at in terms of something good for all time. It makes one yearn for the generosity of law professor Brian Slattery's argument for incorporating Indian law as one of the roots of our constitutional heritage: nowhere in those roots does one find immutability and freedom from evolution as a principle.[26]

At the still, dead heart of the relationship between Canada and aboriginal peoples is the *Indian Act* itself, a Victorian horror insufficiently updated and now in urgent need of replacement. Under the guise of protecting Indians from rapacious frontiersmen in the nineteenth century, the act severely constrains, in the twenty-first, the economic opportunities available to reserve communities and individuals, guarantees substandard housing, gives too much power to Ottawa, perpetuates dependency and encourages the growth of a parasitical Indian industry. It has an almost East German quality to it. There has to be something better.

I have argued for some years that the moral onus for this old horror rests with white Canada. This legislation is not something Indians invented for themselves. It is up to mainstream Canada to grasp the nettle and get on with reform, recognizing that those who benefit most from the rot at the core will resist most vocally. Legislative reform will be a lengthy process. It will require that Parliamentarians—not just bureaucrats—sit down with Indian leadership to discuss subjects principally in the provincial domain and work out new, modern statutes. These laws would cover such areas as education, land and water management, cultural programs, governance, fiscal relations with other levels of government, a regime for laws of general application and more. They would create new institutions whose size and scale answer tomorrow's challenges. When an Indian community is ready to move away from the old *Indian Act,* it would do so by a referendum of its members—but this would be a one-way gate. There would be no going back. Over time, perhaps many decades, the number of bands adhering to the old act would dwindle into insignificance, through their own choice. Government's task is to create attractive options, not to force the choice.

Almost three centuries have passed since a group of Indians, materially poor beyond the imaginings of modern-day Canadians, were persuaded to make a new start thirty miles from Montreal, on land that was promised to them forever but was leached away by people careless of the old promises. This was hardly a unique case: all over North America, from the days of the Spanish conquest in Florida and the American Southwest to current-day British Columbia, Europeans have made and reneged on land-sharing arrangements with the original inhabitants. What made Oka different was the formidable Mohawk resistance, based on a strong ideology and an economic base outlawed by the settler governments, that set them at the sharp edge of aboriginal irredentism. But Mohawk differences with other native groups in this regard are in degree, not in kind. It can be confidently predicted that similar long-standing disputes, if stirred by some careless act of the new majority, will turn virulent. In this post-9/11 world, there will be a temptation to brand the insurgents as terrorists. They are not. They are merely people who did not have the defences, military or microbial, to resist the European onslaught. Their collective grief will not be assuaged, but it can be respected, as can the letter of the historic promises.

CONDOLENCE

IN THE spring of 1991, I was invited—summoned is perhaps the more accurate word—to the reserve of the Oneidas of the Thames, near London, Ontario. Terry Doxtator and Bruce Elijah, who had played such an important role behind the wire at Oka in avoiding bloodshed, wanted me to see what life was like in Oneida country. I was interested in seeing the community that was home to these people, so I readily assented to coming— alone, as requested. I was met at the airport, taken to the reserve and toured through various facilities. I saw a school full of kids hard at work, and a new senior citizens' home, of which the community was rightly proud. We discussed the reserve's water supply and other infrastructural issues. But then things took a new turn. I was to come to the Longhouse. Indeed, the whole community was to come to the Longhouse, for a ceremony of condolence.

The expression of deep sympathy and support for someone who is called on to carry heavy burdens, personal or communal, is one of the most arresting and attractive features of Iroquois culture. As Doug George-Kanentiio explains, "Forgiveness and restoration of *kanikenriio*, the 'good mind,' is stressed as a person who is unburdened by hate may then apply reason and clarity of thought toward the resolution of the matter that has provoked grief or hostility."[1] Until then, the matter had been entirely theoretical for me. But

Bruce Elijah and his colleagues, it slowly dawned on me, felt that I was worth being condoled: an honour beyond words.

I was led into the Longhouse, an inconspicuous wooden building perhaps thirty by eighty feet in size. The central part was an open floor, and seating areas for each clan enclosed by low wooden walls lined the sides. At one end of the long open area was a small wood stove, at the other a single kitchen chair on which I was bade to sit. Community members filed in, silently taking their seats in their assigned spaces. There followed sweetgrass and orations and prayers in Oneida, followed by translations from Bruce Elijah. I was welcomed. The long and honourable history of my hosts was recounted. Friendship was devoutly wished. Then I was asked to stand, while elders prayed that my eyes might be opened and a young girl with an eagle feather lightly brushed my eyes. Another elder prayed that my ears might be cleared, so that I might hear and understand, while another girl with another feather brushed my ears. A third prayed that I might speak only the truth, and my lips were touched with the feather of an eagle. More prayer, and then the whole community lined up in front of me, in two criss-crossing files. One by one, they stopped in front of me, some shaking hands, most hugging me, all condoling me for the burdens of my job.

To this day, I feel immense gratitude to this Oneida community, as well as an obligation to speak the truth as I know it. This whole book comes from that afternoon.

ENDNOTES

CHAPTER 1

1 The account by George-Kanentiio (2006), 1–9, mixes tradition and archaeology as convincingly as any. A recent review of more ancient history is Goebel et al. (2008).

2 Price (1979), 135, thinks these people were related to the Hurons and the Petuns. At Stadacona, they would have been beyond the climatic limits of the Huron-Iroquois corn-beans-squash cultivation, and thus relatively weaker than in their home communities, which Price suggests reabsorbed them after warfare. Trigger and Pendergast (1978) survey all the major hypotheses.

3 Ratelle (1991).

4 Kanienkehaka is the more traditional name; "Mohawk" is derived from the Algonquin word for cannibal. Both terms are used by Mohawks today, with more traditional people seeming to prefer Kanienkehaka. I use both interchangeably.

5 The account is taken from Champlain (1613); the quote is from p. 99.

6 A splendid new biography of Champlain, Fischer (2008), summarizes the first third of the seventeenth century in New France in a way that will not soon be equalled.

7 Dalton (1968), 60.

8 Hunt (1940).

9 Goodleaf (1995), 8–9.

10 Tooker (1978). An oral history of an eclipse coincides with 1451. Mr. Justice Binnie in *Mitchell* prefers "around 1450."

11 Parker (1912).

12 Tooker (1978), 437–40.

13 Parker (1912).

14 Canada. House of Commons, "Minutes of Proceedings and Evidence of the Standing Committee on Aboriginal Affairs" 48 (1991), 24.

15 Thompson (1991), 5.

16 Ibid.

17 Quoted in Thompson (1991), 8; original in Public Archives of Canada, MG 17, CO 42, vol. 66, 52. Minutes of a speech addressed to Sir John

Johnson, Bart., Superintendent of Indian Affairs, by the Principal Chiefs of the Village of the Lake of Two Mountains, assembled in council, dated Indian Department Office, Montreal, February 7, 1787; Augneetha [Agneetha], the Principal Chief, Speaker. The excellent and reliable reviews by Jones and Thompson of DIAND's Claims and Historical Research Centre (1991, 1993) are indispensable.

18 Ibid., 9.

19 Ibid., 10.

20 Ibid., 11–12.

21 The correspondence and conditions are detailed in the land claim of 1977 by the Oka Indian Band.

22 Oka Indian Band (1977), 158. The reasoning is laid out in detail in *Corinthe* [1912].

23 A founding constitutional document of Canada, this unilateral proclamation set out to regulate the conflict between settlers and native peoples by demanding that before Europeans could settle, the Indians must be "treated with" in such a way as to surrender their title and come under the protection of the English sovereign. See George R. (1763).

24 *An Ordinance to incorporate the Ecclesiastics of the Seminary of Saint Sulpice of Montreal*, 2 Vict. ch. 50 and 3–4 Vict. ch. 30, included in the Consolidated Statutes of Lower Canada in 1861 as ch. 42, *An Act respecting the Seminary of St. Sulpice*. Since this act was published two years after its 1839 proclamation, it is referred to in most texts as the Ordinance of 1841. I prefer the year of enactment.

25 The superior in 1715, quoted by Thompson (1991), 8.

CHAPTER 2

1 *R. v. Sioui* [1990], 1 S.C.R. 1025.

2 The convoluted history of treaties, the different meanings ascribed to them by the parties and the subsequent cheating, theft, ill treatment and general sharp dealing by governments is a story for another time, but excellent introductions to a voluminous literature may be found in DIAND publication's (www.ainc-inac.gc.ca/al/hts/index-eng.asp).

3 Toombs and Toombs (2007).

4 *Cherokee Nation v. Georgia*, 5 Peters (30 U.S.) 1, *Worcester v. Georgia*, 6 Peters (31 U.S.) 515.

5 *Corinthe* [1912].

6 J.A. Crear, minister of Indian Affairs, in a letter to the trustees of the commercial property of St. Sulpice, December 10, 1941, quoted in Oka Indian Band (1977), 186.

7 Order-in-council, May 16, 1899.

8 I asked Don Boudria, M.P. for the riding next to Akwesasne and a federal minister under Jean Chrétien, whether Akwesasne Mohawks were politically involved during the 1990s. "No!" he said. "Only the priest voted—there was just one ballot." Interview, November 21, 2008.

9 Reid (2004), 6. The mixing of tribal origins continues today: Bonhomme (1990).

10 Benn (2009); reviewed by Morton (2010).

11 Canada. Natural Resources, Legal Surveys Division, Historical Review, "Kahnawake," Ottawa, n.d.

12 Landsman (1988); York and Pindera (1992).
13 Landsman (1988), Appendix A. From its style, I suspect it was drafted by Louis Hall: Hall (1970).
14 Canada. House of Commons, *Debates*, December 11, 1986, 2043.
15 When I visited Six Nations in the fall of 1987, Chief Bill Montour noted that he had no legal authority to control stray dogs. When I asked how he dealt with the problem, he took his hand from his pocket to show me a bunch of .22 bullets. Water was another problem on the reserve. The community supply came from the Grand River, a heavily used and endemically dirty stream that suffered occasional pulses of gross pollution. The water intake had no closable forebay, and the treatment plant was a pile of cheap galvanized steel, seriously corroded, that was kept in working order only through the heroic efforts of several young Indian technicians. No non-Indian community would have stood for this, and no province would have allowed such a situation to continue under its regulations. But there were no regulations whatsoever dealing with water on Indian reserves, and DIAND's technical advisors, Public Works, "saved" money by buying the cheapest plant on the market. Swain, Louttit and Hrudey (2006) lay out the regulatory problem that persists to the date of writing (though the minister has promised legislation).
16 Oka Indian Band (1975). *Calder* [1973] S.C.R. 313 was the landmark judgement regarding Nisga'a aboriginal title. The judgement went against the Nisga'a, but the dissent by Hall, Spence and Laskin was so powerful as to set aside blanket claims of extinguishment in British Columbia, putting paid to Trudeau's attempt in his 1969 White Paper to end all legal barriers to assimilation and set the country on a new course of modern treaty-making.
17 Oka Indian Band (1977).
18 There is a vast literature on aboriginal rights, some of which is summarized in Oka Indian Band (1977). A contemporary comprehensive view from the other side of the table is in Whitehall (1992).

CHAPTER 3

1 Lamb (1993).
2 Campbell was nothing if not systematic. Every Monday morning she would come to my office for an hour's closed-door discussion about some aspect of Westminster government. What began informally soon became a high point of my work week and kept me on my toes. She referred to these as "Sir Humphrey" moments in her 1996 memoirs. Campbell (1996).
3 Employment equity in the federal government is nowhere more vexed than with respect to visible minorities. Frequently they are not visible—which is the case with many aboriginal people. Unlike in the U.S., where documentary proof of at least 50 per cent native blood is required, in Canada it is up to individuals to declare (or not) their aboriginal status. When preference in hiring and advancement is tied to aboriginality,

there is an incentive for a potential employee to self-identify as such. In practice, there are many employees who want to feel they have succeeded on their own merits and so decline to claim aboriginal status.

4 Tellier told me that he'd had a choice to make in recommending a new deputy minister to the prime minister, between a bright but dangerously inexperienced policy spark and a pair of steady hands with long sectoral and line experience. On balance, he said, he had opted for new thinking—leaving me with the distinct feeling that my administrative performance would be closely monitored. The point was driven home to me by Jack Manion, Tellier's second in command and a greatly experienced and respected deputy minister. With joy at my promotion came a strong sense of the willies.

5 There are normally three sections (or volumes) in a briefing book: summary material about the department, its legislation, spending estimates, locations, biographies of key personnel and the like; a short and highly confidential section on current issues and controversies; and an annex with copies of all the formal tombstone stuff—a volume so heavy and soporific that only the prospect of flubbing something from it in a parliamentary committee gets anyone reading it at all. A wise department keeps such documents in "evergreen" form, as one never knows when a new minister or deputy will show up.

6 Jacques Gérin was not the only one to suffer under this minister. When she was finally demoted, the Environment department broke out in T-shirts with the memorable motto, "I survived Suzy B-G."

CHAPTER 4

1 Jenish (2004), 236–37. Thanks to Rick Van Loon for the reference.

2 Vachon (1979).

3 Austen (1980).

4 By coincidence we lived there at that time. Minneapolis was the urban heart of the only state with two presidential candidates that year, both reacting against the war policies of the previous two administrations. Widespread protest over the Vietnam war, radical campus politics, the rise of the Black Power and Indian movements and the descent of flower power into drugs made this a special time in the Upper Midwest.

5 Mohawk Nation Council of Chiefs (1990).

6 *Seminole Tribe of Florida v. Butterworth* [1981].

7 *Bryan v. Itasca County* [1976].

8 *California v. Cabazon Band of Indians* [1987].

9 Santa Ynez Band of Chumash Indians, n.d.

10 Wilkinson (2005), 335–36.

11 Hornung (1991), 2.

12 George-Kanentiio (2006), 65. This book and Hornung's are filled with first-hand detail, though the reader needs to remain aware of where the author is coming from.

13 Ibid.

14 The collusion of the tobacco companies in these illegal operations was finally settled in court in 2008 with fines to Imperial Tobacco of $200 million and Rothmans of $100 million. "In other words, the companies exported Canadian brand cigarettes into the U.S. in the early 1990s knowing they would be smuggled back into Canada and rigged the coded packages to make it difficult to trace." Marsden and Fowlie (2008). R.J. Reynolds and its subsidiary Northern Brands agreed in 2010 to pay $400 million, and JTI-Macdonald $150 million. Blackwell (2010).

15 *Mitchell v. M.N.R.* [2001]. Mitchell is a remarkable leader, an anti-gambling traditionalist who says he is a citizen of the Haudenosaunee and who has been a key political figure at Akwesasne for thirty years. I first met him at a congress of Indian youth in Ottawa in 1988, when he astonished more than a thousand young people (and me) by singing a long prayer, a cappella, in Mohawk.

16 Mitchell offered to send his counsel around to see me and sweep the cobwebs from my mind. Imagine my surprise when two distinguished lawyers, Jean Chrétien (not then a Member of Parliament or Leader of the Opposition) and his colleague Eddie Goldenberg, showed up at my office one day. We had a pleasant conversation in which I advanced my entirely unscholarly argument—this is one legal opinion for which the Department of Justice bears no fault—and we parted. Of course there can be no relation between this conversation and Mitchell's subsequent basing of his argument principally on aboriginal rights.

17 *Mitchell v. M.N.R.* [2001], 2.

18 The best view of this conundrum is that of Supreme Court Justice Ian Binnie in *Mitchell*, paragraphs 128-30, who adopts the concept of shared or merged sovereignty from the Royal Commission on Aboriginal Peoples: "Shared sovereignty, in our view, is a hallmark of the Canadian federation and a central theme of the three-cornered relations that link aboriginal governments, provincial governments and the federal government. These governments are sovereign within their respective spheres and hold their powers by virtue of their constitutional status rather than by delegation. Nevertheless, many of their powers are shared in practice and may be exercised by more than one order of government ... On this view, to return to the nautical metaphor of the 'two-row' wampum, 'merged' sovereignty is envisaged as a single vessel (or ship of state) composed of the historic elements of wood, iron and canvas. The vessel's components pull together as a harmonious whole, but the wood remains wood, the iron remains iron and the canvas remains canvas ... It represents, in a phrase, partnership without assimilation."

19 Ibid. The Supreme Court did, however, reinforce an important principle of Indian law established in *Delgamuukw*, namely that oral

evidence of prehistoric times may be accepted as any other evidence—tested and allowed or disallowed by a judge according to the ordinary rules of evidence.

20 Cross (1994), George-Kanentiio (2006), York and Pindera (1992), but especially the detailed account by Hornung (1991). None of these sources is without bias, but the accounts were prepared separately and, broadly, tell the same story with respect to weapons.

21 Swain notes (1989).

22 Interview with Pierre Cadieux, December 17, 2008.

23 Johansen (1993), Hornung (1991) and George-Kanentiio (2006).

24 George-Kanentiio (2006), 105.

25 Ibid., 101.

26 Swain notes (1990).

27 Ibid.

28 Winegard (2009), 15.

29 George-Kanentiio (2006).

30 Keene (1990), 4.

31 Lavoie (1991), 10.

32 Winegard (2009), 25.

CHAPTER 5

1 Garry Carbonnell, personal communication, March 24, 2009. Claude Soucie, "Municipality of Oka et al v. Jean-Roch Simon et al: Application of Municipal By-laws to Oka lands," memo to Deputy Minister of Indian Affairs and Northern Development, September 30, 1991. DIAND Legal Services, Hull, Quebec.

2 Oka Indian Band, letter to the Hon. Judd Buchanan, March 27, 1975.

3 Hon. Bill McKnight, letter to Kanesatake chief and council, October 14, 1986.

4 Canada. House of Commons, "The Summer of 1990" (1991), 3-7.

5 Petitioners from groups called the Kanesatake League for Democracy and the Committee for Change had 230 signatures of about 537 adult members of the band, which led to a proposal for another referendum on the form of government. According to Drummie (1991), 37, "The question was struck, arrangements made, the date set, and—the Six Nations Hereditary Chiefs obtained an injunction three days before voting day challenging the authority of the Minister to have such a vote." In the usual timely, helpful way of the courts, the issue was not resolved until 1991. Drummie also remarks wryly that with that resolution, the tenure of a hereditary chief became one year.

6 Canada. House of Commons, *Debates* 47 (1991), 11-12.

7 Canada. House of Commons, "Minutes of the Proceedings and Evidence of the Standing Committee on Aboriginal Affairs" 55 (March 19, 1991), 41-42.

8 Ibid., 59.

9 York and Pindera (1992), 45.

10 Winegard (2006), 124.

11 Ibid., 43.

12 The *Fifth Report of the House Standing Committee on Aboriginal Affairs* cites a 1987 letter from Walter David Sr. to the band council protesting the council's "knowledgeable theft of our title, our clan system and the Great Binding Law, the 'Kayanerakowa,' all of which belong to the Longhouse people." Abiding by the *Indian Act*,

a law of another country, was anathema. Canada. House of Commons, "The Summer of 1990" (1991), 13.

13 Swain notes (1990).

14 Canada. National Health and Welfare (1990). I objected but was told that since the Statistics Canada labour force and family expenditure surveys did not include reserve populations, nothing could be done. The rot went deeper than NHW's briefers.

15 Swain notes (1989).

16 Swain notes (1990).

17 Winegard (2006), 173.

18 Ibid., 177.

19 York and Pindera (1992), 77.

20 Ciaccia (2000), 60.

21 Winegard (2006), 182–84.

22 Ibid., 189.

23 Johansen (1993).

24 "Within a few hours of the killing of Corporal Lemay, word was being circulated at Akwesasne as to who shot the fatal bullet and how it was done. The information was consistent with the results of the formal investigation some months later." George-Kanentiio (2006), 123.

25 It was not until July 26 that anyone in an official position stated publicly that it was not an SQ bullet. Since the statement came from Sam Elkas's executive assistant, John McKenna, it was neither seen as unbiased nor widely reported.

26 Gilbert (1995), 70–72.

27 Ibid., 401–3.

28 Ibid, 195. Author's translation.

29 Québec, Sûreté du (1990).

30 Ibid., 208.

31 Directeur général adjoint Marc Lizotte, ibid., 216. Author's translation.

32 Ibid., 208–10.

CHAPTER 6

1 Parisella interview (2008), 19.

2 In 1969 the federal government published an integrationist White Paper on Indian Affairs which proposed sweeping away the *Indian Act* and all its colonialist cobwebs (Canada. Indian Affairs and Northern Development, 1969). It is often called the Trudeau White Paper but was in fact the result of intensive consultations between Jean Chrétien and Indian leadership across the country. "Mr. Chrétien has told me that what really happened was that the rhetoric from the Indians in the consultation was about the *Indian Act* as a colonial document that should be abolished ... to his disappointment, he discovered after the fact that the Indians never expected him to agree, and when he did so, were taken aback and concerned that maybe if the govt had agreed to their demands that they had made the wrong demands! He thought he had listened in good faith and had proposed radical and progressive reform. Instead they almost immediately accused him of cultural genocide! So he withdrew the White Paper." Goldenberg (2009). But not before the younger Indian leadership had responded with their stinging Red Paper (Cardinal, 1969).

3 Ciaccia (2000).

4 Parisella interview (2008), 5–6.

When Bourassa finally went away
for treatment in September 1990,
there occurred one of those little
crises that so often blow governments off their courses. Quebec
was, with some reluctance and
after a political battle, preparing
to introduce legislation to imple-
ment the Goods and Services Tax.
The day before the legislation was
to be introduced in the National
Assembly, the minister of Revenue
had an attack of conscience, decided
he could not do it and resigned. It
fell to John Parisella to decide that
Gérard D. Lévesque should succeed
the previous minister and to call the
groggy Bourassa in hospital to get
his concurrence.

5 Much of this account of the period
from July 11 to July 21 is taken from
the Drummie manuscript (1991).

6 Kalbfuss (1990).

7 Drummie (1991), 46.

8 Ibid., 46.

9 Siddon interview (2008).

10 *Globe & Mail* (July 19, 1990);
McGillivray (1990). The latter was
a Southam "news" story but was
more opinion than news.

11 Falardeau-Ramsay (1990).

12 Drummie (1991), 55.

13 Ibid.

14 Ciaccia (2000), 106.

15 Canada. National Aboriginal Economic Development Board (1990).

16 Calla interview (2008).

17 Courcy (1990). The CPR bridge is
just west of the Mercier. At one
point during the summer, Mohawk
witnesses told me that a train of
flat cars routinely hauling Leopard

tanks from Gagetown to Petawawa
passed through the reserve and
over the bridge, causing no end of
consternation in Kahnawake. The
army has no recollection of such a
movement.

18 O'Reilly (1990); summarized in
Canadian Press (July 18, 1990).

19 Goodleaf (1995), 6.

20 The formal view of the Department
of Justice was delivered in Hudson
(1990).

CHAPTER 7

1 Canadian Press, July 20, 1990.

2 After July 11, "members of the militant Warrior societies from Kahnawake and the Akwesasne reserve...
began pouring into Oka" (Canadian
Press, July 13). "Warriors who have
come to help at the barricades are
all men. They've come from the
Akwesasne reserve near Cornwall,
the Kahnawake reserve near Montreal and Ganienkeh reservation in
New York State" (*Ottawa Citizen*,
July 13). Somewhat over the top, I
had characterized the Warriors as
a "gang of criminals that is holding the Mohawk community in a
state of armed insurrection"; but
the Akwesasne Mohawk Nation, the
traditional Longhouse government,
had condemned the Warrior Society as "an organization sustained
by criminals engaged in criminal
activities such as smuggling and
gambling" in a May 1990 position
paper. The Warriors boasted to the
Montreal *Gazette* on July 13 that
they could match police firepower:
"We have .50-, .60-calibre, AR-15s,

.45 Thompsons—every kind of automatic weapon you could want . . .
We have mortars, claymores [land
mines], grenades—all the goodies."
"Loran Thompson [an outspoken
member of the Akwesasne War-
rior Society] . . . replaced . . . Ellen
Gabriel as spokesman for the belea-
guered Mohawks . . . [prompting]
one Kanesatake activist to wonder
whether the heavily armed Warriors are taking over" (Montreal
Gazette, July 21). I described the
Warriors as competent and heavily
armed and said that many of them
had previous military experience,
including during the Vietnam
war. On July 20, the *Toronto Star*
said "Some of the older Warriors
are Viet Nam veterans. The younger
fighters got their training in the
U.S. Marines. It's these veterans
who teach the less-experienced
local youth how to booby trap the
forest with barbed wire and how to
assemble pipe bombs. 'They're well
paid for what they do,' said a local
Mohawk . . . He said that profits from
the Mohawks' lucrative border traffic in cigarettes are channelled into
a special Warrior fund that pays
for soldiers' weapons and salaries."
I had said in my backgrounder
that there were seventy-five to a
hundred Warriors at Oka. According to *La Presse* on July 13, "Les
membres du conseil de bande et du
Longhouse de Kanesatake veulent
reprendre les pourparlers avec les
autorités gouvernementales . . . Ces
Indiens représentent les neuf dix-
ième de la population autochtone

d'Oka alors que la faction Warriors
regroupe tout juste une centaine
de personnes. Le hic, c'est que les
Warriors . . . refusent de plier aux
demandes du gouvernement local."
Even the Lubicons and the Assembly
of First Nations said they supported
Indian rights but not violence
(*Edmonton Journal*, July 14).
A *Gazette* editorial of July 21 said,
"[T]he worst people in the affair
remain the grandiosely named Warriors, who have long behaved less
like chivalrous knights than Mafiosi.
They hold their communities—
Kahnawake, Akwesasne and now
Kanesatake—at gunpoint to extort
what they want. What they claim
they want is recognition of absolute
native sovereignty. What they have
most often used their firepower to
get is a sordid empire of illegality:
gambling and sales of smuggled,
duty-free cigarettes. They hold their
communities in such terror that no
one—not the Indian police, not the
white police, not their fellow citizens—gainsay them." For my part,
I concluded that the CBC was more
anti-government than pro-news
and ceased to have anything to do
with them for a decade.

3 One consequence of my briefing was
that I received a number of letters
from across the country, some of
which displayed an uncomfortable
degree of racial animosity. More
typical was a fax from old friend
and sometime tobacco lobbyist Tex
Enemark: "You have simply got to
stop beating around the bush. Being
mealy-mouthed never got anyone

anywhere! Say what you think! Stop being evasive ... Anyway, you might like to know that the Tobacco Institute have had some independent forensic accountants do an assessment of the volume of cigarettes being smuggled. Their number is about $1/2 billion annually."

4 Yurkovich et al. interview (2008), 12.

5 Ibid., 14.

6 Hartt interview (2008), 18.

7 Yurkovich et al. interview (2008), 14.

8 Ibid., 46–47.

9 The video is an example of communications being put to work to achieve an essentially political end. In the words of General Foster, "The demo tape of the .50 cal machine gun served a number of purposes exceptionally well. It brought reality of force in visible terms to politicians and police that had no experience in this kind of violence. It established the Army as the authority and allowed me freedom of action because none of them wanted to be tagged with that kind of responsibility. It showed the uselessness of hiding behind patrol cars and a few sand bags. I achieved much with this demo tape and all of it intended." Foster 2010.

10 As Van Loon recalls (2008 interview, 4), "I think the line that worked best, you know, I was as forthcoming as I possibly could be, I mean I wasn't trying to hide anything, and at the end I said, you know, frankly, we are completely flummoxed about what to do, so that any advice that you could give us would be

gratefully received ... They didn't have a thing to say. But they were very gracious in the first place [and] they were flattered, I think, that somebody would ask them that. I have testified before several parliamentary committees in both Senate and House, and I've never received so many compliments as I did after that one."

11 *R. v. Sparrow* [1990].

12 Shaw (1990).

13 Being sued is part of the job at Indian Affairs. I once asked our lawyers to tally the suits naming me personally or ex officio and was told the quantifiable claims totalled more than $4 billion. This did not include Indian claims to more than 120 per cent of British Columbia. My response to sputtering lawyers soon became, "Take a number."

14 Hartt interview (2008), 11.

15 Ibid., 33.

16 Mulroney (2007), 1.

17 Hartt interview (2008), 20.

18 Stanley Hartt (2008 interview, 8) recalls: "So Ward [Elcock, PCO's Assistant Secretary for Legislation and House Planning—effectively the top PCO lawyer] goes to Manitoba and he shows this [agreement] to the Speaker, and the Speaker says this works. He shows it to the Clerk of the House, and the Clerk says it works. So he goes to sit outside Filmon's office, and seeks an appointment with Filmon, and Filmon let him sit there for three days and never saw him ... [I]t had to do with the fact that Carstairs was against Meech Lake and he had a minority situation, he couldn't

afford any light between her and him."

19 Hartt again (2008 interview, 6): "It is true that Joe Ghiz [premier of Prince Edward Island] called Wells a prick. In fact what he said was, 'You were a prick at Dalhousie, you are a prick now and you'll always be a prick.' And the retraction the next morning said, 'Wells did not go to Dalhousie.'"

20 Hartt interview (2008), 8.

21 Mulroney (2007), 798.

22 Agreement of August 12, 1990.

23 Wells (1990).

24 Bisson (1990).

25 Paterson's involvement is well described in his memoir: Paterson (2005), 122-37.

26 Ibid., 126.

27 Ibid., 128. Paterson evidently had some catching up to do.

28 Ibid., 129.

29 Ibid., 132.

30 Ibid., 132.

31 Ibid., 132-33.

CHAPTER 8

1 This was not universally applauded. Our departmental legal counsel, Michael Hudson, was roundly abused by individuals from the aboriginal law section of the Canadian Bar Association for the prime minister's choice. See Hudson (1991).

2 In January 1993 de Chastelain became Canada's ambassador to the United States. Remarkably, and uniquely, he was recalled as CDS for two years beginning in January 1994. During his second term, the incomplete and ineffective inquiry into the death of Somalian prisoner Shidane Arone blamed de Chastelain for the debacle, saying he had failed as a commander. His offer to resign was turned down, and he went on to play a decisive role in the resolution of the mess in Ulster. He still serves as Chairman of the Independent International Commission on Decommissioning, to the great satisfaction of the concerned governments. He is the only CDS I know who has welcomed visitors to a forces dinner in a kilt, playing bagpipes. As well, he is the author of the military version of Murphy's Law: "All major battles occur at the junction of four maps." Fowler interview (2008), 11.

3 Foster, personal communication, April 23, 2008.

4 de Chastelain (2009), 6.

5 Fowler interview (2008), 11; de Chastelain interview (2008), 23. Fowler went on to become a highly effective ambassador to the United Nations and in retirement was the special envoy of Secretary-General Ban Ki-Moon to Niger, where he was kidnapped in December 2008 by Al Qaeda in the Maghreb. He and his colleague Louis Guay were ransomed four months later.

6 Vice Admiral Chuck Thomas interview (2009), 3.

7 de Chastelain interview (2009), 5.

8 Chief Superintendent Lowell Thomas interview (2008).

9 Frank Vieni, letter to Dwayne White, August 16, 1990.

10 Kerr (1990); Goodwin (1990).

11 Goodwin (1990).

12 Cochrane (1990).

13 Air Defence Anti-Tank System, a mobile all-weather vehicle fitted with radar and Mach 3 rockets.

14 Winegard (2009), 36.

15 Foster, personal communication, November 9, 2008.

16 de Chastelain interview (2009), 17.

17 Ibid., 13-14.

18 The usefulness of military honours should not be downplayed. A critical confidence-building measure had occurred a few days earlier at the Kahnawake barricade. In one of the more disorderly struggles with the Châteauguay mob, a Mohawk flag was seized. The army retrieved it, dusted it off, folded it in the formal triangular fashion and presented it to the Mohawks at the barricade with a salute and a handshake. As always in Indian country, the coin of respect is more valued than all the honeyed words of politicians. The first mixed party across the bridge was led by a military piper.

19 Two years later, "Red Ian" Deans, the chairman of the Public Service Staff Relations Board, who rarely ruled against a grieving employee, ordered Horn to be reinstated, but with no pay for the interim. So the end result was that she paid the price for insubordination—two years' pay—in a way that was salutary for departmental staff. In later years, she resigned and became a polemicist for the Warrior cause; see Horn (1994) an example, or browse www.mohawknationnews.com. In a letter to me dated September 4, 2008, Ms. Horn said that she heard I had also tried to have her killed, which gravely overstates the power of a deputy minister.

20 Doxtator (1990).

21 de Chastelain interview (2009), 8.

22 Ibid., 22.

23 Ibid., 12.

24 Canada. Indian Affairs and Northern Development, "Oka Chronology" (1990), 29.

25 Ibid.

26 The question of allowing more Iroquois behind the barricades was touchy. One evening I got a call from de Chastelain, asking in effect for character references for the three individuals mentioned. I called Gerry Kerr, DIAND's director-general for Ontario, and from his people got the report that while they were Iroquois nationalists, they were peaceful and well-respected men. I passed this on to de Chastelain within the hour, and he made the decision to let them in, on the grounds that their counsel might help achieve a peaceful resolution.

27 Yurkovich et al. (2008), 1-5.

28 Goar (1990).

29 Canada. Indian Affairs and Northern Development, "Oka Chronology" (1990), 31.

30 Foster (2008), 2.

31 Canada. National Defence, "Post-Oka Communications Symposium" (1990), 9.

CHAPTER 9

1 Kershaw (2006).

2 See the correspondence with Cohen and his attorneys in the annexes to Gilbert (1995).

3 Canadian Press (1998).

4 Oliphant (2010).

5 The Beothuks of Newfoundland were gone by 1829, but a half century before the British had attempted to relieve population pressures in Nova Scotia by moving some Mi'kmaq from Nova Scotia to the island province. The resulting Conne River band escaped the long course of Canadian history and became aware that it might have some rights under the *Indian Act* only some time after 1949, when Newfoundland joined Confederation. Those same rights were controversial in a poor province, however, as they could easily lead the Conne River people (now the Miawpukek First Nation) to being considerably better off than their neighbours. Notwithstanding, on their urgent entreaty DIAND made them a band under the *Indian Act* in 1987.

6 On this point I anticipated the conclusion of the Royal Commission on Aboriginal Peoples, which in 1996 said, "The Commission is convinced that before Aboriginal and non-Aboriginal people can get on with the work of reconciliation, a great cleansing of the wounds of the past must take place." RCAP (1996), vol. 1, ch. 1, 6.

7 I made this argument later in a *Globe and Mail* op-ed. This course has been applied in a few instances, notably with the *First Nations Land Management Act*, S.C. 1999, c. 24, but not universally. I wonder whether both Indian and left-wing white resistance to Robert Nault's First Nations Governance bill, swiftly dropped along with the minister by Prime Minister Paul Martin, would have been so vocal if optionality had been a key feature.

8 Mulroney (1990).

9 Gilbert (1995). The SQ, defiant to the last, leaked the report to a friendly journalist a week before publication so that it could spin the story: everybody but the SQ was responsible for Lemay's death. Sossoyan (1998).

10 House of Commons Standing Committee on Aboriginal Affairs (1991).

11 Rochon and Lepage (1991).

12 Ibid., 28–29.

13 Canada. House of Commons, *Debates* 51 (1991), 4–18.

14 House of Commons committees, with the exception of Public Accounts, are usually chaired by someone from the governing side, and seats are allocated in proportion to party standings in the House. There is a small staff to assist the chair and to draft the final report, but in general there is modest or no independent research capacity, nor is the committee aided in its examination of witnesses by counsel. A committee studies an issue by calling witnesses, usually articulate people with an axe to grind (a category that includes ministers and senior civil servants), who are allowed ten to fifteen minutes to make their case. They are then questioned by committee members, who have seven to ten minutes to ask their questions and listen to the answers. There is no capacity

for drilling deeply into any matter, especially since even members of the same party rarely collaborate. Under the circumstances, Hughes and the staff did an excellent job of selecting witnesses and producing a report without partisan dissents.

15 Canada. House of Commons, *Debates* 51 (1991), 4–18.

16 In the spring of 1991, when Canada was still at war with Iraq, the Iraqi ambassador to the U.S., Moham-med al-Mashat, was suddenly sum-moned home from Washington, despite his strident public defence of the Saddam Hussein regime. He flew to Vienna instead and let sev-eral intelligence agencies know that he would like to defect. Canadian security officials determined to fast-track his entry, months ahead of more deserving Iraqis. There fol-lowed a comedy of errors and mixed communications between officials and ministers, interrupted by a cabinet shuffle, with the result that al-Mashat and his wife were legally in Canada before ministers had even heard his name. Sutherland (1991).

17 Until recently, the definitive word on royal commissions and other inquiries came from Nick d'Ombrain, who was godfather to several during his tenure as head of the Machinery of Government sec-tion of PCO (d'Ombrain, 1997), but he has been surpassed by Professor Ratushny (2009).

18 *Order-in-Council* P.C. 1991-1597, August 26, 1991.

19 Canada. *Report of the Royal Com-mission on Aboriginal Peoples* (1996), vol. 1, ch. 1.

20 Widdowson and Howard (2008).

21 Hawthorn (1966, 1967).

22 Burgess (2000).

23 Alfred (1999, 2005, 2006).

24 de Chastelain interview (2009), 22.

25 Foster interview (2008).

26 Swain et al. (2006). Curiously, this standard exists nowhere in law or regulation. It is merely an offhand phrase from a memor-andum to cabinet in 1977. It is no longer a matter of simple government policy, however, as Section 15 of the Charter, on equality rights, extends the concept much farther as part of the Canadian constitution. Canada, *Constitution Act, 1982.*

27 Wente (2008).

28 With respect to water, see Swain et al. (2006), vol. 1, 47–49 and vol. 2, 2–3.

29 Montreal *Gazette* (2008).

30 Paul (2008).

31 www.rcmp-grc/qc.nouv-news/ com-rel/2009/05/090519-eng.htm, May 19, 2009, accessed January 21, 2010.

32 Ha and Perreaux (2008).

33 Moyes (2008).

34 Patriquin (2008).

35 Ivison (2008).

36 Costigan (2008).

37 Becker and Van Natta (2008).

38 Deer (1997).

39 Canadian Press (2008).

40 Galloway (2008).

41 *Pyke v. Cuomo* [2009].

42 Ibid.; upheld on appeal.

43 Diamond (1997) is a fascinating, if bleak, view of the collision of European and native American populations.

CHAPTER 10

1 Harold Calla, personal communication, March 4, 2009. Calla recalls three apposite quotes from the wise old Chief Joe Mathias: "Aboriginal right and title is not worth the life of one Squamish band member." "You can't eat fiduciary duty." "Aboriginal rights and title do not stand still."

2 Russell (2008). One is struck by how many of the establishment players in this drama are, like Russell, Rhodes scholars. Ian Clark, Fred Drummie, John Rayner, Robert Bourassa and Desmond Morton are all branded by the arch-colonialist's gift.

3 Garnett interview (2008), 2.

4 Russell (2008), 42.

5 Linden (2007), vol. 1, 685.

6 Grice (2009).

7 See the series of articles by Christie Blatchford in the *Globe and Mail*, November 2009.

8 Canada. National Defence (1991).

9 de Chastelain interview (2008), 6.

10 Morton (1991).

11 Canada. House of Commons (1991), 32.

12 Craig (1991), 23.

13 Keegan (2003), 370–99.

14 According to Lieutenant Colonel Robin Gagnon, commanding Third Battalion Twenty-second Royal Regiment at Kahnawake, "It would have helped beforehand to be familiar, not only with the underlying reasons for their demands, but also with their culture and traditions. Their outlook is altogether different from ours. Moreover, the chiefs have no decision-making power whatever. They must constantly consult their people and reach a consensus." Baril (1990), 5.

15 Russell (2008), 42.

16 Canada. National Defence (November 16, 1990). "Post-Oka Communications Symposium," Ottawa, unpublished transcript. The distinguished journalists George Bain and Lysiane Gagnon decried the bias and unprofessionalism of much of the media coverage during the same symposium.

17 Bury (1990).

18 Patel (1990).

19 de Chastelain (1990); Foster (1990).

20 As examples: Beauregard (1993), Boswell (1991a and b), Cocking (1991), Eve (1990), Gagnon (1991), Heinrich (1990), House of Commons (1991a and b), Morris (1995), Norris (1990), Osler and MacFarlane (1991), Perigoe (1990), Roth (1990), Skea (1993–94), Valaskakis (1994), York (1990).

21 Thompson (1996), 3.

22 Occasionally, U.S. transborder arming of criminals comes home to roost. Arizona is currently appealing the dismissal of charges against a U.S. gun dealer who had been arming the Mexican drug cartels. McKinley (2009).

23 Richards (2008).

24 Friesen and O'Neill (2008); George-Kanentiio (2008); Canada. RCMP (2007, 2008).

25 Leyne (2009).

26 Slattery (1996).

CONDOLENCE

1 George-Kanentiio (2006), 87.

BIBLIOGRAPHY

CASES

Bryan v. Itasca County, 426 U.S. 373 [1976]
Calder v. British Columbia (Attorney General) [1973] S.C.R. 313.
California v. Cabazon Band of Indians, 480 U.S. 202 [1987].
Cherokee Nation v. Georgia, 5 Peters (30 U.S.) 1 [1831].
Corinthe et al. v. Seminary of St. Sulpice [1912] 5 D.L.R. 263, [1912] A.C. 872.
    Judicial Committee of the Privy Council.
Delgamuukw v. British Columbia [1997] 3 S.C.R. 1010.
Ermineskin Indian Band and Nation v. Canada [2009] 1 S.C.R. 222.
Guerin v. The Queen [1984] 2 S.C.R. 335.
Mitchell v. M.N.R. [2001] 1 S.C.R. 911.
Pyke v. Cuomo, U.S.C.A. 2nd Circuit, 07-0334-cv(L), 07-3524(CON) [2009].
R. v. McIvor [2008] 1 S.C.R. 285.
R. v. Sioui [1990] 1 S.C.R. 1025.
R. v. Sparrow [1990] 1 S.C.R. 1076.
Seminole Tribe of Florida v. Butterworth, 658 F. 2nd 310, U.S.C.A. 5th
    Circuit [1981].
Worcester v. Georgia, 6 Peters (31 U.S.) 515 [1832].

STATUTES

Canada Order-in-Council, May 16, 1899.
Canada Order-in-Council P.C. 1991–1597, August 26, 1991.
Canadian Human Rights Act, c. H-6, amendments of 2008.
First Nations Commercial and Industrial Development Act, S.C. 2005, c. 53.
First Nations Fiscal and Statistical Management Act, S.C. 2005, c. 9.
First Nations Jurisdiction over Education in British Columbia Act, S.C.
    2006, c. 10.
First Nations Land Management Act, S.C. 1999, c. 24.

Indian Act, R.S.C. 1985, C. I-5.

National Defence Act. R.S.C. 1985, C. N-5.

An Ordinance to incorporate the Ecclesiastics of the Seminary of Saint Sulpice of Montreal, 2 Vict. (3) ch. 50 (1839); also 3-4 Vict. ch. 30 (1840).

INTERVIEWS

Boudria, Hon. Don. November 21, 2008.

Cadieux, Hon. Pierre H. December 17, 2008.

Calla, Harold. December 17, 2008.

Cardinal, Ruth. July 10, 2008.

de Chastelain, Gen. (ret.) A.J.G.D. November 21, 2008. Rev. March 30, 2009.

Drummie, Frederic R. April 20, 2008.

Flemming, Jeanne. July 8, 2008.

Foster, LGen. (ret.) Kent, and Frederic R. Drummie. April 23, 2008.

Fowler, Robert R. November 20, 2008.

Garnett, VAdm (ret.) Gary. October 7 and November 4, 2008.

Gélinas, Nathalie. August 6, 2008.

Graham, John. November 21, 2008.

Hartt, Stanley. November 11, 2008.

Inkster, Comr. (ret.) Norman D. November 10, 2008.

McCue, Harvey and Sharon. July 9, 2008.

Morden, Reid. November 5, 2008.

Mulroney, Rt. Hon. Brian. November 20, 2008.

Parisella, John. July 8, 2008.

Rayner, John S. July 9, 2008.

Santi, Roberta. November 12, 2008.

Shannon, Anne Park. March 20, 2009.

Siddon, Hon. Thomas E. June 15, 2008.

Tellier, Paul M. November 24, 2008.

Thomas, VAdm (ret.) Chuck. March 23, 2009.

Thomas, CSupt (ret.) Lowell. July 8, 2008.

Van Loon, Richard. July 3, 2008.

Wilson, Hon. Michael H. November 5, 2008.

Yurkovich, Susan, Jacquie Prokopanko, Joseph Whiteside and Ray Castelli. November 6, 2008.

REFERENCES

Alfred, Taiaiake. *Peace, Power, Righteousness: An Indigenous Manifesto.* Don Mills: Oxford University Press, 1999.

———. *Wasáse: Indigenous Pathways of Action and Freedom.* Peterborough, Ont.: Broadview Press, 2005.

——— and Lana Lowe, "Warrior Societies in Contemporary Indigenous Communities," 2006; background paper for Linden (2007).

Anonymous. "Four Men Caught with Drugs, Guns," *Gazette*, Montreal, October 11, 2008.

Austen, Ian. "Troopers Keep Peace in Mohawk Dispute," *Globe and Mail*, Toronto, June 16, 1980.

Baril, Maj. Gérald. "Mission Accomplished," *Sentinel*, vol. 6 (1990), 2–8.

Beauregard, Claude. "L'intervention Militaire à Oka: Stratégie, Communication et Couverture de la Presse/the Military Intervention in Oka: Strategy, Communication and Press Coverage," *Canadian Military History* vol. 2, no. 1 (spring 1993), 23–47.

Becker, Jo and Don Van Natta Jr. "For McCain and Team, a Host of Ties to Gambling," *New York Times*, September 28, 2008.

Benn, C. *Mohawks on the Nile: Natives among the Canadian Voyageurs in Egypt, 1884–1885*. Toronto: Dundurn Press, 2009.

Bisson, Bruno. "Les Cinq Signataires de l'Entente de Dimanche Sont Tous Liés Aux Warriors," *La Presse*, Montreal, August 15, 1990.

Blackwell, Richard. "Tobacco giants to pay \$550-million settlement," *Globe and Mail*, Toronto, April 14, 2010.

Blatchford, Christie. Series of articles in the *Globe and Mail*, Toronto, November 2009. "Just how sensitive is Canada's native file?" (Nov. 10), "Government preoccupied with how suit seen by natives" (Nov. 11), "Finally, the weak have a voice against the strong" (Nov. 12), "A couple terrorized in a 'war zone' while police stood by" (Nov. 13), "Two standards of policing failed the residents of Caledonia" (Nov. 14), "With a shotgun and his dog, he tried to defend his Caledonia home" (Nov. 17), "A false date, a shotgun fixation and a fumbled cross-examination" (Nov. 19), "A reign of terror, a trail of OPP inaction" (Nov. 20), "Abandoned, unprotected, afraid. Afghanistan? No. The heart of Ontario" (Nov. 21).

Bonhomme, Jean-Pierre. "Les Amérindiens de Kahnawake sont bel et bien propriétaires de leur territoire. Mais ils ne sont pas tous Iroquois, loin de la," *La Presse*, Montreal, July 19, 1990, A3.

Boswell, Randy. "A Clash of Perspective," *Content*, March/April 1991, 18.

———. "Oka: Crisis in Journalism," *Content*, January/February 1991, 16–17.

Burgess, Diane. "Kanesatake on Witness: The Evolution of CBC Balance Policy," *Canadian Journal of Communication*, vol. 25, no. 2 (2000), 17.

Bury, Charles. "Oka 1990: Covering the Crisis Wasn't Easy," Ottawa: Department of National Defence, 1990.

Cairns, Alan C. *Citizens Plus: Aboriginal Peoples and the Canadian State*. Vancouver: UBC Press, 2000.

———. *First Nations and the Canadian State: In Search of Coexistence*. Kingston, Ont.: Queen's University School of Policy Studies, Institute of Intergovernmental Relations, 2005.

Campbell, Kim. *Time and Chance: The Political Memoirs of Canada's First Woman Prime Minister*. Toronto: Doubleday Canada, 1996.

————. "The Warriors and the Criminal Law," *Canadian Speeches/Issues*, vol. 4, no. 6 (1990), 68–69.

Campbell, Robert M. and Leslie A. Pal. "Feather and Gun: Confrontation at Oka/ Kanesatake," in *The Real Worlds of Canadian Politics: Cases in Process and Policy*. Peterborough, Ont.: Broadview Press, 1991.

Canada. *Constitution Act, 1982*, being Schedule B to the *Canada Act, 1982* (U.K.), 1982, c. 11.

————, House of Commons. *Debates.* [*Hansard*]. Ottawa, 1991.

————, House of Commons. "Minutes of Proceedings and Evidence of the Standing Committee on Aboriginal Affairs," Ottawa, Supply and Services, 1991.

————, House of Commons. "The Summer of 1990," *Fifth Report of the Standing Committee on Aboriginal Affairs*, Ottawa, 1991.

————, Indian Affairs and Northern Development. "Oka Chronology," unpublished manuscript, Ottawa, 1990.

————, Indian Affairs and Northern Development. *Statement of the Government of Canada on Indian Policy*, Ottawa, 1969.

————, National Aboriginal Economic Development Board. "Memorandum to the Minister of State (Small Businesses and Tourism)," Ottawa, 1990.

————, National Defence. "Eastern Region after Action Report: Operation Salon," St. Hubert, 1991.

————, National Defence. "Operation Salon Highlights," Ottawa, 1990.

————, National Defence. "Post-Oka Communications Symposium," unpublished transcript, November 1990.

————, National Health and Welfare. "Medium-Term Review of Social Issues," Ottawa, 1990.

————, Natural Resources. Legal Surveys Division, Historical Review, "Kahnawake," Ottawa, n.d.

————. *Report of the Royal Commission on Aboriginal Peoples*, Ottawa: Queen's Printer, 1996.

————, Royal Canadian Mounted Police. *Contraband Tobacco Enforcement Strategy*, Ottawa, 2008.

————, Royal Canadian Mounted Police. "Current Trends in Firearms Trafficking and Smuggling in Canada," Criminal Intelligence Brief, November 23, 2007.

————, Royal Canadian Mounted Police. "Kahnawake," Ottawa: RCMP, 1989.

Canadian Press. "Quick Facts," July 18, 1990 (CP 1952ED 18-07-90).

————, "Man acquitted before defence heard," September 22, 1998.

————, "Organized Crime Targeted in Eight Pre-Dawn Raids," *Globe and Mail*, Toronto, December 11, 2008.

————, untitled article, July 20, 1990.

Carbonnell, Garry. Personal communication, March 24, 2009.

Cardinal, Harold. *Red Paper on Native Development,* Indian Chiefs of
    Alberta, 1969.

Ciaccia, John. *The Oka Crisis: A Mirror of the Soul.* Dorval, Que.: Maren
    Publications, 2000.

Clark, Keith. "The Collision of the Recognition Act and the New Relationship,"
    Business in Vancouver, November 4–10, 2008, 20.

Cochrane, Janice. "B.C. Blockades Update," briefing note, Department of Indian
    Affairs and Northern Development, Vancouver, August 14, 1990.

Cocking, Marie. "More of the Same: Editors Reluctant to Change Native
    Coverage Even after Oka," *Content,* May/June 1991, 18–19.

Cook, Curtis and Juan D. Lindau, eds. *Aboriginal Rights and Self-Government:
    The Canadian and Mexican Experience in North American Perspective.*
    Montreal and Kingston: McGill-Queen's University Press, 2000.

Costigan, Christopher. "Canada Targets Kahnawake Online Gambling,"
    Gambling911.com, March 6, 2008, www.gambling911.com/Canada-
    Kahnawake-030608.html.

Courcy, Denis. Letter to John Ciaccia, July 18, 1990.

Craig, E.P. "In Light of Oka: A Need to Re-Examine Aid of the Civil Power,"
    National Defence College, 1991.

Cross, R. and H.S. *Lasagna: The Man Behind the Mask.* Vancouver:
    Talonbooks, 1994.

Dalton, Roy. *The Jesuit Estates Question, 1760–1888.* Toronto: University
    of Toronto Press, 1968.

de Champlain, Samuel. *Voyages of Samuel de Champlain.* Trans. Charles
    Pomeroy Otis. Reprint of Prince Society ed., Boston, 1880, vol. 11, Burt
    Franklin: Research and Source Works Series #131. New York: Burt Franklin,
    1966. First pub. 1613.

de Chastelain, A.J.G.D. "Statement by the Chief of the Defence Staff,"
    Department of National Defence, Ottawa, 1990.

Deer, Kenneth. "Coroner's Report Critical of SQ," *Eastern Door,* vol. 4,
    no. 28 (1995).

———. "RCMP Carry Out Sting Operation on South Texas Ranch," *Eastern
    Door,* vol. 6, no. 33 (1997).

Diamond, Jared. *Guns, Germs and Steel: The Fates of Human Societies.* New
    York: W.W. Norton, 1997.

Dionne, Paul G. "Rapport d'Investigation du Coroner." Montreal: Gouvernement
    du Québec, Bureau du Coroner, 1991.

d'Ombrain, Nicholas. "Public Inquiries in Canada," *Canadian Public
    Administration,* vol. 40, no. 1 (spring 1997).

Doxtator, Terry. "Press Statement." Oneidas of the Thames reserve, Ont.: Six
    Nations Confederacy (Haudenosaunee), 1990.

Drummie, Frederic R. Manuscript. 106pp. Ottawa, 1991.

Eve, Doni. "The Value of a PR Strategy." *Content,* November/December 1990, 21.

Falardeau-Ramsay, Michelle. Letter to Thomas E. Siddon, July 18, 1990.

Fischer, David Hackett. *Champlain's Dream.* Toronto: Knopf Canada, 2008.

Flanagan, Tom. *First Nations? Second Thoughts.* Montreal and Kingston: McGill-Queen's University Press, 2000.

Foster, Kent. "LGen Foster Announces Direct Military Action at Oka and Kahnawake," Department of National Defence, Ottawa, 1990.

———. Personal communication, November 9, 2008 and May 4, 2010 (email).

Friesen, Joe. "CSIS Turning to Natives in Search of Information," *Globe and Mail,* Toronto, November 29, 2008.

Friesen, Joe and Katherine O'Neill. "Armed Posses Spreading Violence across Prairie Communities," *Globe and Mail,* Toronto, May 9, 2008, A12–13.

Gabriel-Doxtator, Brenda Katlatont and Arlette Kawanatatie Van den Hende. *At the Woods' Edge: An Anthology of the History of the People of Kanehsata:ke.* Kanesatake, Que.: Kanesatake Education Centre, 1995.

Gagnon, Lysiane. "Tripping the Light Fantastic," *Content,* January/February 1991, 18.

Galloway, Gloria. "Canada Falls Short on Tobacco Control: Report," *Globe and Mail,* Toronto, November 7, 2008, A10.

George R. *A Proclamation.* Court of St. James, London, October 7, 1763.

George-Kanentiio, Douglas M. *Iroquois on Fire: A Voice from the Mohawk Nation.* Westport, Conn.: Praeger, 2006.

———. "It Wasn't Supposed to Be This Way," *Ottawa Citizen,* November 19, 2008, A15.

Gibson, Gordon. *A New Look at Canadian Indian Policy.* Vancouver: Fraser Institute, 2009.

Gilbert, Guy. "Rapport d'Enquête du Coroner Guy Gilbert sur les Causes et Circonstances du Décès de Monsieur Marcel Lemay: Annexes," Montreal: Gouvernement du Québec, Bureau du Coroner, 1995.

Globe and Mail, editorial. "Ottawa's conspicuous absence from Oka," July 19, 1990.

Goar, Carol. "Siddon Redeems Image with a Sensitive Speech to Irate Native Chiefs," *Toronto Star,* September 15, 1990, 1.

Goebel, Ted, Michael R. Waters and Dennis H. O'Rourke. "The Late Pleistocene Dispersal of Modern Humans in the Americas," *Science,* vol. 319 (2008).

Goldenberg, Eddie. Personal communication, April 7, 2009.

Goodleaf, Donna. *Entering the War Zone: A Mohawk Perspective on Resisting Invasions.* Penticton, B.C.: Theytus Books, 1995.

Goodwin, Donald K. "Long Lake #58 Indian Band—Railway Blockade," briefing note, Department of Indian Affairs and Northern Development, Ottawa, 1990.

Grice, Craig. Personal communication, 2009.

Ha, Tu Thanh and Les Perreaux. "Guilty Pleas Reveal Mob's Thuggish Montreal Ways," *Globe and Mail*, Toronto, September 19, 2008, A1, A4.

Hall, Louis Koroniaktajeh. *Rebuilding the Iroquois Confederacy*, 1970. Reprinted by Mohawk Nation Kahnawake Branch, 1998.

Hawthorn, H. B., ed. *A Survey of the Contemporary Indians of Canada: Economic, Political, Educational Needs and Policies*, 2 vols. Citizenship and Immigration, Ottawa, 1966, 1967.

Heinrich, Jeff. "Media Solidarity? Not When There's a Good Story to Be Had." *Content* September/October 1990, 14.

Horn, Kahentinetha (Kahntineta). Letter to Harry Swain, September 4, 2008.

———. *Mohawk Warriors Three: The Trial of Lasagna, Noriega & 20-20*. Kahnawake, Ont.: Owera Books, 1994.

Hornung, Rick. *One Nation Under the Gun: Inside the Mohawk Civil War*. New York: Pantheon, 1991.

Hudson, Michael. "Review of Six Demands by Mohawks of Kanesatake," memorandum for the deputy minister of Indian Affairs and Northern Development, DIAND Legal Services, July 24, 1990.

———. "Canadian Bar Association (Ontario) Joint Meeting Native Justice/ Civil Liberties Section 'Oka—Constitutional Aftermath,'" memorandum for the deputy minister of Justice, DIAND Legal Services, March 27, 1991.

Hunt, George T. *The Wars of the Iroquois: A Study in Intertribal Trade Relations*. Madison: University of Wisconsin Press, 1940.

Isaac, Thomas and Keith Clark. "Legal Observations Concerning the 'Discussion Paper on Instructions for Implementing the New Relationship,'" unpublished memorandum, Vancouver, March 9, 2009.

Ivison, John. "Ottawa Targets Gaming: Native Reserve Hosts Illegal Online Poker Sites," *National Post*, March 5, 2008.

Jenish, D'Arcy. *Epic Wanderer: David Thompson and the Mapping of the Canadian West*. Lincoln: University of Nebraska, 2004.

Johansen, Bruce E. *Life and Death in Mohawk Country*. Golden, Col.: North American Press, 1993.

Jones, M.J. "Research Report on the History of Disputes at Oka/Kanesatake," Part II of *Materials Relating to the History of the Land Dispute at Kanesatake*. Indian Affairs and Northern Development, Claims and Historical Research Centre, Ottawa, September 17, 1993.

Kalbfuss, Elizabeth. "Department Heads on Holiday When Sûreté Sent In," *Gazette*, Montreal, July 13, 1990.

Keegan, John. *Intelligence in War: Knowledge of the Enemy from Napoleon to Al-Qaeda*. Toronto: Key Porter, 2003.

Keene, Capt. Tony. "Guns among the Mohawks," *Sentinel*, vol. 4 (1990), 2-4.

Kerr, Gerry. Briefing note for Fred Drummie, August 13, 1990.

Kershaw, Sarah. "Through Indian Lands, Drugs' Shadowy Trail," *New York Times*, February 19, 2006.

Lamb, Mary Anne. *Journey of Many*. Hull, Que.: Indian Affairs and Northern Development, 1993.

Landsman, Gail H. *Sovereignty and Symbol: Indian-White Conflict at Ganienkeh*. Albuquerque: University of New Mexico Press, 1988.

Lavoie, Lt. Roland. "Behind the Scenes at Op Salon," *Sentinel*, vol. 1 (1991), 8-10.

Leyne, Les. "While Grown-Ups Talk, the Kids Wait," *Times-Colonist*, Victoria, April 8, 2009.

Linden, Sidney B. *Report of the Ipperwash Inquiry*, 4 vols. Toronto: Queen's Printer for Ontario, 2007.

Marsden, William and Jonathan Fowlie. "Province Wins in Tobacco Lawsuit," *Times-Colonist*, Victoria, August 1, 2008.

McGillivray, Don. "Natives Want More Than Ottawa's Trinkets," *Gazette*, Montreal, July 19, 1990.

McKinley, James C. Jr. "Prosecutors Seek Appeal in Dismissal of Gun Case," *New York Times*, March 20, 2009.

McKnight, Hon. William. Letter to Kanesatake Chief and Council. October 14, 1986.

Mohawk Nation, Canada and Quebec. "Agreement between the Mohawk Nation and the Government of Canada and the Government of Quebec," Kanesatake, Que., 1990.

Mohawk Nation Council of Chiefs. "Mohawk Sovereignty Security Force, Mohawk Nation Office at Kahnawake," Akwesasne Mohawk Nation, 1990.

Morris, Martin J. "Overcoming the Barricades: The Crisis at Oka as a Case Study in Political Communication," *Journal of Canadian Studies*, vol. 30, no. 2 (1995), 74-90.

Morton, Desmond. "Bayonets in the Streets: The Canadian Experience of Aid of the Civil Power 1867-1990." *Canadian Defence Quarterly* (1991): 30-36.

———. "Navigating Imperial Rivers," *Literary Review of Canada*, January/February 2010.

Moyes, Mark. "Fort 'Hawks," *Driven*, October 2008, 30-31.

Mulroney, Brian. *Memoirs 1939-1993*. Toronto: McClelland & Stewart, 2007.

———. "Notes for an Address to the House of Commons, September 25, 1990," Prime Minister's Office, Ottawa, 1990.

Norris, Alexander. "Gazette Reporter Singled Out for Abuse," *Content*, September/October 1990, 12-13.

Obomsawin, Alanis. *Kanesatake: 270 Years of Resistance*. National Film Board, Ottawa, 1991.

Oka Indian Band. Letter, March 27, 1975.

Oka Indian Band. "Oka Indian Land Claim Submitted to the Government of Canada," 1977.

Oliphant, Jeffrey. *Report of the Commission of Inquiry into Certain Allegations Respecting Business and Financial Dealings Between Karlheinz Schreiber and the Right Honourable Brian Mulroney*, Ottawa, May 31, 2010.

O'Reilly, James. Letter to John Ciaccia, July 18, 1990.

Osler, Andrew and Andrew MacFarlane, "How Eleven Canadian Newspapers Reported Oka," Canadian Communications Association, Kingston, Ont., May 30, 1991.

Parker, Arthur C. *The Code of Handsome Lake, the Seneca Prophet,* New York State Museum Bulletin 163, 1912; reprinted by IroQrafts, Ohsweken, Ont., 2000.

———. *The Constitution of the Five Nations or the Iroquois Book of the Great Law.* New York State Museum Bulletin 184, 1916; reprinted by IroQrafts, Ohsweken, Ont., 2006.

Patel, Tara. "Whither Oka?" *Between the Lines,* Nov. 30-Dec. 13, 1990.

Paterson, Alex K. *My Life at the Bar and Beyond.* Montreal: McGill-Queen's University Press, 2005.

Patriquin, Martin. "The New Face of Online Gambling," *Maclean's,* March 17, 2008.

Paul, Ryan. "Kanesatake Police Audit Raises 'Concerns,' says Day," *Intertribal Times,* May 2, 2008.

Perigoe, Ross. "The Media and Minorities: Native Concerns Ignored Unless There's a Conflict," *Content,* September/October 1990, 10-12.

Pertusati, Linda. *In Defence of Mohawk Land: Ethnopolitical Conflict in Native North America.* Albany: State University of New York Press, 1997.

Pothel, Claude. "Rapport Medico-Legal (Amende)," Montreal: Gouvernement du Québec, Ministère de la Sécurité Publique, Laboratoire de médecine légale, 1991.

Price, John A. *Indians of Canada: Cultural Dynamics.* Scarborough, Ont.: Prentice Hall, 1979.

Québec, Sûreté du. "Opération Doré 90-4 'Oka,'" St.-Eustache, Que., 1990.

Ratelle, Maurice. "Étude sur la Présence des Mohawks au Québec Méridional de 1534 à nos Jours," Ville du Québec: Gouvernement du Québec, 1991.

Ratushny, Ed. *The Conduct of Public Inquiries: Law, Policy and Practice.* Irwin Law: Toronto, 2009.

Reid, G.F. *Kahnawake: Factionalism, Traditionalism, and Nationalism in a Mohawk Community.* Lincoln: University of Nebraska Press, 2004.

Richards, John. "Closing the Aboriginal/non-Aboriginal Education Gaps," C.D. Howe Institute *Backgrounder* 116, October 2008.

Rochon, Monique and Pierre Lepage. *Oka-Kanesatake, Summer 1990: A Collective Shock,* Quebec Human Rights Commission, April 1991.

Roth, Lorna. "The 'Mohawk Crisis': Reflections on French, English and Mohawk Media Coverage," manuscript, Concordia University, Montreal, November 1990.

Russell, Peter. "A Betrayal of Trust," *idea&s,* vol. 1 (2008), 36-43.

Santa Ynez Band of Chumash Indians. "History of Native American Gaming,"
n.d., www.santaynezchumash.org/gaming_history.html (accessed March
23, 2009).

Schneider, Stephen, "Our Healthiest Industry? Organized Crime is Flourish-
ing in Canada, Just As it Always Has," *Literary Review of Canada,* January/
February 2010, 20–22.

Shaw, Richard G. "Status Report of Litigation Involving Kanesatake," briefing
note for the deputy minister of Indian Affairs and Northern Development,
DIAND Legal Services, Ottawa, August 10, 1990.

Siddon, Tom. "The Fateful Turning Point at Kanesatake Standoff," *Canadian
Speeches/Issues,* vol. 4, no. 6 (1990), 63–67.

Skea, Warren H. "The Canadian Newspaper Industry's Portrayal of the Oka
Crisis," *Native Studies Review,* vol. 9, no. 1 (1993–94), 15–31.

Slattery, Brian. "The Organic Constitution: Aboriginal Peoples and the Evolution of Canada," *Osgoode Hall Law Journal,* vol. 34, no. 1 (1996), 101–12.

Sossoyan, Matthieu. "Le silence des Mohawks ... ou des medias?" *Recherches
amérindiennes au Québec,* vol. 28, no. 2 (1998), 85–93.

Sutherland, S.L. "The Al-Mashat Affair: Administrative Accountability in
Parliamentary Institutions," *Canadian Public Administration,* vol. 34,
no. 4 (winter 1991), 573–603.

Swain, Harry. "How to Get Out of the Indian Act Mess," *Globe and Mail,*
Toronto, November 9, 2005.

———. "Whatever Happened to Indian Agents? Preparing DIAND for the
1990s," speech to Treasury Board management, Ottawa, 1992.

Swain, Harry, Stan Louttit and Steve Hrudey. *Report of the Expert Panel on
Safe Drinking Water for First Nations.* Ottawa: Indian Affairs and Northern
Development, 2006.

Thompson, John. "A History of the Mohawks at Kanesatake and the Land
Dispute to 1961," Part I of *Materials Relating to the History of the Land
Dispute at Kanesatake,* Indian Affairs and Northern Development, Claims
and Historical Research Centre, Ottawa, 1991.

Thompson, John. *The Long Fall of the Mohawk Warriors.* Toronto: Mackenzie
Institute, 1996.

Tooker, Elizabeth. "The League of the Iroquois: Its History, Politics, and
Ritual," in Bruce G. Trigger, ed., *Northeast,* vol. 15 of W.C. Sturtevant, ed.,
Handbook of North American Indians. Washington, D.C.: Smithsonian
Institution, 1978, 418–41.

Toombs, Robert and Isabelle. *That Sweet Enemy: The French and the British
from the Sun King to the Present.* New York: Knopf, 2007.

Trigger, Bruce G. "Early Iroquoian Contacts with Europeans," in Bruce G.
Trigger, ed., *Northeast,* vol. 15 of W.C. Sturtevant, ed., *Handbook of North
American Indians.* Washington, D.C.: Smithsonian Institution, 1978,
344–56.

Trigger, Bruce G. and James F. Pendergast. "St. Lawrence Iroquoians," in Bruce G. Trigger, ed., *Northeast*, vol. 15 of W.C. Sturtevant, ed., *Handbook of North American Indians*. Washington, D.C.: Smithsonian Institution, 1978, 357–61.

Tugwell, Maurice and John Thompson. *The Legacy of Oka*. Toronto: MacKenzie Institute, 1991.

Vachon, Robert. "Invasion Chez Les Mohawks à Akwesasne (St-Regis)," *Recherches amérindiennes au Québec*, vol. IX, no. 3 (1979), 4.

Valiskakis, Gail. "Rights and Warriors: First Nations, Media and Identity," *Ariel*, vol. 25, no. 1 (January 1994), 61–71.

Vernet, Sylvia du. *An Indian Odyssey: Tribulations, Trials and Triumphs of the Gibson Band of the Mohawk Tribe of the Iroquois Confederacy*. Islington, Ont.: Muskoka Publications, 1986.

Vieni, Frank. Letter to Dwayne White, Emergency Planning Committee, Mohawk Council of Kahnawake, August 16, 1990.

Wells, Paul. "Chief Questions Authority of 5 Who Signed Accord," *Gazette*, Montreal, August 14, 1990.

Wente, Margaret. "Hey, It's Just Indian Country," *Globe and Mail*, Toronto, March 6, 2008, A15.

Whitehall, Ivan G. "'This Land Is Our Land—and We Want It Back': Aboriginal Land Claims—an Overview," in Frank McArdle, ed., *Selected Papers Based upon Lectures Delivered at the Conference of the Canadian Institute for Advanced Legal Studies, The Cambridge Lectures 1991*, Cambridge University, England. Montreal: Editions Y. Blais, 1992.

Widdowson, Frances and Albert Howard. *Disrobing the Aboriginal Industry: The Deception behind Indigenous Cultural Preservation*. Montreal and Kingston: McGill-Queen's University Press, 2008.

Wilkinson, Charles. *Blood Struggle: The Rise of Modern Indian Nations*. New York: W.W. Norton, 2005.

Wilson, Edmund. *Apologies to the Iroquois. With a Study of the Mohawks in High Steel by Joseph Mitchell*, 1949. London: W.H. Allen, 1960.

Winegard, Timothy C. "The Court of Last Resort: The 1990 Oka Crisis and the Canadian Forces," MA thesis, Royal Military College, 2006.

———. "The Forgotten Front of the Oka Crisis: Operation Feather/Akwesasne," *Journal of Military and Strategic Studies*, vol. 11, nos. 1 and 2 (2009).

York, Geoffrey. "In Defence of the Truth: Reporters behind Oka Barricades Weren't 'Agents of Propaganda,'" *Content*, November/December 1990, 18–20.

York, Geoffrey and Loreen Pindera. *People of the Pines: The Warriors and the Legacy of Oka*, 2nd ed., Toronto: Little, Brown, 1992.

ACKNOWLEDGEMENTS

MANY PEOPLE helped me put this story together. At the top of the list is my old colleague Fred Drummie, associate deputy minister of Indian Affairs in 1990, now retired and living in New Brunswick. With great generosity Fred gave me not only his extensive records of the period but also the manuscript of his memoir, on which I have drawn freely. On the western side of the country, LGen (ret.) Kent Foster offered me contemporary notes, photos and reminiscences and introductions to old military comrades. I have also benefited enormously from interviews with Joanne Aubé, the Hon. Don Boudria, the Hon. Pierre H. Cadieux, Harold Calla, Ruth Cardinal, Ray Castelli, Gen. (ret.) A.J.G.D. de Chastelain, Jeanne Flemming, Robert Fowler, VAdm (ret.) Gary Garnett, Nathalie Gélinas, John Graham, Eddie Goldenberg, Stanley Hartt, Commissioner (ret.) Norman Inkster, Richard Labelle, Harvey and Sharon McCue, Reid Morden, the Rt. Hon. Brian Mulroney, John Parisella, Jacquie Prokopanko, John Rayner, Roberta Santi, Anne Park Shannon, the Hon. Tom Siddon, Norman Spector, the Hon. Paul Tellier, VAdm (ret.) Chuck Thomas, Chief Superintendent (ret.) Lowell Thomas, Richard Van Loon, Joseph Whiteside, the Hon. Michael Wilson and Susan Yurkovich. Transcripts of these interviews, which covered much more than Oka, now reside in the National Archives. Garry Carbonnell, Chief

Steve Bonspille, and, in a different way, Kahntineta Horn, brought me up to date on Kanesatake twenty years after the events of this book. Ian and Marjorie Clark shared some of the early moments of my own involvement. Harvey Schipper, Karen Minden, Richard and Jean Van Loon, and Jennifer and Don Moulton provided rest along the way. Charlotte Stenberg, in addition to preparing the transcripts, was the very model of a multilingual research assistant. David Bond, Kathleen Shoemaker, Fred and Madeleine Drummie, and Charlotte Stenberg read parts of the manuscript and made many valuable improvements. Scott McIntyre is everything a publisher should be, and Barbara Pulling, my editor, is an expert in the making of silk purses. None, of course, are responsible for the remaining errors, which are mine alone.

It is conventional also to say something about one's long-suffering spouse. Well, not only would this book not have been written without Julie, I don't think I would have got through the summer of 1990 without her, either. Her affection for and acceptance within Indian communities has been a joy to us both.

INDEX